D1569298

Understanding Stepmothers

Understand Epigenetics

Elizabeth Church, Ph.D.

Understanding Stepmothers

Women Share Their Struggles, Successes, and Insights

HarperCollins*PublishersLtd*

HarperCollins Publishers Ltd
2 Bloor Street East, 20th Floor
Toronto, Ontario, Canada
M4W 1A8

www.harpercollins.ca

National Library of Canada Cataloguing in Publication

Church, Elizabeth A. (Elizabeth Ann), 1955–
Understanding stepmothers : women share their struggles, successes and insights / Elizabeth Church. – 1st ed.

ISBN 0-00-200660-X

1. Stepmothers. 2. Parenting. 3. Stepfamilies. I. Title.

HQ759.92.C49 2004   646.7'8   C2004-900336-4

DWF 9 8 7 6 5 4 3 2 1

Printed and bound in Canada
Set in Bembo and Antique Olive

Contents

Introduction

Why is it so hard to be a stepmother? This question may appear to be small, but it has puzzled and vexed many thousands of women. It is also a question that I had to confront. When I met my partner twenty-three years ago, I was twenty-five and living the footloose life of a graduate student, while training to become a clinical psychologist. My partner's daughter was eight and his son twelve, just a year younger than my youngest brother. There was even a slight connection between the two boys, because both had been in the same Grade 1–Grade 2 class five years earlier.

Like many stepfamily households, mine has been fluid. When I met my stepchildren, they lived with their mother and stayed with their father on alternate weekends. A year later my stepson decided that he wanted to be with his father and moved in. He and his sister spent weekends together at either their mother's or their father's. Shortly after that, I moved in with my partner and his son, and the three of us lived together until my stepson graduated from high school and went away to university. My partner and I were on our own for about a year until our eldest daughter was born. Eight months after my daughter's birth, my stepdaughter, then age sixteen, chose to move in. Our household then had to accommodate the often opposing habits and schedules of a young baby and a teenager. My daughter would be clamouring to be lifted out of her crib at 5:30 a.m., while my stepdaughter was often happy to sleep until mid-afternoon. My stepdaughter lived with us for two years until she finished high school and went off to university, just before my second daughter was born. In the space of nine years, the composition of our household changed seven times.

I stepped into stepmothering with little hesitation or forethought. I had always enjoyed being around children. I had chosen to study child psychology and worked with children in summer camps and group homes. I assumed that my relationships with my stepchildren would be as straightforward and relaxed as those with my youngest brother and other children I knew. Instead, I was bewildered and hurt at the response I encountered. Even what I considered benign comments would be met with wariness or blank faces. If I asked the children how their mother was, for instance, I would rarely get an answer. It was only much later that I realized that it was easier for them to keep their two households separate. They had one life with their father and another one with their mother.

My life shifted radically. I went from living on my own, and pleasing myself, to running a complicated household. When my stepson gave me his pants to mend, I was flabbergasted. It hadn't occurred to me that I would be taking on these kinds of domestic responsibilities. My partner assumed I would fit in easily. During one argument in which I was voicing my frustrations, he shot back that, as a psychologist, I should be more understanding. I was furious at his assumption that it was up to me to adapt, but his comment stung, because I, too, believed that I should be managing better. I was ashamed of my reactions, particularly when family and friends seemed unaware of the complexity of my predicament.

Gradually I realized that I was woefully unprepared to be a stepmother. Before meeting my partner, I had had little contact with stepfamilies. I grew up in a two-parent family with my three brothers. No one in my extended family had been divorced or remarried. Only one of my friends in elementary school had divorced parents. Her father had remarried, but since she lived with her mother and rarely saw her dad, her stepmother was not a presence in her life. And my parents had had little experience with stepfamilies. I can remember only one friend of my parents who became a stepmother, when she married a widower.

Probably one reason I knew so few stepfamilies when I was growing up in the 1960s is there *were* a lot fewer. Since divorce laws relaxed in the 1960s, the number of stepfamilies in North America has rapidly increased. Currently, 50 percent of all marriages in the United States are remarriages for at least one spouse, about one-third of U.S. children will live in a stepfamily at some point, and 40 percent of adult women will be part of a stepfamily. In Canada, the numbers are less dramatic because divorce and remarriage rates are lower. Nevertheless, by the mid-1990s, only about one-third of Canadian children were born into a "traditional" family where there were two married parents who had not lived together prior to marriage and 8.6 percent of Canadian children under age twelve lived in a stepfamily. In Canadian remarriages, 26 percent of men and 15 percent of women are stepparents. These figures underestimate the actual number of stepfamilies in Canada and the United States, since researchers usually count only families where the couple is legally married. It is increasingly common for couples with children to live together without marrying, particularly if they have been divorced before.[1]

Initially, I knew few other stepmothers and felt very isolated. I began to seek out other stepmothers, often friends of friends. If I met a stepmother, I would drop a few trial comments, to see if she wanted to talk about her experiences. Most were as eager as I was to tell their stories. It was enormously relieving to discover that these women were struggling too, that I was not alone. An immediate affinity often sprang up, grounded in our shared experiences. Later, in my clinical practice as a psychotherapist, I worked with many stepfamilies who were under stress. Sometimes I saw stepmothers individually, sometimes the children or the biological parents, and at other times the whole stepfamily. While many people in the stepfamilies felt out of their depth, the stepmothers often were the most conflicted and unhappy.

All this distress and confusion started me thinking in broader terms, and I began tracking down what has been written about stepmothers. I dug up lots of evidence—clinical, anecdotal, and empirical—that stepmothers have more difficulty adjusting than do stepfathers. They also tend to be less satisfied with their relationships with their stepchildren than are stepfathers.[2] Researchers have proposed several explanations for stepmothers' discontentment. Some suggest that stepmothers may feel more burdened because they often bear greater responsibility for the household than do stepfathers. Others argue that stepmothers, desiring greater closeness with their stepchildren than do stepfathers, may feel disappointed with the arm's-length relationship that develops with stepchildren. Another hypothesis is that stepmothers may be judged more harshly than stepfathers, since women are expected to do more in families than men. Despite an acknowledgement that stepmothers are more stressed, they have been studied much less than stepfathers. Consequently we understand a lot less about them.[3]

My reading confirmed my experience but also left my original question—why it is so hard to be a stepmother?—unanswered. I wanted to find out how others felt about being a stepmother. I embarked on my own study of stepmothers and did intensive audiotaped interviews with 104 stepmothers. I was curious whether their experience shifted over time, and if so, how. I sought out brand-new stepmothers, those who had been stepmothers for many years, and even some who were stepmothers for a second time. I also wondered how having children of their own affected stepmothers, so I included both childless stepmothers and those with biological children, whether from previous relationships or current ones.

The stepmothers who volunteered for my study proved enthusiastic participants. They knew their interview was confidential, and for many, it was the first time they felt they could speak freely. It was clear that these women wanted to be good stepmothers.

They wanted their stepfamilies to work and often felt thwarted and bewildered in their attempts to accomplish this. I found their stories fascinating and absorbing. Just when I had decided that I had heard every possible variation, the next stepmother would add a new patch to the complex quilt I was assembling.

Most interviews lasted about two hours. Although each was anchored by a set of prepared questions, which addressed many aspects of stepmothering, I encouraged each stepmother to elaborate as much as she wished. The interviews ranged widely. Most women had spent a great deal of time reflecting on—and agonizing over—their experiences and often had astute comments about the experience of being a stepmother. I offered to tell my story after the interview and to share what I had learned from my research. All were interested to hear this, as they wanted to find out whether others had had similar troubles. Many also hoped to gain some insight into their own situation. Their thirst to understand more about stepmothering further motivated me to write this book. During the long research process, I talked more casually with hundreds of other stepmothers. My study was like a magnet for stepmothers. If I was in a social situation and the topic came up, stepmothers would gravitate to me and relate their stories.

The interviews were transcribed and all identifying names and details were altered. I spent many, many hours reading, studying, and analyzing the transcripts in order to identify those themes that occurred frequently across the interviews. My goal was to capture and represent these women's perspectives, to develop a picture of what it is like to be a stepmother today. A number of recurring and fundamental challenges for stepmothers started to emerge, and I identified seven main sources of stress for stepmothers—the spectre of the wicked stepmother, unrealistic initial expectations, the idea of the perfect mother, dealing with the "ex," lack of authority vis à vis stepchildren, unsupportive partners, and for childless stepmothers, their partner's unwillingness to have more children. In Part One of this book, I examine each of these stressors in detail.

At the same time, my initial preconceptions—often ideas from my experience or from conversations with stepmother friends—were turned upside down. I interviewed a number of stepmothers who to my surprise (and initial consternation) did not have the same conflicts as I had. Some had breezed into stepmotherhood with little distress or trauma. Their expectations, emotions, and ideals were so distant from mine that we could have been living on different planets. The first few times I encountered these step-mothers, it was easy to dismiss them as anomalous or to suspect they were telling only half of their story. As I did more interviews, I learned that these women were not just exceptions. Rather, step-mothers react to, and comprehend, their situation in diverse ways. Not all stepmothers battle with the same issues or in the same manner. There seemed to be five distinct approaches to stepmoth-erhood. In Part Two, I describe the five models, which I have called Nuclear, Biological, Retreat, Couple, and Extended. These relate not only to how stepmothers define their place in the step-family, but how they regard relationships inside and outside the stepfamily, the conflicts they run up against, and emotional reac-tions such as guilt and jealousy.

In Part Three, I report on what stepmothers gain through expe-rience. Almost without exception, stepmothers told me that, if they could start again, they would take a very different tack. Both their attitudes and actions often altered significantly. I share here their hard-won knowledge. I also introduce a special group of stepmothers, those who had previously been part of a stepfam-ily—either as a stepchild or a stepmother. Their experiences give them a unique and valuable perspective on stepfamily life.

I devote one chapter to stepmothers' assessment of help they sought, whether it was therapy, self-help, or support from other stepmothers. Many of the women went for professional help, either for themselves, their stepchildren, their relationship with their part-ners, or the whole family. Some therapists were instrumental in untangling problems and developing new perspectives. Others were ignorant about the stepfamily dynamics, and their advice often exacerbated an already troubled situation. In the last chapter, I offer seven principles that guide the actions of stepmothers who are the happiest and have the most harmonious relationships within their stepfamilies. At the same time, I believe that stepmothering cannot be reduced to a simple set of rules. Stepfamilies are complex. What is relevant for one situation will not necessarily transfer to another. What is appropriate in a long-established stepfamily may backfire at the beginning. I also caution that stepmothers must not be the only ones to assume responsibility. Stepmothers cannot make their stepfamilies work in a vacuum. There must be other supports and structures—both inside and outside the family—if stepmothers and stepfamilies are to flourish.

Throughout the book I weave the voices and stories of the stepmothers with whom I talked. In order to preserve their anonymity, I have changed the names and some identifying details. Their stories are essentially unaltered, however, and the quotations are all their words. Rather than interrupt their stories with a detailed report of the study, I give this information in the Appendix. The stepmothers' narratives illuminate the disappointments, conflicts, and joys (yes, those exist too) associated with being a stepmother. I introduce stepmothers, like Gail, who tried to mould their stepfamily into their ideal family and ran into resentment rather than gratitude; childless stepmothers, like Betsy, whose partners refused to have children with them; stepmothers like Martha, who considered themselves wicked because of ambivalent feelings toward stepchildren; stepmothers like Deborah, who realized that, no matter how hard they tried to be mothers to their stepchildren, this goal was unattainable; and stepmothers like Sheila, who initially had huge trepidations about becoming a stepmother and ended up having a lot of fun.

As I listened to the stepmothers' stories, my perception of myself as a stepmother shifted. When other stepmothers described feeling hurt at being excluded, my own hurt felt less childish. I noticed myself comparing their actions and reactions against my own. Why didn't I try to be a mother to my stepchildren when so many other stepmothers had? How were some stepmothers able to strike the right balance with their stepchildren from the start? Through this process of self-examination, I became both more aware and more forgiving of myself. I hope that reading these stories will offer other stepmothers similar insights and comfort.

PART ONE

Why Is It So Hard to Be a Stepmother?

The seven chapters in Part One paint a bleak picture of stepmothers' lives. After reading them, one might wonder why any woman would choose to become a stepmother, or if she unwittingly falls into stepmotherhood, why she doesn't run away at the first opportunity. My aim in this part is to answer the question of why it is so hard to be a stepmother. The seven obstacles I describe—the tyranny of the wicked stepmother; stepmothers' unrealistic expectations; the burden of motherhood; overbearing ex-wives; precarious, strained relationships with stepchildren; unsupportive partners; and disempowered childless stepmothers—offer ample evidence of why so many stepmothers feel so stressed and miserable. It is a rare and unfortunate stepmother who has to contend with all seven, however. Most stepmothers wrestle with only a few. And for some, one stress will be offset by something more positive. One stepmother may be dumped with all the housework, but a friendly relationship with her stepdaughter mitigates her resentment. Another may start out believing she will become her stepchildren's mother and may become hurt when her stepchildren rebuff her efforts. If her partner mediates between her and the children, she may realize that their reaction is not a rejection of her but of that role. They do not want another mother but might welcome an interested adult. As we will see later, life does improve over time for most stepmothers. Nevertheless, all the stepmothers I interviewed struggled with at least one of these seven challenges, and their first few years as a stepmother were often bumpy and arduous.

Chapter 1

The Wickedest of Them All:
The Image of the Wicked Stepmother

What is the first word you associate with "stepmother"? If you are like most people, it is probably "wicked," or "evil," or "witch." And, if you were asked to describe your picture of a stepmother, it might sound something like this: "A stepmother was a really mean person, probably with warts all over her face. Ugly. And dangerous to the children, because she wanted to get rid of them. Not just mean, but murderous."

From early childhood, we are steeped in images of wicked step-mothers in fairy tales and films. "Wicked" seems to fit as naturally with "stepmother" as "innocent" does with "children." Certainly the many stepmothers with whom I spoke linked stepmothers with wickedness. Although you might expect stepmothers to rebel against this characterization of them as evil, cruel, and malevolent, only a minority of the women I interviewed actively rejected it. In fact, the above portrayal of the stepmother as wart-covered, ugly, mean, and murderous came from a stepmother herself. Almost without exception, the women with whom I spoke referred to wicked stepmothers in fairy tales—most often those in "Cinderella," "Hansel and Gretel," or "Snow White," and the image of the wicked stepmother was very much alive for them.

Mirror, Mirror on the Wall, Who's the Wickedest of Them All?

Wicked stepmothers are ubiquitous in folk literature—they show up throughout history, across cultures, and within many religious traditions. We can find one as far back as 1500 BCE in an Egyptian folktale in which a wicked stepmother persecutes her blameless stepson. In the nineteenth century, 345 variations of "Cinderella" were identified in cultures as diverse as China, India, Japan, and France. And the wicked stepmother persists today. Many of our most familiar fairy tales—"Hansel and Gretel," "Cinderella," "The Six Swans," "Snow White"—feature wicked stepmothers, and two of these—"Snow White" and "Cinderella"—were turned into movies by Disney, one of our most powerful purveyors of mass culture.[1]

By contrast, good stepmothers appear rarely in folk tales and literature. Even in the book *Politically Correct Bedtime Stories*, written in 1994, in which the author spoofs the idea of political correctness by recasting nasty figures from fairy tales into a more sympathetic light, the stepmother retains her cruel form. The fact that the author does not alter the stepmother's character suggests that he, like many others, cannot imagine a stepmother as anything other than evil.[2]

Wicked stepmothers act out their evil powers in many ways. Some are what have been called "lustful" stepmothers because they attempt to seduce their innocent stepsons. Others, like Snow White's stepmother, attempt to murder or poison their stepchildren. The murderous stepmother was so common in Classical Roman literature that the word for stepmother in Latin, *noverca*, became almost synonymous with "cruel" and "harsh."[3] Wicked stepmothers are often jealous or envious. Snow White's stepmother, for instance, wants to be the "fairest of us all" and tries to kill Snow White, who, as the more beautiful, thwarts her ambition. Wicked stepmothers also show up as witches, employing their magical powers to harm their stepchildren. In one Japanese story, the stepmother transformed herself into a serpent in order to pursue her stepson across the ocean.

Finally there is the kind of wicked stepmother with whom we are most familiar—the bad mother. Cinderella's stepmother treats her punitively and harshly, Snow White's envies her stepdaughter's youth and beauty so much that she tries to kill her, and Hansel and Gretel's abandons her stepchildren in the forest in order that she not starve. Taken together, these women represent the opposite of everything that mothers are supposed to be: unconditionally loving, accepting, and selfless.

The wicked stepmother's malevolent power is heightened in these stories because she always represents the negative pole of a dualism. The wicked stepmother is all bad, while everyone else is all good. There is never any hint, for example, that Hansel and Gretel's father should be held accountable for abandoning his children in the forest. At the end of the story, the children run happily home into his arms, the stepmother having conveniently died in the interim. Nor is there any indication that Cinderella might not be entirely innocent, that she might be angry and resentful as often happens in real stepfamilies.

The Grimms' fairy tales make for a fascinating example of this splitting. Although the popular image of Jacob and Wilhelm Grimm is that they gathered folk tales from peasants, their stories came from a middle-class and largely literate group. They also made substantial alterations to the tales through the various editions of their books. The figure of the stepmother changed significantly. In the original version of "Hansel and Gretel," it was a mother and a father who abandoned their children. In later editions, the Grimms removed the father from the centre of the story and changed the mother into a stepmother so that all the nastiness was seen to emanate from her. The Grimms believed that folk tales should be used as an instrument to educate children and modified the stories to epitomize the values they believed children should acquire. In their scheme, mothers were not supposed to be cruel and unfeeling. How much easier to accept such behaviour from a stepmother.[4]

The Disney movie versions of *Snow White* and *Cinderella* only intensified the trend begun by the Grimms: the father is more absent, the mother has completely disappeared, and the stepmother becomes the repository of all malice and evil. In his planning notes for *Cinderella*, Disney clearly regarded the stepmother as the true villain. He said: "I feel that the stepsisters are under a domineering mother. They are spoiled brats, but it's the mother who is forcing them."[5]

Why are there so many wicked stepmothers in folk and fairy tales? Although they may represent ambivalent feelings that step-mothers may have about their stepchildren, it would be naive to think they are accurate portrayals of stepmothers' behaviour. Step-mothers do not chop up their stepchildren and serve them in a stew to their father for supper, as described in a particularly grue-some Grimms' tale, "The Juniper Tree." And, despite the murderous stepmother's ubiquity in Roman literature, there is no evidence that Roman stepmothers went about killing their stepchildren.

Images of wicked stepmothers convey messages about how women should *not* act and feel—jealous, angry, unloving toward children. The wicked stepmothers are often the only women in the fairy tales to exert any power, albeit as witches. By contrast, the heroines are always modest and passive. These wicked stepmothers offer potent negative models. Since the stories always end with the stepmothers suffering, they can be interpreted as cautionary tales for women who may be tempted to overstep the boundaries of acceptable behaviour.

As I mentioned earlier, good stepmothers rarely appear in litera-ture. After a great deal of searching, I did discover a few. One is in an old Icelandic folk tale, "The Tale of Hildur, the Good Step-mother." I also came across two contemporary examples, one in a children's storybook, "The Good Stepmother," written in 1992, and the other in a recent movie featuring the ever-present Olsen twins, Mary Kate and Ashley, *It Takes Two* (1995). Although the first tale emerges from a very different culture and time period than the others, the three share a number of attributes.[6] First, all the mothers are dead. Although you might expect this with the older story, one would think it would be less common today when most stepfamilies result from divorce. In all three examples, the child, not the father, selects the stepmother, and the stepmother-stepchild relationship is more central in these stories than the husband-wife bond. The stepmother acts as a kind of servant to her stepchild. In "The Tale of Hildur," for instance, Hildur's condition for marrying the King is that she and her future stepdaughter, Ingibjorg, live on their own for three years. Although Hildur is herself a princess, in a curious reversal of roles, she cares for Ingibjorg and frees her from three curses cast by Ingibjorg's dying mother. All three stories end with the wedding. Technically, then, these women are not really stepmothers. Perhaps they would not appear quite so wonderful after a few years of marriage!

These stories can be interpreted as a kind of wish fulfilment for children. In the push-and-pull of divorce and remarriage, children rarely have much say about who will be their new stepparents. Here they take control. They are the important ones. On another level, these stories paint a dismal picture for a woman who strives to be a good stepmother. In order to fulfil the "Hildur syndrome," she has to subsume her desires into caring for her stepchildren. She has no agency, no power of her own. Instead of Cinderella serving her stepmother, we have the good stepmother dancing attendance on her stepchildren. This model is as untenable as that of the wicked stepmother, but, as we will see, a number of stepmothers try to be Hildur to their stepchildren.

Under the Spell

For many of the stepmothers I interviewed, fairy tales were their only source of knowledge about stepmothers prior to becoming one themselves. The image of the wicked stepmother made the prospect of stepmotherhood daunting for some women. Lina was twenty-five when she met Jake, whose two sons were only ten and twelve years younger than she was. She had never known anyone who lived in a stepfamily and was apprehensive about what role she could play in their lives. Adding to her uneasiness was her image of stepmothers, which was lifted directly from fairy tales: "I don't like the name stepmother, because I think of a woman with a big ugly nose and a witch's hat. That's my mental image of a stepmother. And a wart on the end of her nose." Scared by this picture, Lina started scouring bookstores trying to discover something to counter it: "As I stood in that bookstore, I saw myself that way, and I was frightened. I thought, 'Oh, I'm not sure I'm going to like this role. Because it's such a bad one.'"

No Escaping

Like Lina, some stepmothers feel victimized by the association with the wicked stepmother, as though they are at the mercy of the image. Others are able to distance themselves from the image. One stepmother watched a little girl in her stepdaughter's daycare recoil on hearing that she was a stepmother: "One self-possessed little three-year-old asked me, 'Who are you?' I said, 'Well, I'm Clara's stepmother.' And her eyes got very big, and she sort of sat back a bit, her back straightened, and she said, 'You mean, just like in Cinderella?'" While the stepmother was amused with the little girl's comment, her stepdaughter was not: "And it was interesting, because later when I would introduce myself as 'I'm Clara's stepmother,' Clara would pull my hand and say, 'No, don't tell them that.'"

Adults may be more sophisticated and less direct than young children, but the image still evokes a predictable response. While doing this research, I frequently had people say to me—"Oh, you must be wicked then!" After all, not only was I writing about stepmothers but I was one too. I prefer to assume these comments are meant in jest, and that most adults, unlike young children, do not picture me as the wicked queen in Snow White. Their knee-jerk reaction does suggest, however, that stepmothers continue to be stereotyped by this image.

Yet, within the stepfamily itself, a stepmother is rarely called wicked to her face. Only two of the 104 stepmothers I interviewed had ever been accused of wickedness by their stepchildren. The fear of being labelled remains, however. Even if nothing is said, some stepmothers are convinced that their stepchildren, partners, or in-laws regard them as evil, particularly if they are the disciplinarians of the household. One stepmother described how the image of the wicked stepmother has created a double standard: "There have been times when I've got upset over things the boys were doing. I would get upset and shout. But if [my partner] was upset and shouted, it was looked at in a totally different light. I would be looked at as the wicked stepmother, but he would just be a parent getting upset." Although no one ever used the dreaded word, she believed the perception existed.

Stepmothers often try to avoid being labelled as wicked by refusing to be called a stepmother at all: "I don't like the word stepmother. It reminds me of Cinderella and the ugly stepmother. So, I said to [my stepchildren], 'Don't you dare introduce me as your stepmother.' They asked me what I would like. And I said, 'Just say Audrey, my dad's wife.'" Others sidestep the issue. Tina always introduces her stepdaughter, Caterina, as her daughter, because "I've heard of stepparents not treating the child as his child or her child so I introduce her as my daughter." This, however, creates another bind for Tina: "[I'm] a Christian and very strong in my faith. When people ask how long I have been married, and I say two years, and Caterina's five years old, I have to explain that, because the idea of having a child out of wedlock to me is embarrassing."

I Didn't Want Them to Think . . .

Worrying that they may appear wicked prevents some stepmothers from speaking out. Rather than show anger or annoyance, they will bite their tongues. They also restrain themselves from asking their stepchildren to do chores around the house, such as picking up clothes off the floor or making their beds, even if the mess is driving them crazy. If their stepchildren are rude or belligerent, they will pretend not to notice. One stepmother felt humiliated when her teenage stepson would ignore and dismiss her in front of family and friends, but she avoided confronting him: "Maybe I should have been wicked, been angry, and expressed my frustration at how he was speaking or that he was so sullen and arrogant. . . . I have been so guarded against being a bad stepmother that I have no relationship with the child, other than providing the nurturing physical environment." Note how this stepmother equates being angry with being wicked.

Stepmothers are often cautious around others as well. One woman became a stepmother at age twenty-four to two children aged ten and nine. The children spent their summers with their father, but since he was often away on business, she was left to care for them. The children were charming and affectionate, but totally undisciplined. As a part-time father, her partner wanted his time with his children to be fun, so he had never established rules or limits. The stepmother's mother-in-law took her aside and suggested that she be firmer with the children because they were too wild and needed some routine. Although the stepmother agreed, she did not say anything: "Sometimes I felt frustrated at not being able to get the kids on a schedule. I couldn't talk to him about it, because I didn't want him to think I thought any less of his kids, or that I was complaining. And I didn't want to talk to his family about it either. I didn't want them to think I thought his kids were awful. I didn't want to appear, you know, the wicked stepmother."

This self-silencing leaves stepmothers without support. While mothers let off steam by commiserating with one another about their adolescents' outrageous behaviour, stepmothers often do not allow themselves this liberty. They worry that if they criticize their stepchildren, others will label them as wicked. Some, like the stepmother quoted above, do not even unburden themselves to their partners. The stigma of the wicked stepmother is an effective gag.

The Thoroughly Modern Wicked Stepmother

How do stepmothers themselves define the wicked stepmother? Some consider a stepmother wicked if she does not *act* like a mother to her stepchildren. As one stepmother said, "An uncaring person and maybe cruel. Not physically cruel, but emotionally cruel—reminding them constantly that 'I'm not your mother,' and comparing them maybe to your own children." The "physically cruel" fairy-tale stepmother who poisons or abandons her stepchildren has become an "emotionally cruel" one. And the emotional cruelty lies in reminding her stepchildren that she is not their mother (which of course she is not). The woman quoted above has both biological children and stepchildren. Her relationships with the two sets of children are very different, and this creates an internal conflict for her, because she believes they *should* be the same.

Stepmothers also brand a stepmother as wicked for the perfectly natural feelings of ambivalence toward her stepchildren. The stepmother does not even have to act on her feelings. As one stepmother remarked, "[She] has let the jealousy and competition and sense of powerlessness take over. . . . Maybe the wicked stepmother is actually doing a lot of good things for the child." Doing "good things" is insufficient. The stepmother must be loving both inside and out.

There are also what I call "sins of omission." A stepmother becomes wicked, simply because she fails to act—doesn't love her stepchildren, doesn't include them in her life, doesn't listen to them. The stereotyping extends even further. A stepmother is considered wicked if she exerts power (just like in the fairy tales).

Some stepmothers vilify other stepmothers for interfering in a father's relationship with his children. As one stepmother commented, "A wicked stepmother doesn't let the child have access to the father or the father have access to the kid." Like the fairy-tale depictions of fathers as powerless and blameless in face of virago stepmothers, this view absolves the father of his responsibility to take charge of the situation.

Despite the pervasiveness of the wicked stereotype, I was still surprised at how easily some stepmothers assume the mantle of wickedness. In order to feel wicked, they do not have to deprive their stepchildren of food, or beat them, or send them into the woods. They just have to feel angry, or jealous, or resentful toward their stepchildren. Some embrace the "Hildur syndrome," condemning themselves to wickedness if they consider their own needs at all.

Maddy is a remarkably dedicated stepmother. When her stepdaughter Jane, age eleven, moved in, Maddy re-arranged her work schedule and dropped out of her weekly volleyball games so that she could be home with Jane. For Evan, Jane's father, it was business—and pleasure—as usual. Maddy was delighted to make the adjustments as Jane has been a bonus in her life. It took Maddy only one incident to feel she was slipping into murky territory. Evan had planned a fishing weekend with his friends, and Maddy saw a opportunity for some free time, so she arranged for Jane to stay at her mother's house. Although Jane and her parents were fine with Maddy's request, Maddy felt guilty: "Evan was going away, and Jane wasn't planning to go to her mother's for the weekend. I said to Evan, 'I'd like her to go to her mother's, because I just want to go out with my friends and let loose.' . . . I felt—not that Jane ever realized what had happened—I felt very selfish." Even though Evan is the biological parent, Maddy never suggests that he is selfish for wanting time off. She holds herself to a higher standard and believes she failed by placing her desires ahead of her stepdaughter's.

Stepmothers are more likely to feel wicked if their partners are lax about discipline or if the limits of their authority are unclear. One stepmother described how she felt caught in this role: "I felt like I was a wicked stepmother just by trying to run the house. . . . I'm always saying things like 'Rinse off your plate before you put it in the dishwasher' and 'Take that upstairs' or 'Get your shoes off.' They're just little things that a preteen or teen absent-mindedly wouldn't think of necessarily. But I'm the only one who points it out." It can be hard for stepmothers to know what they can legitimately demand. Is it okay to discipline their stepchildren? Ask them to clear the table? Fasten their seat belts? If a stepmother is uncertain about her role, asking her stepdaughter to rinse off her plate may feel tantamount to telling her to sleep among the cinders.

I Was a Wicked, Wicked Person

In many ways Martha, age forty-four, typifies the struggles of stepmothers who become ensnared in the wicked stepmother's web. She and Wilf married six years ago. Before she first met him at a party, Martha had heard from mutual friends that Wilf's wife had died of cancer the previous year. He was overwhelmed with trying to care for his three children, Sean, Mark, and Alicia, who were ten, eight, and six at the time she met them. By contrast, Martha had relished her five years as a single parent. She and her daughter, Sarah, then age eight, had a close, companionable relationship. Sarah visited her father every weekend, so Martha had guilt-free time for herself.

There was an immediate attraction between Martha and Wilf. Within three months, they were already planning marriage. In retrospect, Martha acknowledges that she and Wilf were so caught up with their own joy that they did not really consider that the children might not share their excitement: "Right from the beginning, my husband and I have been very intentional about our own relationship. The whole thing is based on our relationship. It wasn't like two families coming together. We fell in love and we wanted to be together. And that is still the case, very much, which is wonderful. But, I don't think either of us knew how difficult it would be to put the two families together."

Before marrying Wilf, Martha was enthusiastic about the prospect of the expanded family she and Wilf were forming together with their two sets of children. The four children hit it off from the start, particularly Sarah and Alicia. Martha had a great deal of compassion for her stepchildren because their mother had died. As a social worker in a hospice for AIDS patients, she worked with families who were grieving. The children had never spoken about their mother since her death. Wilf was at a loss about how to help them and looked to Martha, who also believed she could encourage them to talk: "It's my job, it's what I do all the time, working with people who are dying, working with families who have someone who is dying, both before, around, and after death. Most of my time is spent with talking to patients. And I do that easily, and they talk to me easily. So I thought I could give these kids that kind of support." Very quickly, she realized that her good intentions were a "*big* mistake." Not only did her stepchildren rebuff Martha's attempts to talk about their mother, but they shrugged off any other overtures she made.

Martha "got right into the whole wicked stepmother syndrome. I ended up feeling like I was a wicked, wicked person." This label did not originate with her stepchildren. Even though they are still sullen and uncommunicative, they have never been openly angry or rebellious. Her own daughter is much more defiant: "My own daughter is terrible. I'll tell her to do something five times and it still may or may not get done. My stepchildren will often do what I tell them to do." Although Sarah is much ruder to her mother than her stepsiblings have ever been, Martha has never felt like a wicked mother. Her perception of herself as a wicked stepmother is linked to how she feels inside, to her hurt feelings when her stepchildren continually push her away: "I think for me, the most devastating thing was being rejected. Nothing prepared me for that. And I felt totally rejected. Every time I reached out, tried to do something for these kids, I felt totally rejected. That was the beginning of the devastation; then I found myself rejecting back, and being mean back."

Martha felt haunted, for instance, that she had once hung up the phone while her stepdaughter, Alicia, was talking to her friend. Martha had needed to call her office and had asked Alicia to get off the phone. When Alicia ignored her, Martha was furious and grabbed the phone out of Alicia's hand. Martha apologized afterwards, but she continued to feel ashamed, that her actions were unforgivable. While Martha's reaction was extreme and certainly did not help improve her relationship with her stepdaughter, it seemed to me to be less dire than she interpreted it. Certainly she had been angrier than that with Sarah on occasion and did not agonize over this. The difference with her stepchildren was her internal reactions: "I felt like this other person came over me" or "I could just feel myself exploding" or "I got into such an awful, awful feeling." On the outside, she was usually restrained and polite with her stepchildren, but on the inside, she was consumed with hurt and anger.

The unequal distribution of household work created some of the tensions. At the beginning, Wilf and Martha agreed that they would take equal responsibility for housework and child care. The problem was that Wilf travelled a great deal in his job as a salesman, so Martha was left alone with the four children, sometimes four nights a week. Throughout the interview, Martha stressed that Wilf was willing to take on his share. It was obvious, however, that this had not happened. Because they believed they shared the housework, the fact that Martha did more was never acknowledged. Martha ended up reproaching herself for resenting the extra work.

Martha also became the enforcer. While he was a widower, Wilf had had a full-time live-in housekeeper. His children were accustomed to being waited on. Martha had also fallen into the habit of pampering Sarah while the two of them lived on their own. She and Wilf decided that all the children should take more responsibility around the house. They drew up a schedule for chores—taking out the garbage, setting the table, emptying the dishwasher, etc.—which they posted on the refrigerator door. With Wilf often away, Martha was left to implement the new regime. Not surprisingly, both Martha's daughter and her stepchildren were less than thrilled with the increased work. Nagging them about chores and battling their opposition only heightened her feeling of being overbearing and arbitrary. Again, since the family myth was that Wilf and Martha were equal partners, Martha's role as the heavy was not validated.

In order to accommodate the six of them, Martha and Wilf sold their houses and moved into a larger one. The transition was a shock for Martha: "I had a house of my own with my daughter—the whole house was mine—and it felt like my retreat from the world. I'd been there for five years and I had made it my house, and I really liked it, it was a very comfortable place for me. . . . So I moved into this new house with four new people and of course I was now sharing a bedroom, which I had not done for a long time. I didn't have one corner of that house that was mine." Not only had she lost her own space, but the house was overflowing with the clutter and noise of four children. As she walked home after work each day, she "could just feel [her] whole mood and [her] whole self sinking." Confronted with a heap of children's schoolbooks, coats, and shoes on the hall floor, she would have to fight back her desire to hurl the children's possessions down the stairs. Her method of coping was to lock herself in her bedroom until she could face the children calmly. The intensity of her reactions only confirmed Martha's belief that she was "acting crazy," "feeling like a basket case," that she had become a "wicked, mean person."

Further poisoning this potent brew was jealousy: "One of the reasons why I ended up feeling like this wicked stepmother was because part of me was jealous. And it made no logical sense." The first pangs appeared on her honeymoon. She and Wilf had planned a Caribbean holiday for the two of them. Sarah was to stay at her father's and her three stepchildren with their grandparents. At the last minute her mother-in-law became ill, and her stepchildren came along. Wilf and Martha had no time to themselves. While Wilf was occupied with entertaining the children, Martha was left to stew. Few women would want to share their honeymoon with their stepchildren, yet Martha chastised herself for resenting them.

Martha's self-condemnation was compounded by her belief that her stepchildren needed a replacement mother. Initially, she tried to include them in the activities she and Sarah enjoyed together, such as hiking, biking, and swimming. Either they refused or came along so grudgingly that she gradually stopped inviting them. She and Sarah continued their excursions. This threw her into another conflict. If she bought Sarah a treat, she would guiltily hide it from her stepchildren and Wilf. Her view of herself as a surrogate mother led her to expect she should act exactly the same with her stepchildren as she did with Sarah, although her stepchildren gave no sign that they welcomed this.

To a large extent, Martha's self-hatred was exacerbated by the ambiguity in her situation. She thought she should be a mother and others urged her in the same direction, yet her stepchildren did not welcome her in this role. Although she had the responsibility for the household, she did not have the necessary authority. Her misapprehensions about how to be a stepmother caused her to believe she was exercising tyrannical power over her stepchildren when she was demanding less from them than from her own daughter. During the interview, Martha even tried to convince me that she was a wicked stepmother—"I did have more power than these kids, I mean I do realize that!"—although she never recounted any incident that I could recognize as evil. From my perspective, I saw quite a different landscape. To me, Martha—and the other self-identified wicked stepmothers—appeared more oppressed than oppressors: they had subjugated themselves to the myth of the wicked stepmother, which led them to view themselves as hateful.

Chapter 2

Crashing Mirrors: Unrealistic Initial Expectations

Many women enter their stepfamilies with high hopes and admirable intentions. They imagine an easy transition into the stepfamily, close relationships with stepchildren, and a harmonious home life. Most quickly become disheartened, however, and find themselves boiling over with hurt, anger, guilt, resentment, jealousy, and feelings of estrangement. Unexpected conflicts spring up with stepchildren and partners, and with people they had never anticipated being part of their new lives, such as a partner's ex-wife. On top of these frictions, stepmothers often feel disillusioned—even that they have failed—when they cannot achieve their initial ideals.

When stepmothers look back from the vantage point of experience, most agree that they were hopelessly naive about the complexity of their new situation. Some were so entranced by their relationship with their partners that they did not stop to consider how radically their lives would be overturned. From the moment Priscilla met her partner, Terry, she was swept up into a romantic whirlwind. Priscilla was twenty-two—half Terry's age—and had just moved out of her parents' house after graduating from university. She had no intention of becoming involved with anybody, but fell "crazily in love" with Terry. Both were avid runners, hikers, and kayakers and started their relationship by training for a marathon together. Terry had two teenaged children, Steven and Natalie, who lived with their mother and stayed with him every second weekend. Since he saw his children infrequently, he wanted to devote the whole visit to them. Priscilla was content to keep herself busy with friends and activities on those weekends, but this meant she barely knew the children before she and Terry married: "Oh my God! I didn't even have any expectations of becoming a stepmother, I mean I didn't want Steven and Natalie. I just wanted Terry. . . . It never occurred to me that I was getting stepchildren—and I didn't really even think of myself as a stepparent."

Priscilla was not hostile to her stepchildren. They simply did not appear on her radar: "It's not that we ignored the fact that he had kids. It's just not something that we spent a lot of time thinking about." A couple of months after the wedding, Steven told his father he wanted to move in, and Priscilla found herself living full-time with the commotion and mess of a teenaged boy. When I met with her, she was still reeling from how her life had been turned upside down.

You might think that things would have been better if Priscilla had had some expectations, ones based on a realistic assessment of how stepmothering would change her life. Yet stepmothers who invest a tremendous amount of energy imagining their place in their stepchildren's lives often are caught off balance as much as, or more than, Priscilla. Priscilla was unusual in that she had few expectations. Most stepmothers suffer from the opposite problem. Before becoming stepmothers, they have built up an idealized image of life in their new stepfamily. While they sense there may be complications, they believe they have them under control. Reflecting back on their initial assumptions, experienced stepmothers often shake their heads. One stepmother commented: "Well, I was really naive. I wasn't a mother yet. I knew nothing about what being a mother meant. And I guess I thought little kids are so cute, that you just love them and live happily ever after. I really didn't realize what it meant—emotionally and practically." This woman landed in a situation very different from what she had anticipated—an interfering ex-wife, resentful stepchildren, and a partner who absented himself at the sign of any conflict.

Often we try to make sense of our lives by projecting ourselves into the future, by imagining possible scenarios and directions. These projections become plans for how we want to proceed. While this type of thinking can help to direct and focus oneself, the process can also be deceptive. We may construct an idealized future that bears little relevance to our lives, and our expectations may be wildly out of sync with the people around us.

The vast majority of the stepmothers with whom I spoke believed, at first, that they had an accurate idea of stepfamily life. They quickly discovered that their assumptions did not match the reality of their situation. Six expectations caused stepmothers the most turmoil. The first four are the sorts of ideas that appear in Hollywood movies or television. One is a *Brady Bunch* notion, that simply getting remarried will immediately create a big happy family. Another is that stepmothers and stepchildren will instantly and magically love one another. A third expectation, and one of the most common, is similar to the idea of the fairy godmother—that the stepmother can rescue her stepchildren from their miserable situations. A small group of women begin with the reverse expectation—they envision the stepfamily fulfilling the missing elements in their own lives, that the stepfamily will rescue *them*.

The two other expectations appear, at least on the surface, to be more realistic. Here stepmothers ground their projections in previous experience and assume they can predict the future based on their pasts. Thus the fifth expectation: the new stepfamilies will be like the families they grew up in. With the sixth, stepmothers sometimes assume that, because they get along well with children, their relationships with stepchildren will also run smoothly. Planning one's future based on the past can be a sensible strategy. A tactic that works in one place can often be used successfully again. The problem for most stepmothers is that the stepfamily is unfamiliar territory. They are attempting to apply old categories to a new situation. Some stepmothers have only one expectation. Others load themselves down with several. As we will see, both the apparently fictional and the apparently realistic expectations require extensive revision and rethinking.

Expectation One: No Friction, No Tensions, No Stresses: My Stepfamily Will Instantly Be a Happy Family

Stepmothers often assume that remarriage will automatically create a new family. They imagine that everyone will get along well and immediately feel close to one another. To their chagrin, they discover that their stepchildren are already part of a family and may not want to alter that dynamic. The more the stepmother tries to create a family, the more the children may resist. Realizing that their stepchildren—and often their partners too—do not share their vision is crushing for some stepmothers.

Paulette's first husband had pretty much disappeared when her two children were only six and eight. She had been a single parent for eight years when she married Richard, who had three children. She and Richard had actually met through their children. Paulette's son, Anthony, was best friends with Richard's son, Scott, throughout school. Because Scott's mother worked long days, he often ate dinner at Paulette's, and her house became a second home for him. Paulette had been excited about becoming a stepmother. She envisioned the seven of them united into a strong, loving family, with Richard as a father to her children and with her as a mother to his. In order to accommodate everyone, Paulette and Richard decided to pool their resources and build an enormous new house. All the children had their own rooms and were allowed to decorate them as they wished. While her own children were enthusiastic about the new space, her stepchildren were lukewarm: "I expected the stepchildren to be, I guess, more appreciative of being a part of a big family, and everybody being very congenial, no friction, no tensions, no stresses. But I found that they were not really appreciative."

Paulette loved running and organizing a household and was proud of her domestic and culinary skills. By contrast, she believed her stepchildren had missed out on a lot because their mother was so preoccupied with her job as an advertising executive. Her plan was to make up for this: "I was naive when I became a stepparent in thinking that the stepkids were going to think, 'Oh, this is great! Isn't this wonderful!' You know, because I try to run a very organized home and my career is homemaking. I don't put anything ahead of that, and I expected them to see it as wonderful."

Their first Christmas together, Paulette ended up in tears. Christmas had always been a huge family event for Paulette, and she was eager to have the two families celebrate together. She envisioned them all decorating the Christmas tree together, but her stepchildren refused to leave their rooms when the time came. Though she dedicated many hours to picking perfect presents for her stepchildren, they ripped them open and shoved them aside with the barest of acknowledgements. Dinner was a similar disaster. Paulette had gone out of her way to cook their favourite Christmas foods, but the children bolted down their dinner without a word of thanks and headed off to watch TV in the den.

In retrospect, Paulette wonders if her skills in the kitchen and the house might have exacerbated tensions by making "their mum [seem] less than perfect." Although she does consider her stepchildren's mother inadequate and selfish, she recognizes that her stepchildren do not share her perception. She also realizes that her efforts to win over her stepchildren may have backfired—the more she did, the more they felt they had to defend their mother. At the same time, it has been distressing that her stepchildren seemed "to resent the fact if I try to have things nice." After two years as a stepmother, Paulette has tempered her expectations. When I asked her for advice for a new stepmother, she cautioned, "Don't expect too much too fast."

Expectation Two: I Will Love Them Automatically

Some stepmothers assume that because they love their partner this love will transfer easily to his children, and that the children will reciprocate. It is hurtful to realize that, far from loving their stepmothers, stepchildren often resent and even hate them, particularly at the beginning when the balance of power and distribution of affection and attention are shifting dramatically. The new stepmothers in turn discover that it is hard to feel affection for someone who is glowering at them across the dinner table. Failing to love their stepchildren, particularly if others expect this too, often makes stepmothers feel guilty and ashamed. If they also react angrily, it is a short walk into the dark woods of the wicked stepmother.

One striking example of this is Deborah, who had married John, a widower. John's first wife had died when his daughter, Emma, and son, Luke, were both under age two, and he and Deborah married within twelve months. They believed that the children would develop best within the security of a two-parent family, so they told the children that Deborah was their mother. Family and friends were sworn to secrecy. Until a cousin inadvertently leaked the truth when the children were adolescents, Emma and Luke believed Deborah was their biological mother.

Deborah had been only twenty-four when she became a stepmother and had spent little time around children. Immediately following the wedding, Deborah quit her job as a lab technician and assumed total responsibility for the household and the care of her two young stepchildren. Everyone—family and friends and Deborah herself—assumed that Deborah would not only act like a mother, but that she would also "naturally" love her stepchildren: "I knew I was expected to look after them. I did it because I wanted to do it. . . . I thought that I could be a good mother to them. I could give them love and affection and caring."

It was not so straightforward, however. Even though her

stepchildren believed she was their mother, Deborah was always at loggerheads with her stepdaughter, Emma. Deborah thought that Emma, having been indulged after her mother's death, was spoiled and wilful. When Deborah tried to establish regular routines for bedtimes and meals, or if she made Emma eat her vegetables before dessert, Emma would stamp her foot and run to her father complaining that Deborah was mean. More often than not, John would overrule Deborah and let Emma have what she wanted. Emma would smirk and dance off. Deborah was left seething.

After Deborah and John's son, Steven, was born, the situation worsened. Emma, then age eight, was jealous of the new baby and accused Deborah of favouring the baby over her. John would often take Emma's side in these disputes. Although Deborah resented Emma's manipulations, she felt guilty because it was easy to care for Steven, who welcomed Deborah's love and attention, while Emma was so prickly and complicated. When Emma and Luke, by then thirteen and twelve years old, respectively, found out that Deborah was not their mother, the recriminations and battles with Emma escalated. It became increasingly difficult for Deborah to feel positively, let alone lovingly, toward her stepdaughter. Although her relationship with her stepson, Luke, was more harmonious, with Steven's birth it became apparent to her that she did not feel like a mother toward either stepchild. She did not confide these feelings to anyone, because she worried that others would see her as nasty. Keeping this secret inside took its toll, however, and in the interview with me, she wept as she related her story for the first time. Looking back, she is convinced that her belief in automatic love added to her burden.

Expectation Three: I Will Rescue My Stepchildren

Many stepmothers enter their stepfamilies with a mission: to rescue their stepchildren (and often their partners as well) from misery and give them happy lives. Instead of falling into the trap of the wicked stepmother, such stepmothers cast themselves as fairy god-mother. They assume their stepchildren have been damaged by their parents' divorce or their mother's death and need the step-mother to swoop down and make it all better. Often they pity their stepchildren, seeing them as woebegone, neglected, or unhappy. One stepmother recounted her initial reaction to her stepchildren: "I felt so bad for them, that they had been gypped. They were so young and needed so much. . . . They deserved a home, and I think I saw myself as giving them a childhood rather than a daycare." Some stepmothers are habitual rescuers. The stepfamily offers yet another opportunity to repair and fix. Others jump in because they identify with their stepchildren. One stepmother, Hallie, who mar-ried Tristam, a widower with a three-year-old daughter, was drawn to the little girl because of the parallels with her own childhood: "My mother died when I was two years old. And I could see my own self in that little child. I felt so sorry for her, and I did every-thing under the sun that I could do."

These rescuers commit an enormous amount of time and energy redressing what they consider the deficiencies in their stepchildren's lives. They re-organize the house, set routines and rules in place, work with the school to improve their stepchildren's academic performance, arrange for counselling and therapy, plan elaborate birthday parties and holiday extravaganzas, and even cut back on their own work in order to be there when their stepchil-dren come home from school. Although initially it is often gratify-ing to see their stepchildren benefit from their efforts, most discover that their task is more demanding than that of a fairy god-mother. A wave of the magic wand does not, in the end, transform the environment. Some partners and stepchildren are grateful. More often, however, the rescuing backfires. Children do not always want their lives transformed. Some resent their stepmothers' attempts to help and are actively hostile. Even if they tolerate their stepmothers' efforts, they rarely acknowledge them. Although the stepmothers' partners are usually more appreciative, often they too resist change. Stepmothers frequently feel taken for granted, abused, angry, and burnt out.

A large part of Harriet's initial attraction to Dave was her desire to help him and his children. Dave's wife, Penny, had committed suicide two years earlier. He was struggling along on his own, trying to balance his job with caring for his two children. Harriet describes herself as a fixer: "It's ridiculous, you know, I go through the world thinking I can save things." Even before her death, Penny had often been in hospital for depression. Harriet felt that the children had never really known a true mother's care. Harriet herself had gone through a bitter divorce and wanted to re-make a family for her eight-year-old son, Nathaniel. Her mission was "to create a nice healthy family out of divorce and suicide." She believed the children needed a parent devoted full-time to their care, so she took an extended leave from her job as an arts administrator. In order to give her stepchildren stability and continuity, she and Nathaniel moved into the house that Dave had shared with his first wife. Storing most of her own belongings in the basement, she lived with the first wife's decor, even though she found it oppressive. Her stepchildren were both doing poorly at school, and Harriet committed many hours to helping them with schoolwork. Her philosophy was to give and give without expecting anything in return.

After a year, Harriet felt she was drowning. Her task had turned out to be much bigger than she had anticipated: "I remember the first time I thought, 'Wow, this is really hard.' I was doing the ironing in the basement and I began to weep because of what had happened that day." While she was in the kitchen making lunch, she had overheard her stepchildren discussing her. Far from being grateful, they were resentful and angry. They saw her as meddling and attempting to control and take over their lives. What was perhaps most devastating was hearing her stepson sarcastically refer to her as a "wicked stepmother." From her stepdaughter's knowing laugh, she could tell this was not the first time they had labelled her this way.

As her stepchildren became adolescents, they became openly rebellious and defiant. Harriet realized that she could not make it all better. She withdrew and started taking comfort in the small changes she was able to effect, for instance, getting her stepson involved in kayaking, which he loves. Now, eight years later, Harriet's "romantic attitude" has contracted into something more "practical." The best she can hope for with her stepchildren is civility and superficial politeness.

Expectation Four: I Will Be Fulfilled by This Stepfamily

A small group of stepmothers view the stepfamily as their chance to compensate for what they have missed in their own lives. Although they are usually not conscious of this expectation, some imagine that the stepfamily will become the ideal family they never had. Some childless stepmothers see their stepchildren as giving them a chance to be a mother. I spoke with a few women whose biological children had died and who hoped their relationships with stepchildren could be a kind of reparation. The problem, of course, is that their stepchildren may not want their stepmothers as part of their families, nor do they usually regard them as mothers. Some do not even want to be touched by their stepmother. She is a stranger. Their stepchildren's responses often feel like a slap in the face. Often only through this rejection do these women realize how they have constructed a fantasy stepfamily.

Take Hallie for example. Being motherless herself, she wanted to take the place of her stepdaughter's mother. At the same time, this new stepfamily represented Hallie's dream of being part of a loving family. After Hallie's mother had died, her father became more and more distant and finally drifted away. Hallie was bumped from relative to relative, the perpetual outsider. She mourned the loss, not just of her mother, but of the family she could have had. She was drawn to Tristam for his commitment and protectiveness toward his daughter, Stephanie. She imagined the three of them as a close family. In reality, Stephanie did not want to share her father. Tristam was often so focused on Stephanie that he did not notice that Hallie was pushed to the margins. Far from this family making up for her childhood, it became an eerie repetition.

Expectation Five: This Stepfamily Will Be Just Like My Family

Stepmothers often assume that because they have grown up in a family or are mothers themselves, they understand what it means to be part of a stepfamily. They believe that their rules and traditions will easily transfer to the new situation. If they are accustomed to gathering around the table for a lengthy, talkative dinner conversation, they may expect their new stepfamily to behave similarly. Like the stepmothers who fall prey to the image of the *Brady Bunch*, these women overlook the reality that their stepchildren and partners already form a unit. In fact, they have usually already lived together in two different kinds of families—first a two-parent family and then a single-parent one. In both these, they have established routines, customs, and patterns of interacting and are often reluctant to learn yet another set.

Manners often become a focus of conflict. Stepmothers frequently describe their stepchildren's manners as "terrible." When you examine these statements, the stepmothers are usually referring to a difference in standards. Their stepchildren's behaviour is not the same as the behaviours the stepmothers learned in childhood or what they have taught their own children. A stepmother who raises her children to be at ease in adult company may feel irritated and ashamed if her stepchildren mumble and look at the ground when introduced to adults. If she insists that they start shaking hands when they meet adults, she may meet with resentment.

The problem of expectations is also compounded by divorce. Inexperienced stepmothers routinely assume that a stepfamily will operate like a non-divorced family. Children who have experienced their parents' divorce and move back and forth between two households usually have a different notion of family than children who have always lived with two parents. Stepfamily bonds may be looser and more elastic than those in non-divorced families.[1] Not understanding this, a beginning stepmother is sometimes highly critical if the stepfamily does not have the same tight alliances that she experienced. A stepmother's initial expectations can make her feel frustrated, hurt, and angry: frustrated because she is powerless to change the stepfamily, hurt when her efforts are spurned, and angry with others for not sharing her ideals about family.

While still in her early twenties, Stacy became involved with Mike, who shared joint custody of his three young children with his ex-wife. Stacy threw herself into her role with great enthusiasm—baking, cooking, sewing, volunteering for school trips, taking her stepchildren on outings, helping with their schoolwork—all while juggling her own business as a consultant. Mike, who was feeling overwhelmed by the responsibility of caring for three children and maintaining a demanding law practice, was grateful for Stacy's energy and commitment. Her stepchildren's response was mixed. While they enjoyed going swimming with their stepmother, they were less happy about weekly trips to the library. In Stacy's family, book learning was prized and everyone loved reading. Her stepchildren, by contrast, never picked up a book unless forced to. Stacy's quest was to win her stepchildren over to reading, but the more she pushed books, the more they resisted, and the more frustrated she became.

Family celebrations were also a source of tension. These were defining events in Stacy's family, while in Mike's they were often perfunctory: "Birthdays are celebrated in my family and you're the king of the day. We have a social event, party, gifts, those kinds of things. Yet in Mike's family, birthdays are not such a big deal. Sunday dinners were also a big thing in my family life. . . . I had some expectations about Sunday dinner but it was not one that [Mike and his children] wanted to meet." Initially, Stacy knocked herself out planning elaborate family events and then became annoyed when her stepchildren would show up late or disappear halfway through: "Particularly the boys can't really handle somebody else's birthday happening. So I often got angry and would say, 'Why can't you stay at the table and at least wait until we have the cake, and open the gifts.'" At first, she was so irritated that she considered dropping everything. Over time, Stacy has realized that not only did her stepchildren "not grow up with these traditions originally," but that this stepfamily could not sustain the same closeness that she wanted: "At one time I was going to pack it all in and say to hell with it. But I decided not to, I decided just to not make a big deal about it. We give money to the kid who is having the birthday and wish them happy birthday. I'm a little more relaxed and I don't make the meals so fancy and so long. I don't expect that they're going to cut off all their social occasions. We make the dinner from 6 to 8 rather than like my family dinner, which went from 6 o'clock until midnight." Although Stacy did not set out to impose her values on her stepfamily, she later recognized how her anger stemmed from her stepchildren's unwillingness to live up to her ideal family—her own.

Expectation Six: I Get Along Well with Children

Many stepmothers enjoy being around children. When they meet their stepchildren, they are confident that the same pattern will be maintained and frequently feel blindsided by their stepchildren's guarded reactions. Running up against recalcitrant or hostile stepchildren can shake a stepmother's sense of herself and make her question her abilities and competency. Lacking an understanding of stepfamily dynamics may translate into naive expectations about relationships with stepchildren. And having biological children is not always an advantage if mothers assume that their experiences with their own children will apply to their stepchildren.

Patricia, age fifty, related a particularly dismal tale about her relationship with her teenaged stepdaughter, Amy. She had begun with very high hopes. Patricia considers herself a no-nonsense, straight-ahead kind of person. Handed a task, she will figure out how to accomplish it efficiently and with little fuss or hand-wringing. A high school English teacher for twenty-five years, she still enjoys working with adolescents. Patricia welcomed the prospect of having a girl in her life since she had only twin teenaged boys, Aidan and Bill, from her first marriage: "I like children and I get on amazingly well with my two sons. . . . My relationships with them are extremely close, and I was really quite looking forward to a girl, to mother her a bit. But it never really worked out like that. I was actually very sanguine and a lot of people said to me at the start, 'You like children and you get along so well with your own, you get on so well with all their friends.' I had always got along extremely well with the students I've taught."

When Patricia first met Jeff four years ago, Amy, then fourteen, lived with her mother and visited every second weekend. Although Amy was not friendly, initially she was not overtly hostile either. Patricia was unperturbed by Amy's lukewarm reaction as she anticipated that their relationship would strengthen over time. Although, unlike some stepmothers, she did not want to be a mother to her stepdaughter, she did imagine that they would develop a relaxed, comfortable relationship. About a year after Patricia and Jeff met, Jeff, who is a chemistry professor, was offered a position at a prestigious university in another country. Patricia was mixed about the idea of being uprooted. On the one hand, she and Jeff would have a chance to start on their own, but on the other, she was torn about leaving her job and her sons. The boys were in their last year of high school and elected to stay with their father so that they could graduate with their class. In the end, Jeff accepted the job and he and Patricia moved. The first few months after the move, Patricia was adrift. Jeff was immersed in his work, but she could not find a regular teaching position since her credentials were not recognized in the new country. With her usual determination, she set out to upgrade her qualifications.

Just as her plans were starting to get in focus and she was making new friends, she and Jeff received a late-night phone call from Amy announcing that she had had a fight with her mother and she was planning to come to live with them. Patricia's troubles began at this point. From the moment Amy moved in, she made it clear she was only interested in her father. She ignored Patricia almost completely. This was most glaring at dinner time. Amy was very adroit at engaging her father's attention, so Patricia would sit silently at the table as Amy chatted away to her father. Patricia's response was to try harder: "I thought if I keep doing my best over a long period, she will get better, and she will see that I am a real person and not just a person to be left alone in the kitchen making three-course dinners and washing them up. I felt a little bit left out because it's never been like that at all with my own children."

Patricia found herself extending herself more and more for her stepdaughter, cooking individual meals for Amy, who was a vegetarian, buying her expensive presents that she could not afford, until it dawned on her that she "was doing more work for Amy than [she'd] ever done as a mother." Although Patricia's efforts were wearying, Amy's total rejection was far more distressing. Amy deigned to notice her stepmother only when she wanted something—a drive to the mall, her skirt ironed, an advance on her allowance. Patricia felt she was being treated, as she said, "no better than a servant." She was not accustomed to this kind of contemptuous dismissal: "I've never had to face much in the way of rejection really or awkwardness either, for that matter. I've had pretty good relationships throughout my life." Patricia's conflict with Amy led her to becoming depressed and undermined her work, marriage, self-confidence, and generally optimistic take on life.

Stepmothers' unrealistic expectations are rarely challenged before they become stepmothers. One reason for this is that often they do not check with their partner to see if he has a similar vision of the new family. Perhaps because they are confident that they know what they are getting themselves into—a confidence they later describe as naiveté—they assume they and their partners have shared plans. It is a big shock if they discover their partner has other ideas about the stepfamily.

Multiple Expectations

While many stepmothers start off with one or two of these six unrealistic expectations, some are burdened with four or five. Their initial adjustment to stepmotherhood is often even more turbulent. When I met Gail, she had been married for only six months. She had embarked on her new role with numerous ideas for her new stepfamily. Perhaps because her disillusionment was still fresh, she was very articulate about how her expectations had caused, and were still causing, her to feel hurt and disregarded and had led to friction with her stepchildren and her partner, Dennis. Gail, age thirty-one, had been single for many years and was ready to settle down. Dennis, by contrast, had been married twice before and had children from both marriages—two teenagers from his first and a seven-year-old daughter from the second. Dennis was extremely cautious about making another commitment. For the four years before they married, he kept his relationship with Gail so secret that his children discovered just before the wedding that Dennis and Gail were a couple. Understandably, they were unprepared for a new stepmother and sulked throughout the wedding, particularly the older two, who already had had one stepmother. Gail had had lots of time to imagine this new family and was bursting with plans.

First, she believed she could right all wrongs and heal all miseries (Expectation Three: I Will Rescue My Stepchildren). She had set out to rescue Dennis. When they met, he had assured her that, because of his history of "failed relationships, he couldn't love, shouldn't love, had a heart of stone." Gail's reaction was "Nonsense! Nobody truly has a heart of stone, or at least not one that I couldn't soften up." Although she won Dennis's heart, she was less successful with her other project: to mend Dennis's relationship with his son, Mark. Originally, all of Dennis's children had lived part-time with him. As Mark became a teenager, he and Dennis began warring over Mark's lacklustre performance at school. When Mark shrugged off Dennis's demands that he focus on his studies, Dennis retaliated by cutting off Mark's allowance. Their relationship deteriorated to the point that Mark moved in full-time with his mother. He rarely saw his father. Gail encouraged Dennis to phone Mark, but Dennis was obdurate. Gail said, "I believe that Dennis loves his son and isn't particularly good at processing emotional experiences. . . . Occasionally I bump into issues in conversation with him. It's like I'm opening some protected boxes of information and he gets angry. Or he says things like 'Mark is no more than $400 a month to me.'" The more Gail pushed Dennis to approach Mark, the more he dug in his heels. After Dennis accused her of meddling in what she did not understand, Gail decided it was time to retreat.

Gail hit another wall when she changed household routines. She was appalled that Dennis and his children ate dinner in front of the television. In her family "mealtime was sacred, a time for discussion," and it made her "blood boil" to see them glued to the TV while they ate. Gail started cooking family dinners as a way of drawing everyone to the table (Expectation Five: This Stepfamily Will Be Just Like My Family). Dennis was receptive. Her stepchildren were not. They protested when their regular television routine was interrupted. They also objected to Gail's attempts to expand their repertoire of foods. They liked french fries and hamburgers and were not pleased to see them replaced by eggplant and pesto. Mealtimes were often stiff, a far cry from the spirited conversations Gail had anticipated.

Although Gail did not want to have children herself, she was delighted that Dennis came with three. In particular, she thought she would have the same kind of close, affectionate relationships with her stepdaughters that she had with her nieces: "I wanted them to have a daughter-like role in my life. I was very happy with the idea that Dennis came with daughters. I don't want to have children of my own, or most of me doesn't want to have children of my own, so I was really happy that he had already taken care of that part of life for me because I like having children in my life." She assumed that Dennis's children would meet her need to be around children (Expectation Four: I Will Be Fulfilled by This Stepfamily). Mixed into this projection was Gail's belief that she would have the same kind of relaxed and fun relationships with Dennis's children that she had with her many nieces and nephews (Expectation Six: I Get Along Well with Children): "I had this notion that children were automatically loved and would automatically love me, because children do that. I'm very easy with children. But this is just a whole different situation. . . . This assumption led to behaviours on my part that the [stepchildren] should be a certain way with me and they're not."

Very quickly, Gail realized that not only did her stepchildren not love her, but they considered her an alien in their family. Her new meal regime did not win her any allies, and whenever Gail proposed an activity with her stepdaughters, she was politely, but definitely, turned down. Her inability to make any headway with her stepchildren was distressing because Gail had assumed that they all would be close (Expectation One: No Friction, No Tensions, No Stresses: My Stepfamily Will Instantly Be a Happy Family). Gail spends a huge amount of time with her family and she envisioned her stepfamily being the same way.

Most upsetting, though, was discovering that Dennis also did not view them as a family. Like many stepmothers, Gail had assumed she and Dennis had the same ideals. Gail had been planning a big family Christmas dinner for both hers and Dennis's extended families. Dennis had shrugged off her attempts to discuss this. One conversation erupted into an argument with Dennis yelling, "We're not a family. You can think of us as a family if you want, but we're not a family." Gail was devastated. Her reaction helped her become aware of how she had built up an idealized image: "[I felt] horrible because I've been infused with family from my family of origin. I didn't even realize I was so full of this notion of family. I felt like I had lost a husband, I felt like I lost a daughter, I felt like I lost that sense of family as a safe place."

Gail could not even get sympathy from her own family, because they assumed, as she had, that Gail's stepfamily was like their family. When Gail's teenaged stepdaughter, Melinda, was deliberately rude to Gail at a family party, Gail's sister advised Gail to lay down the law: "My sister would say things like 'What Melinda needs is . . .' Because she would have some notion about how she'd shape one of her kids up if they treated her the way Melinda treats me. . . . Then I would have to explain that I'm not her mother and I can't do those things." Gail's mother gave her similar lectures. Rather than getting the support she craved, her family's lack of understanding meant that Gail had to educate them, as well as herself, about stepfamily dynamics. She felt more and more isolated.

Although Gail had been confident when she first married, six months later when we talked, she recognized how her well-meant, but misguided, assumptions about Dennis and his children had impeded her integration into this new stepfamily. In part, she attributed her difficulties to a lack of direct experience: "I didn't have any material to draw from. There aren't any stepfamilies in my family." Becoming a stepmother forced Gail to confront many of her unquestioned beliefs about families. She thought she perceived this family accurately but really she was looking at reflections of her projected ideas. When Dennis denied they were a family, her stepchildren complained about eating at the dining room table, or her stepdaughter stepped away from Gail's hug, these mirrored images started to splinter: "Some of the hardest points in this whole process were my notions of what family is. I would project on big mirrors, huge mirrors, and I didn't even know I had these mirrors in my mind. The mirror would crash, and it was devastating."

Gail is beginning to acknowledge that this family's patterns and customs may have some value. To her stepchildren's surprise, recently she was the one to suggest they order a pizza. She now sees how television draws this family together, that conversation takes place while watching TV: "We'll order a pizza and watch a video together. And those things all come together, the video, the food, the television, because it's a kind of bonding point."

Not all stepmothers' experiences are as crushing as Gail's. Some do realize their initial expectations—their relationships with their stepchildren are loving and close from the start and their stepchildren and partners welcome being rescued. Most discover, however, that they are ill-prepared for stepfamily life. One of their biggest stumbling blocks is faulty expectations. They believe they know what they are getting themselves into, but their plans and beliefs are based on erroneous or incomplete information. Except for stepmothers who grew up in a stepfamily, stepmothers rarely look to existing stepfamilies as a source of information. Instead, they draw on their childhood experience, which, for most of them, was in a nuclear, non-divorced family. They want to be successful, but arming themselves with unrealistic ambitions often means their efforts are thwarted. The resulting disillusionment can be shattering.

Chapter 3

Motherhood: The Impossible Ideal

The wicked stepmother is not the only image looming over stepmothers. They also have to contend with the ideal of the good mother. While this image is apparently more benign, its effect on stepmothers can be as pernicious. Mothers, motherhood, and mothering were constant themes in my discussions with stepmothers. A number referred to their name as an indication of their role, that they should "step into a mother's shoes." According to the Oxford English Dictionary, however, "stepmother" derives from old English and means "one who becomes a mother to an orphan." Almost half the stepmothers I talked with believed that a good stepmother should be the same as a good mother. Even if they did not equate good stepmothering with good mothering, they drew on ideas of motherhood to form their ideal stepmother. For instance, some thought they should care for their stepchildren as they would for their own children. Their responses were puzzling to me, because only a handful actually believed that they could ever replace their stepchildren's mother.[1] On the contrary, they often went to considerable lengths to avoid usurping the mothers' position.

This discrepancy between the ideal of motherhood and the actual experience of stepmothers creates tension and dissonance for many stepmothers. Their inability to attain this impossible goal leads some stepmothers to feel ashamed or guilty and to view themselves as failures. In this chapter, I examine the heavy weight of the good mother on stepmothers.

A Saint

Despite all the changes in Western women's lives over the last fifty years, motherhood is still considered the most positive role for women. Whether or not they have children, in our culture, all women have to contend with the idea of the good mother. Women without children often feel stigmatized as deficient, deviant, or selfish.[2] We consider maternal love so basic that we call it a natural instinct. Even though many writers have refuted this notion of a maternal instinct, it continues to dominate our thinking.[3] Mothers who are abusive or neglectful are often judged more harshly than fathers who act similarly.[4] In our current ways of thinking, good mothers are supposed to be completely available to their children. They should be loving and giving, respond completely to their children's emotional and physical needs, and place their children's needs ahead of their own. They are also responsible for shaping their children's achievement and behaviour. Middle-class mothers are expected to provide constant creative and educational opportunities to maximize their children's potential. Mothers are also held accountable for problems their children may have. If a child is rude or emotionally troubled, this will frequently be attributed to poor mothering. Often this blaming has more to do with notions of what mothers *should* do rather than being based on any evidence. Until recently, for instance, mothers were thought to cause schizophrenia and autism in their children.

The mother's needs are totally absent in this model. Her desires are supposed to have been subsumed into her children, and she is expected to feel completely fulfilled by her mothering. Resentful, angry, or even ambivalent feelings toward children are not permitted. It is as though motherhood strips women of negative emotions. Even if her child hurls objects at her and screams "I hate you, I hate you," the mother is supposed to remain loving and accepting. This image of the good mother exerts huge pressure, not only on actual mothers, but on many stepmothers who feel they should aspire to the same self-sacrifice and devotion.

The Martyr

Most of the stepmothers I talked to had adopted the conventional idea of the good mother. They described good mothers as emotionally available and supportive, nurturing, providing physical care, offering educational opportunities and moral direction, and loving their children unconditionally. Only a handful referred to any needs a mother might have. This ideal is pretty much unattainable for biological mothers. For stepmothers, it is even more unfeasible. One reason is that the rewards of motherhood are frequently absent. Mothers are often sustained through taxing times with their children by the affection and love that is, or has been, present between them and their children. If they daily face a sullen teenager, they can recall the sunny three-year-old who pressed on them innumerable hugs and kisses. Particularly at the beginning, stepmothers cannot draw on a store of positive memories to counterbalance the scowls.

Some stepmothers put themselves in the untenable position of a martyr—trying to be a good mother without expecting anything in return. In Chapter 1, you met Maddy, who felt guilty about arranging a weekend off from caring for her stepdaughter, Jane. Recently Jane's mother has been pressuring Jane to move back in with her. Maddy, who is very attached to Jane and who has invested a huge amount of time caring for her, is upset about this, but she feels she has no right to these feelings: "A good stepmother is the same thing [as a good mother] except that a really good stepmother would be able to accept the other mother and wouldn't need anything back from the child. If Jane wanted to spend time with her mother, that would be okay, and if Jane wanted to stay with us, that would be okay too." This sounds a lot like Hildur, the good stepmother in the Icelandic tale. While not

41

all stepmothers demand so much of themselves, most assume at least one aspect of a mothering role, either acting like a mother, feeling like a mother, or conforming to others' expectations of mothering.

Acting Like a Mother

Maternal work is multi-faceted. It often encompasses the *physical* chores of cleaning, shopping, and preparing meals; the *emotional* work of attending to everyone's needs—for instance, comforting children after a nightmare; the *organizational* responsibility of making sure the household runs smoothly—for instance, that children have regular dental visits; and what has been called the *kinship* work of keeping family members connected through, for instance, holiday celebrations.[5]

Stepmothers usually assume at least some of these responsibilities. Most often they do the bulk of the physical work, whether it is cooking or laundry or housecleaning, but some take on all four facets of the household.[6] Even stepmothers who consciously reject the mother role usually do some domestic work. You might expect stepmothers to be resentful or to question why they are doing so much. On the contrary, most seem to accept these duties as part of their job. Their motivations for taking on the household are complex. Many slip into this role without any forethought. It feels natural to them. When I asked these women how they felt about being responsible for running the household, they often seemed taken aback, as though it never occurred to them that their partners could do more. Others throw themselves into the domestic realm more consciously, both because they enjoy it and it gives them a place in the family. In the previous chapter, I described Paulette's disappointment at her stepchildren's negative response to her efforts. This was in part because her domestic accomplishments are a big part of her identity: "To me it's important to be a homemaker. I think the home should be a place where no matter what happens out there in the run of the day, it's a retreat to come home. It's pleasant. It's somewhere that they can feel warm and protected. That's my goal as a mother, to make a good home."

Other stepmothers step in because the domestic situation is chaotic and they believe someone needs to take charge. Their partners are unable or unwilling to organize the household and the stepmothers believe the children are suffering. Often these women are rescuers. Betsy, age thirty-four, has always sought out challenges. She plays squash competitively and, as an engineer, has been successful in the male-dominated arena of construction. When she fell in love with Mick three years ago, she did not hesitate about plunging into a relationship with a man who had three children, even though many of Mick's friends took her aside and warned her that his children were spoiled, lazy, and undisciplined. At the time she met Alasdair, Olivia, and Simon, they were thirteen, twelve, and seven. Mick and his ex-wife, Angela, had separated two years before that, and he had stayed in the family house while she moved into a new condo. The children shuttled back and forth between their parents' houses.

Mick warned Betsy that housework was not his forte, but she was still left open-mouthed by the mess she encountered on her first visit to the house: "The family room, you couldn't even open the doors any more there was so much junk that had accumulated over the years. The living room, you couldn't see the couch. You could only see this two-foot piece of carpet. The rest was covered with newspapers and clothes, dishes and just junk. It was absolutely disgusting." Both Mick and his ex-wife were pack rats. Since they had moved into the house thirteen years earlier, every child's drawing, every broken toy, all the children's baby clothes had been saved and stored in the basement.

Betsy, by contrast, is a compulsive organizer and cannot abide clutter. She knew that she could not live in this disorder. Before she moved in, she swept through the house like a cyclone, pitching out boxes and boxes of papers, odd socks, and old junk. She scrubbed the entire house and set up a schedule for the house with weekly chores for all three children. Although Betsy's stepchildren appreciated the regular meals and clean clothes, they grumbled about having to clean their rooms before they received their weekly allowance. Betsy was astonished that Mick was incapable of being consistent with his children. He would tell them to pick up their clothes and dirty dishes off the floor, but if they objected or left their belongings lying around, he would not confront them. He would either step around the mess or pick up after them. The complete disarray that Betsy witnessed on her first visit was the consequence of Mick's inability to establish clear rules and routines with his children.

How much a stepmother does around the house often depends on her partner's willingness to be involved. Sometimes stepmothers, like Martha, whose partner's job meant he was often away three or four days a week, are landed with the household work because their partners are not around. Other times their partners gradually hand over their responsibilities and the division of labour becomes more and more unequal. Some stepmothers are unhappy with this imbalance. For instance, in retrospect, Martha believes that she and Wilf too readily fell into traditional male and female roles: "There's no question that I was an overfunctioner. I was taking far more responsibility for the household than I should have. And Wilf let me do that because, I think a lot of men let women do that. If [women are] going to do it, then [men] won't." Most stepmothers, however, do not expect their partners to be equal participants around the house. Martha came to this insight only after a therapist pointed out how little Wilf contributed, even though three of the four children in the house were his.

Stepmothers' frustrations about "acting like a mother" relate less to the actual labour involved and more to feeling their work is not acknowledged or that others are hindering their ability to do it. Although some find the extra responsibilities wearing and onerous, most want the opportunity to care for their stepchildren. It is upsetting if their efforts fall on stony ground. As we saw in the previous chapter, Paulette wanted to create a home for her stepchildren, something she felt their mother had not done. Before she met Richard, she already knew Richard's son, Scott, well through his friendship with her son, Anthony. Paulette expected she would become closer with Scott after she and Richard married, but, paradoxically, Scott pulled away and became more distant. Her stepchildren's lack of appreciation was baffling and disappointing. Richard's youngest child, Tammy, was twelve when Paulette came on the scene. Paulette knew that Tammy had been babysitting herself after school since she was eight, so Paulette made an effort to be home every day when Tammy finished school. Just as she had with her own children, Paulette made breakfast and lunch for Tammy each morning and drove her to school. While Paulette did not expect elaborate thanks, she was accustomed to an occasional "Thanks, Mum" from her own children. Tammy gave nothing. After Richard talked to Tammy about this, Tammy acknowledged that she resented her stepmother. While, on one level, Tammy knew Paulette was doing a lot for her, she told her father that Paulette sometimes "irritated" her. Paulette was upset: "When I realized that she had resentments and she didn't appreciate the things I was doing, it really hurt." Although Paulette can now understand how Tammy's loyalty to her mother complicates her response to Paulette, she still feels "terrible that I haven't been successful in what I tried to accomplish."

The other big stumbling block to acting like a mother is not having enough authority. This is a huge issue for stepmothers, and we will look at it in more detail in Chapter 5. While a stepmother might be doing a mother's work, usually she does not have a mother's clout. She might be preparing dinner every night, but will have no say over whether her stepchildren arrive home in time to eat it. If, like Martha, a stepmother is left to run the household because her partner is absent, she may be in the unenviable position of telling her stepchildren to do chores when her right to enforce them has not been established.

Stepmothers also feel that others sometimes hinder their ability to run the household. Their partners, the biological mothers, or even their in-laws will overturn the stepmothers' plans without consultation. A stepmother may organize a family dinner, only to have the mother claim her rights and whisk the children off to her parents'. All this often leaves stepmothers feeling undermined. They may feel their powerlessness more acutely in the domestic realm, because this traditionally is women's realm. Their inability to direct the household highlights the tenuous nature of their position.

Acting like a mother generally presents less of a conflict for stepmothers than trying to feel like a mother or living up to others' expectations regarding mothering. When their efforts are appreciated, they often feel a great deal of satisfaction. Betsy took pleasure in seeing the house take shape, and she was delighted when her youngest stepson, Simon, confided that he liked coming home to a tidier house. Taking on the domestic responsibility also allows them to claim a place for themselves and to have some control. Like Betsy, they can put their stamp on the household by throwing out all the clutter. They may have to live with never hearing "thank you" from their stepchildren, but at least they can cook meals that they like to eat. Over the long term, however, stepmothers like Betsy, Martha, and Paulette realize that they have tried to do too much too soon. As we will see in Part Three, stepmothers often learn to step back.

Feeling Like a Mother: A Double Bind

Believing that they should *feel* like a mother leads stepmothers into two deep pits. On the one hand, some stepmothers interpret this as a requirement that they love their stepchildren as a mother loves her children. If they cannot achieve this, they feel guilty. On the other hand, stepmothers who do feel like mothers to their stepchildren become distressed when they discover they can never become their stepchildren's actual mother.

Some stepmothers believe that good stepmothers must feel maternal love for their stepchildren. As we saw in the previous chapter, they assume that, because they love their partners, they will automatically love their stepchildren. When I asked these women what a stepmother should do if this love does not emerge naturally, some suggested that she should just try a little harder: "I really think you can learn to love them . . . over the years, and the way you do things, the way you treat them. I think you can." They do not question whether it is possible to make yourself love someone who does not love you and may even hate you. The responsibility for loving rests with the stepmother.

Some stepmothers up the ante. They aspire to feel the same love for their stepchildren as they have for their children. This creates an even wider gap between their ideal and the reality of their situation, because none of the stepmothers I talked to ever said that they loved their stepchildren exactly the same way they loved their children. And why should they? They have borne their children, been with them since birth, and been able to direct their values and behaviour to a great extent. They inherit their stepchildren. These children already have a history, may have very different values and habits from the stepmother, and may act with suspicion, hostility, or wariness, particularly at the beginning. Nevertheless, their inability to attain this ideal causes some stepmothers considerable anguish.

Tina epitomizes the devoted stepmother and has acted like Caterina's mother in every possible way. From the first time Tina saw her future stepdaughter, she was drawn to her. Tina, then age twenty-nine, worked in the daycare that Caterina attended. Although Caterina was a lovely-looking little three-year-old, she often was bedraggled and ill-kempt. Caterina's parents shared custody and she alternated houses on a daily basis. The constant switching made for chaos. Caterina would arrive at daycare without her coat or mitts because they had been forgotten at the other parent's house. Often she was still eating breakfast as one of her parents hustled her into daycare. Tina had great sympathy for Caterina's father, Jake, who was obviously very attached to his daughter but not managing well. By contrast, Tina had nothing but scorn for Caterina's mother, Beth, who would breeze in airily to the daycare, often the last parent to pick up her child.

Tina believed that Caterina needed a full-time mother at home: "She needed a mummy and I was going to be it!" Neither of Caterina's parents were interested: Beth had no intention of putting her career as a travel consultant on hold, and the option of Jake staying home was never considered. It was Tina who left her job and discontinued her university studies in early childhood education to care for Caterina. Tina is a devout Christian and believes that divorce is not just morally wrong but harmful to children. Jake and Beth had split up, at Beth's instigation, when Caterina was one and a half. It was unfathomable to Tina that a mother would do this to her child. Tina believed Caterina suffered from her parents' divorce and from the subsequent upheaval.

Tina set out to right all wrongs. She was convinced that Caterina's development has been hindered by the lack of regularity, and she called on her studies in early childhood education to help Caterina catch up. Unlike some stepmothers, Tina had everyone's support. Jake was delighted to have Tina relieve him of all his domestic responsibilities. Beth was busy with her career and appreciated the new flexibility she had. Jake's parents, also strong Christians, had been critical of Beth's cavalier attitude and were thrilled with Tina. Tina had felt protective toward Caterina since they first met at the daycare and this rapidly segued into a mother-daughter relationship. Tina considered herself Caterina's mother and Caterina reciprocated by calling her "Mummy" (to distinguish her from her biological mother, whom she referred to as "Mama").

Six months ago, Tina and Jake's daughter, Hannah, was born. On the surface everything appeared perfect. Jake and Tina had wanted to have a child together and now had a beautiful baby. Caterina, now age five, was excited about the new baby and showed no signs of jealousy. Tina was already at home so there were few domestic adjustments to make. The snag was Tina: "I sat down in tears at the end of the first week of being home, because I knew that I felt differently about Hannah. And I was scared to death that Caterina would know. Even that Jake would notice it." Tina felt an immediate bond with, and connection to, Hannah that she did not experience with Caterina. Ashamed of her reaction, Tina attempted to bury it. She was determined to be a mother to both girls and she did not consider it acceptable to have stronger feelings for her biological daughter than for her stepdaughter. Now, half a year later, Tina has not resolved the issue. Although she can logically explain the intensity of her attachment to Hannah—the intimacy of breastfeeding Hannah, the fact that she does not have to share Hannah with another mother, and that Hannah does not have any of Caterina's quirks—Tina still believes she should love Caterina and Hannah identically.

Tina is afraid that Caterina will perceive this: "I don't ever want to treat Caterina differently. I don't want to feel differently about Caterina. It bothers me, because I don't want her to ever pick up on it, think that she's not as good as Hannah, or whatever, or Mummy doesn't love her as much." Tina has not told anyone else her guilty secret because she fears being judged as harshly as she judges herself. One reason she volunteered for my study was to find out if other stepmothers experience this tension as well.

Rather than accepting that their feelings for a child they have borne and cared for since birth will likely be different than those for a child whom they have inherited and share with another mother, some stepmothers, like Tina, torture themselves. The motherhood imperative ensnares them, making them believe that their care, attention, and affection for their stepchildren counts for nothing if it is not underpinned by maternal love.

Stepmothers who do feel like mothers toward their stepchildren often confront the opposite problem when they discover that they can never *become* their stepchildren's mother. No matter how much they may love their stepchildren, the final step is blocked. The barrier is the biological mother. Even if the mother is dead or out of the picture, she is a presence to her children. This can be a painful realization for some stepmothers. They have fallen in love with their stepchildren and want to be their mother and then become aware that their stepchildren will never reciprocate. Although childless stepmothers usually feel this split more intensely, stepmothers with biological children can also experience it. Beata has both a ten-year-old son, Michael, and a twenty-two-year-old stepdaughter, Zoe, to whom she is extraordinarily close. Before Zoe went away to university, she lived with Beata and her partner for seven years. Beata is Zoe's confidante, and Zoe will call her before she contacts either of her parents. The conditional nature of their relationship became apparent recently, however. Zoe is engaged and has started planning her wedding. Anna, Zoe's mother, has been an on-again, off-again parent, but has taken over the wedding preparations. Beata has been shunted to the sidelines. When I asked her what has been most difficult for her as a step-mother, she replied, "The hardest thing? Probably that, as much as I'm expected to be a mother and to give the love and everything of a mother, I'm not the mother. It's a replacement role or a fill-in role. When push comes to shove, Anna's her mother, not me. Zoe may love me as a mother, and respect me as a mother. I know she does. But the bottom line is—Anna's the mother." Beata has not told anyone that she is upset, because she doesn't feel she has the right: "[I feel] hurt. But I think unrealistically so. I mean I know I'm not her mother. It's just that when you put so much into a relationship, it's hard." Here we have another stepmother strug-gling with the martyr syndrome: she should give and give without expecting anything in return. Trying to feel like a mother is dou-ble-edged for stepmothers: either they feel guilty for not loving their stepchildren as a mother, or if they can make this commitment, they discover its impossibility.

Others' Expectations about Mothering

Stepmothers also face outside pressures to mother their stepchildren. Their partners, stepchildren, in-laws, friends, family, total strangers, and even their partners' ex-wives assume that—as women—they will *naturally* feel maternally toward their stepchildren. If everyone in the stepfamily shares this aspiration, the stepfamily usually looks a lot like a nuclear family. This kind of unanimity is unusual. More often, expectations clash. Either the stepmother wants to be a mother but runs into resistance from others or she does not want to be a mother but feels pushed into it. In the latter case, stepmothers usually feel guilty. Martha, the "wicked stepmother," felt enormous pressure from outside. This did not come from her partner or stepchildren, but from people who were more removed, her in-laws, friends, and even some professionals: "Because [my stepchildren's] mother had died, I think it was more natural for people to assume, as I did, that I should play the mother role. My daughter, Sarah, still had a father, so Wilf didn't need to be a father to her. I think if these kids still had a mother, I wouldn't have felt so much pressure." Martha's belief that she should love her stepchildren, coupled with her friends' advice, intensified her shame: "I felt pressure from inside me, but also I had friends who said to me, 'Martha, you just need to love them more, you need to mother them more.' . . . They'd all talk about these poor innocent things who were so hurt by their mother's death. I just felt like the worst thing that was walking the face of the earth. It was hell." Worrying that they will appear unfeeling and horrible, stepmothers often shrink from admitting that they do not want to become mothers to their stepchildren.

I Thought I Could Be the Good Mother

Julie is a stepmother for whom the image of motherhood has created many complications and conflicts, both self-inflicted and imposed from outside. She is now so furious at her partner, Gordon, that she is contemplating leaving her marriage. Looking back, Julie could never have imagined that things would sour so badly. Julie met Gordon six years ago. One of the reasons she was attracted to him was his daughter, Rachel, then age six: "She came tumbling down the stairs, a beautiful little girl—she's absolutely stunning . . . and a nice, nice little girl." At twenty-five, Julie was ready to start her own family. Gordon's devotion to Rachel suggested to Julie that he would be an excellent father. Rachel symbolized the first step in building their family.

Julie also felt a lot of compassion for Rachel, whose early childhood had been bumpy. Gordon had been in a casual relationship with Rachel's mother, Melanie, when she became pregnant and they had never lived together. Melanie was only seventeen when Rachel was born and unwilling to settle down. She drifted through a series of relationships, never stayed at a job for more than two or three months, and Gordon suspected she had a serious drug problem. Gordon, on the other hand, poured all his energy into starting up a computer graphics business. Rachel lived with her mother, seeing her father on weekends. Clear signs that Rachel was being neglected started to emerge. Rachel's school contacted Gordon because she had missed two months of kindergarten. More than a few times, Gordon would drop by Melanie's and find Rachel, then age five, home alone during the evening. Gordon petitioned to gain full custody but was unsuccessful.

Gordon's parents had never approved of Melanie and had tried to pressure Melanie to have an abortion when she became pregnant. Melanie's lifestyle alarmed them. They tried to compensate by taking a special interest in their granddaughter, having her at their cottage for a month in the summers and making sure she had decent clothes to wear. They pushed Gordon to redouble his efforts to get full custody of Rachel.

Four years ago Julie and Gordon had their first child, Tyler. A month after the baby was born, the situation with Melanie exploded. She and her then boyfriend were arrested for drug trafficking, and it became apparent that Melanie was addicted to heroin. Rachel, then age eight, was first taken into care by Social Services and then handed over to her father. Julie welcomed her stepdaughter's arrival. She had worked with troubled adolescents and believed she could turn things around for Rachel. Quickly Julie realized she had underestimated the challenges of caring for a newborn and an eight-year-old who missed her mother and was bewildered and frightened by the rapid changes in her life. Julie and Gordon discovered that Rachel was more troubled than they had imagined: "She had seen an awful lot of rotten stuff. She couldn't go through a day in school, she couldn't sit in a class. She'd never had to do homework at home, never had rules to follow, she didn't have any discipline. So she needed her hand held, to be taken to school. The school was in constant contact because of behaviour problems."

Although Gordon was happy to have custody of Rachel, he did not intend to alter his life at all: "He thought I would take over." His attitude was "I want this daughter, but I brought this daughter in for my wife to take care of and raise and do everything, while I go off and work fourteen-, sixteen-, eighteen-hour days." Since Gordon left for work before the children woke up and often returned after they were in bed, Julie was left in charge of everything, from the daily care of the children, to meeting with Rachel's teachers, attending the school concerts, and organizing the children's birthdays. Two years ago Julie and Gordon's daughter, Esmé, was born, and Julie returned to work as an administrative assistant in a government office.

As a working mother with three children, Julie feels exhausted most of the time. Yet she is happy to care for Rachel as she feels

Rachel needs the stability. What upsets her is Gordon's refusal to recognize her efforts: "I feel I should have a pat on the back once in a while, be told, 'Hey, you're terrific, I love you. I think it's great you're doing all this for my daughter. Too bad I can't.'" Instead, she gets "scrutinized, questioned, if I discipline her." It is not just Gordon who monitors Julie, but her in-laws as well. Having been very involved with Rachel since she was little, they feel they can wade in with their opinions. Although Julie is expected to act like Rachel's mother, she is not granted the authority. At family dinners, her mother-in-law will quiz Julie about her handling of various issues while Rachel is sitting there listening. Rachel, now age twelve, has, not surprisingly, become skilled at playing Julie off against her father, grandmother, and mother. Rachel's mother was released from prison a year ago. She went through a drug rehabilitation program and is turning her life around. Recently Rachel arrived home from her mother's with a new lipstick. When Julie told Rachel she could not wear it to school, Rachel immediately got on the phone to complain, first to her mother and then to her father that Julie was "yelling at her and being mean." Gordon overruled Julie and Rachel now wears lipstick to school.

Julie contrasts this to the situation with her biological children: "No one questions what I do with Tyler and Esmé. No one would cross me. I certainly take criticism, but no one's going to talk about my parenting skills while Tyler and Esmé are sitting at the dinner table." As a biological mother, her authority is unassailable. As a stepmother, she is fair game. Rachel's reactions and behaviours also feel alien to her in a way that her own children's do not. Conflict between Julie and Rachel has worsened, and school is the major battleground. Rachel's attention problems have continued and she has been suspended twice this year, for forging Julie's signature on her report card and for physically attacking another girl. Julie finds the constant calls from the school wearing and humiliating: "I find it increasingly difficult to deal with her problems at school, because I don't see any similarities in her and myself. As a student at school, I was always trying to excel and do well." Julie wonders if part of the friction stems from her trying to instill values that clash with Rachel's early upbringing. "We didn't raise Rachel. So much of your upbringing is in those first few years and we weren't there for that. . . . I always say, 'Well, if she was my child, she wouldn't be acting this way,' even though my kids might turn out a hundred times worse!"

Julie worries she is beginning to "look like Cinderella's stepmother." Julie knows that her standards are high but her rules are equally strict for Rachel and for Tyler and Esmé. As Rachel inches closer to adolescence, she is balking at Julie's regime. For her part, Julie is wearying of the constant struggles. "I'm beginning not to like her very much, unfortunately, and she's beginning not to like me very much because I am the heavy." The rare times Gordon is around, he is the indulgent father. Rachel has also developed a renewed closeness with her mother: "They have a very wonderful relationship now, which I am getting jealous of, because that should have been our relationship if we were still on the weekend thing. Melanie's not the real mum any more. The roles have reversed."

As if all this were not complicated enough, Julie castigates herself for not *feeling* like a mother as well. When Julie first met Rachel, she believed that she "loved Rachel and that I could feel the same way about her [as toward my biological children]. I really felt all those things. The day Tyler was born, I knew that wasn't right. That I couldn't." Like Tina, Julie feels guilty about this and believes that she must be wicked for not loving Rachel unconditionally. She has been reluctant to reveal this to anyone, even to her family, who is very supportive, because she worries how they will perceive her.

Recognizing that her relationship with Rachel is deteriorating, Julie is taking a new tack. She is extricating herself from the maternal role and encouraging Rachel to spend more time with her mother. Although she feels jealous of Rachel and Melanie's new closeness, she hopes that Melanie can offer Rachel the nurturing and love that has become so complicated with Julie. Rachel has responded enthusiastically, but Gordon is furious with Julie: "[He] has real mixed feelings toward [Rachel's] mother and feels she's still a negative influence. . . . I don't think they've ever resolved their problems, or ever will. He just hates her and he will never see any good in her." Although he is unwilling to take more responsibility for his daughter, he wants Julie to continue as before. A few days before Julie's interview with me, she tried to convince Gordon that the status quo was impossible. Her proposal was that either Melanie assume greater responsibility for Rachel, or that Gordon, Julie, and Melanie jointly agree "on some kind of parenting style or some rules that we're all going to stick by, so there's some kind of uniformity." When Gordon refused to consider either option, Julie became enraged. Their discussion erupted into a huge row, and there has been a frigid silence between them since then.

Julie recognizes that the situation has to change. Although initially she could act as Rachel's mother, neither she nor Rachel are comfortable with that now. At present, Julie cannot envision a positive relationship to replace their current one. She still struggles with what it means to be a good stepmother: "A good stepmother is someone who is able to treat the child the same as her own children. Oh dear, I want to say she feels the same way about her stepchildren as her other children. I think that's right, but I don't know if that's possible, because I don't feel like that."

Motherhood casts a long shadow over stepmothers. Both stepmothers who embrace it and those who don't feel its influence. Underpinning this mandated role is the assumption that women are naturally maternal and loving with children. The reality is different. We cannot command love at will. There needs to be an environment in which it can grow. As we will see, some stepmothers do manage to sidestep the trap of motherhood, but for many, the ideal of the loving mother becomes a heavy and painful burden.

Chapter 4

Who's the Real Mother in This Family?
Dealing with the "Ex"

Fairy tales would lead you to believe that the stepmother-stepchild relationship is the most vexed relationship in the stepfamily. I found something quite different. Although stepmothers have much less direct contact with their partners' ex-wives than with their stepchildren, they often consider ex-wives a much bigger irritant in their lives. In many ways, the stepmother-mother relationship is the most fraught and complex of all relationships in the stepfamily. In this chapter, I explain why this is the case.

When Hillary thinks about her partner Stefan's ex-wife, Marika, she starts to fume. Hillary, now age forty-six, has been a stepmother for two years. Before she met Stefan, also age forty-six, she had lived on her own, following her divorce eight years earlier. As a single, childless woman, Hillary found that stepmotherhood demanded many adjustments. Marika has been the biggest challenge. It is not that there is any direct hostility: "The only contact I ever have with her is when she phones. Every time, she says, 'Hello Hillary, this is Marika speaking,' and she says it in a very formal way as if she's got to reintroduce herself every time. Then she asks to speak to the kids. We basically have no relationship."

What annoys Hillary is that Marika has the "power and control." Marika and Stefan have joint custody and the two children—Emily, age thirteen, and Peter, age ten—live half-time with each parent. Technically, the two parents should have an equal voice, but Marika sets the agenda: "It was clear in their interactions when I met them that she saw herself as *the* parent. Stefan was the money-maker—he would give her money. She didn't want him more involved with the children. She felt she was capable of making all the decisions about their lives."

At the time Hillary arrived on the scene, Marika would make decisions without consulting Stefan. Hillary and Stefan would then have to live with the consequences. During Hillary's first summer as a stepmother, Marika enrolled Peter in an intensive, and expensive, hockey camp. Although she did not discuss this plan with Stefan and Hillary, they were expected to foot the bill and also to drive Peter all over the city for his games. While Hillary supported Peter's enthusiasm for hockey, she was annoyed at Marika's high-handed behaviour.

Stefan's passivity in relation to his ex-wife also annoys her. Hillary wants him to stand up to Marika, but he tends to acquiesce to whatever Marika proposes. Hillary considers herself an excellent organizer and resents that Marika tries to direct her too. Much to her chagrin, Hillary found herself deferring to Marika. Hillary had offered to take Emily school shopping. She suggested that Emily first check with her mother in case Marika already had plans. When Marika vetoed the outing for no apparent reason, Hillary was furious. Emily had finally shown a flicker of interest in doing something with her and Hillary hoped she was making headway. Hillary was also annoyed at herself: "After I had talked to Emily about that, I realized I really only needed to check with Stefan because he's a co-parent, but I somehow viewed the mother as having this sort of all-powerful control over the children."

For Hillary, this aborted shopping trip symbolized how Marika has blocked Hillary's relationships with her stepchildren. With Marika as the central figure, it has been hard for Hillary to carve out her place. Peter and Emily listen to their mother first, their father trails a distant second, and Hillary is not even in the race. There has been much discussion, without any resolution, about what Hillary should be called. Hillary considers herself their stepmother. The other three resist this. If pressed to explain who she is to their friends, the children refer to her as Daddy's girlfriend. But they also confided to their father that they don't know what to call her. Stefan is also ambivalent on the subject. Hillary says, "I feel as if they're all saying to me, the kids have one mother and they can't have any other person in their lives with the designation 'mother' in it. . . . Stefan will agree that I am, quote 'parent,' but he really objects to the designation of stepmother or mother of any sort. . . . He says that it's hard to define, that because the kids have a mother, I can't also be called a mother." Hillary is frustrated, because she is already doing a lot of "mothering" things—"all the way from any nurturing things I do, to the interest I show, to being involved in their activities, to disciplining them, to worrying about them, to discussing them with Stefan, to spending money on them." Her lack of a title accentuates the tenuous nature of her position in this stepfamily.

Hillary sometimes wonders how she got into this situation. While she knows that she tends to want to arrange things her way, before she met Stefan, she considered herself a reasonable person. Now she often feels like a petulant child, demanding constant attention, or like a virago, nagging Stefan into appreciating her perspective. Hillary feels pulled into a rivalry with Marika: "I feel in a constant state of competition with their mother. Whether I want to be or not, I feel that it's just kind of part of the landscape of a stepfamily. . . . I'm always trying to catch up to a place that I can never catch up to." Hillary knows this contest is futile because she can never win. She also feels ashamed: "You say to yourself, 'I'm an adult, so why should I be jealous of this other woman who is the mother, the parent? What right do I have to see myself as in the same league as her?' "

Hillary believes that Marika also feels competitive with her and obstructs Hillary's relationships with Peter and Emily because she feels threatened. A recent situation confirmed Hillary's suspicion. Hillary has taught English as a Second Language to international students for the last twenty years. She was startled to hear that

Marika has embarked on the same path. "When Peter told me she was training to be a second language teacher, I could feel my blood pressure go up about thirty points. . . . The first year I met Stefan there was certainly no talk of her working in ESL!"

To add salt to her wounds, Hillary is unimpressed with Marika's parenting. Stefan and Marika had agreed that it was important for Marika to stay home with the children while they were young. Marika "holds herself up to be this really involved, wonderful person," but Hillary views her as selfish, and believes that Marika places her own interests ahead of her children's: "She's become increasing less available to the children because she's doing all this studying. They're alone Monday, Tuesday, and Thursday nights, and they're with us Wednesday night. It makes me so angry. She's got all day to go to classes, why does she go in the evening?" Marika is often not available on weekends as well, because she attends yoga workshops then.

Although most mothers do not adopt the same career as the stepmother, Hillary's story is not atypical. Her feelings of illegitimacy, jealousy, impotence, competition, and frustration are common reactions to their stepchildren's mother. Many consider their partner's ex-wife their biggest challenge, sometimes even when they have little actual contact with her. Some stepmothers believe that life would improve if the mother would just fade away or even die: "If we could just get rid of her, everything would be great. She has thrown a wrench into the situation. I would like just Randy [my partner] and Stevie [my stepson]. It would make life so much easier also for Stevie, he wouldn't have to deal with this. But, oh, what a thing to say! . . . Ultimately—and I'm being very honest about this—I really wish Mary [his ex-wife] didn't exist."

Why Is the Stepmother-Mother Relationship So Vexed?

At first I attributed the animosity between stepmothers and ex-wives to some stepmothers being stuck with particularly cantankerous first wives. They described their partners' ex-wives as emotionally unstable, manic depressive, depressed, unfit, abusive, or as selfish and self-absorbed. It does appear that some stepmothers are encumbered with ex-wives who delight in making the stepmother's life miserable or whose psychological problems create many headaches for the stepfamily.

There are other stepmothers, however, who contend with equally difficult mothers and feel compassion, rather than anger or resentment, toward these women. Julie, whose story I told in the last chapter, has a lot of admiration for how her partner's ex, Melanie, has pulled her life together since she was arrested for drug trafficking: "She went into rehab and she has made remarkable strides. She has all my support and admiration, because I know how difficult it is for people to get over an addiction. Now she's back at school studying." Julie's reaction toward Melanie is remarkably generous considering how much her life was complicated by Melanie's problems. It appears that stepmothers' antipathy toward the ex often relates less to how dysfunctional the mother is and more to how the relationship is structured. There are a number of obstacles to stepmothers and mothers developing friendly, or even neutral, relationships. I outline the six most common.

Obstacle 1: The Omnipresent, Omnipotent Mother

Most stepmothers do not anticipate that their partner's ex-wife will figure in their lives. While their expectations about their stepchildren may be rosy and unrealistic, their partner's ex-wife rarely merits a thought: "The kids' mother is there as well, and I guess that's part of what I hadn't really expected. I hadn't met her until they all had chicken pox and I was delivering Vanessa [my stepdaughter] that Saturday to her place. That was my first exposure to her. Her presence and her influence and her existence were really something I had kind of completely ignored beforehand."

The discovery that their stepchildren's mother will be an active part of their lives is an often unwelcome surprise. Whether or not they actually see the mother, she usually has a major effect on the stepmother's life. Some ex-wives are intrusive. One stepmother came home to find her husband's ex-wife in the bathtub. Another discovered that the ex had come into the house while the stepmother was away and re-arranged the kitchen cupboards. A third was infuriated because her partner's ex-wife called whenever anything broke in her house, and her husband rushed over to fix it. When the stepmother protested, her husband explained that he was doing it for his children, not for his ex-wife. Despite his reassurances, this woman felt pushed into second place.

Inexperienced stepmothers frequently expect that their partner's previous relationship will be left in the past. As stepmothers struggle to find their place at the beginning, the ex-wife's existence may highlight the precariousness of the stepmother's position. If a stepmother feels insecure, she may feel threatened by any claims made by the ex-wife. Even if a stepmother intellectually accepts her partner's prior relationship with his ex-wife, she may not be psychologically prepared to see her partner head over to the ex's house, toolbox in hand.

Stepmothers frequently complain about the mother's ability to wreak havoc in their lives. Scheduling is a frequent bone of contention. Working out when children come and go can be complex and involve the wishes and demands of many people, some of whom the stepmother may never have met. The first year Kay was married, she discovered that, in order to plan her vacation, she had to juggle six work schedules—hers, her ex-husband's, her current husband's, her husband's ex-wife, the ex-wife's new partner, and the new partner's ex-wife. Each time she drew up a plan, it clashed with someone else's. Finally they settled on the last two weeks of July. When, a week later, her partner, Craig, got off the phone and said that those dates were out because his ex-wife's new partner's ex-wife had booked something already, Kay hit the roof. Who was this woman, whom she had never seen, throwing Kay's holiday into disarray. While, over time, some stepmothers set some limits and rules—for instance, that the mother cannot drop by for a bath or cancel well-established plans—it is frequently a shock for step-mothers to discover how much power the ex-wife will have over their lives.

Obstacle 2: Boxing in the Dark

Stepmothers and mothers rarely get to know one another well. Some stepmothers shy away from the ex. Other times it is the mother who avoids the stepmother. The relationship between the former spouses may also create an impediment. If the ex-spouses are locked in an antagonistic relationship, it may be impossible for a stepmother to initiate even superficial contact with the mother. For instance, Julie believed it would benefit her stepdaughter, Rachel, if she, her partner, Gordon, and Rachel's mother, Melanie, all cooper-ated in the care of Rachel. Gordon was so angry at Melanie for her neglectful behaviour when she was addicted to heroin, however, that he rejected Julie's idea that the three of them meet.

Some stepmothers' only source of knowledge about the mother is their partners. Not surprisingly, their partners' opinions about their ex-wives are not always laudatory and may be extremely crit-ical. If a stepmother unquestioningly accepts her partner's negative portrait, she may end up demonizing the mother on the basis of very little evidence. Stepchildren may help to stir the pot a little too. Stepmothers will learn that their stepchildren have passed along information to their mothers that, if it is not a complete fab-rication of what the stepmother has said, is certainly a distortion. Since many stepmothers do not have open communication with the mother, it can be difficult to straighten out misunderstandings or even to know if one has occurred. One mother called her ex-husband in a fury after the children returned home from their visit. Her daughter had complained that the stepmother had refused to let the girl use the computer but had given unlimited access to her own son. The reality was the stepmother's son had a project to complete that weekend, while the girl wanted to play computer games. The ex was not mollified by her ex-husband's explanation and accused the stepmother of favouring her own child.

If the stepchildren are adults or are peripheral to their father's life, a nonexistent or strained relationship between the stepmother and mother presents less of a problem. When the children move back and forth between their parents' houses, however, it can create tensions because of the possibility for misunderstandings.

Obstacle 3: If She Is the Real Mother, Where Does That Leave Me?

Although stepmothers may chafe at the mother's power over their lives, they rarely dispute her status as the "real" mother. They acknowledge the mother's prerogative to come first. Nevertheless, stepmothers become frustrated when they do much of the work, but the mother receives all the glory. Even if a mother disappears, her children will tend to idealize her, while the stepmother's efforts will be overlooked or dismissed with contempt. Intellectually, a stepmother may understand that her stepchildren will be more attached to their mother and that, in order to ward off criticisms, they may feel the need to defend her even more ferociously if she has opted out. At the same time, it is hurtful to have one's work disregarded. Two years ago Babs took over the full-time care of her two young stepchildren, then ages four and five, when Pam, the mother, decided she wanted more freedom. Babs already had two small children of her own, then aged three and five. Although caring for four preschoolers represented a huge commitment, Babs was willing to assume this. What drove her crazy was Pam. Pam regularly quizzed her children about their diet, and the children would relay their mother's messages: "Mummy says you should give us more fruit for our lunches," or "Mummy says that you shouldn't give us so much junk to eat." Then the children would return from their weekly visits at their mother's with sacks of candy. When Babs would limit the amount they could eat, she became the evil witch. She has overheard her stepchildren complaining to their mother and she knows Pam fuels this: "Pam has very much set them up—'Babs's not your mother. She's just a babysitter.' That's what they were told for a little while—'She's just a babysitter!'" Although Babs seethes inside, she bites her tongue because she knows her comments will create a conflict for the children. "I'm always there for them, but kids don't thank you for being there, they only notice when you're not there. They might realize it when they're thirty, and have kids of their own. . . . No matter how badly she treats them, and no matter how badly she hurts them and they cry and they're upset, they so badly want to please her, and want her to love them."

Stepmothers' attachment and commitment to their stepchildren can also be discounted by outsiders. Julie has had complete responsibility for her stepdaughter, Rachel, because her partner, Gordon, works long days and Rachel's mother, until recently, was in a drug rehabilitation program. When Rachel was hit by a car while riding her bike, it was Julie who rushed Rachel off to the hospital. She was stunned at the response she received. "The doctor came over and said, 'Are you her mother?' And I said, 'No.' And I wasn't in the picture any more. He just started talking to Gordon and dealing with Gordon like I didn't even exist. And then he wanted to take her into an observation room, and he said, 'You can wait here.' You know, he just pointed to a place where I could sit. And I couldn't even go in with them. And I remember thinking, 'God, you've got to be kidding.' It really hit me in the face. I wasn't of any importance because I wasn't her mother."

The doctor's dismissal was a reminder that no matter how many lunch boxes she had filled, how many bedtime stories she had read, and how many birthday parties she had organized, in the eyes of the world she was unimportant. Often small and apparently innocuous incidents accentuate stepmothers' marginality. Their stepchild may be asked to draw a family tree for a homework assignment but there is no space on the sheet for the stepmother and her family. The school may ask for a parent meeting and exclude the stepmother, who is the one helping her stepchild with homework every night.

Stepfamilies generally lack validity and recognition. Although they make up a significant proportion of families today in Canada and the United States, they are often invisible. In the last Canadian census in 2001, for instance, respondents were not asked whether they were part of a stepfamily. In stating who lived in their household, stepparents had to list their stepsons and stepdaughters as sons and daughters. In almost all constituencies in Canada and the United States, stepparents have no legal rights in relation to their stepchildren, even if they have the day-to-day responsibility.[1] This lack of recognition is painful for those stepmothers who want to be a presence in their stepchildren's lives. They may see themselves as central, but the world does not.

Obstacle 4: Competition Between the Stepmother and the Mother

What happens if there is room for only one mother but two women are doing the mother's job? Not surprisingly, stepmothers like Hillary often feel drawn into competition with the mother. Stepfamilies are fertile breeding grounds for jealousy, envy, and rivalry. Jealousy typically arises in triangular relationships where one person is jealous of the relationship between the other two and becomes afraid that he or she will be pushed out. Triangular relationships are ubiquitous in the stepfamily. One triangle involves the stepmother, the father, and the child, with the stepmother and child battling to win the father. A second triangle is stepmother–mother–child. Here the stepmother and mother are rivals for the child's affection. Finally, there is the stepmother–partner–ex-wife triangle, with the partner in the centre and the other two vying for his attention. Notice that the stepmother is always on the outside and never the central object of attention. This makes her more vulnerable to jealousy.

Another key ingredient of jealousy is insecurity. People who feel unsure of themselves or of their place in the relationship may be more worried about losing their relationship. If another person captures the attention of their loved one, the conditions are ripe for jealousy. Stepfamilies are often rife with insecurities, especially at the beginning. Some stepmothers become jealous of their partner's relationship with the first wife (the stepmother-partner-ex-wife triangle). They feel that they can never catch up because they came second. These women are jealous of the past, of the relationship they imagined their partner had with the first wife. One stepmother tortured herself with thoughts of her partner's closeness to his ex-wife when his first child was born: "When I was pregnant, this old voice would pop up and say, 'Well, you're not special, you're number two.' . . . Because I knew that he had been there for [my stepson's] labour and delivery, and I would have all these fantasies like when you are seeing a movie and there's this birth scene, and the mother and father are all so ecstatic wrapped around the baby. . . . [My partner] said that it couldn't have been further from the truth. He was eighteen years old and found the whole thing extremely awkward." Other stepmothers become jealous of the mother's close relationship with her children, because they want to have that relationship with their stepchildren (this is the stepmother-mother-child triangle). Hillary, for example, feels she has become drawn into a contest with Marika: "I think there can be incredible competition around who's the better mother. . . . The stepmother always tries to overdo and always has the fresh-baked cookies so that the children see this."[2]

As part of this dynamic, stepmothers often closely scrutinize the mother's performance. Stepmothers' conclusions are rarely favourable. They often feel that they are, or could be, a better mother than the mother. Most of the stepmothers with whom I talked disapproved of the mother's parenting skills. Only a small group believed the mother was a good mother or felt they shared similar values with the mother. Most commonly, they criticized the mother for not providing enough stimulation, not being involved enough with her children, feeding them too much junk food, being too lax about discipline, dressing them poorly, not teaching them manners, or being more focused on her own needs than on her children's.

Since stepmothers live with the consequences of the mother's parenting, and usually have little power to alter the situation, it is understandable that they would be preoccupied with the mother's skills as a parent. At the same time, they often judge her against the impossible societal ideal, enumerating the ways she falls short of the ideal mother who is constantly available, attuned, and striving to create the perfect environment for her children. Sabine takes a dim view of her stepchildren's mother because Sabine believes the mother has placed her career ahead of her children. When Sabine's children were little, she quit her job as a teacher to stay home with them: "[Their mother] is never available. The kids can't even phone her at work, they're not allowed to interrupt her. At one point, the little one said to me, 'My mummy cannot do this because she's not home.' And I said, 'Your mummy has a choice, she can choose her job or she can choose her family.'" Sabine sees signs that her stepchildren are suffering from their mother's preoccupation with work. Like many stepmothers, she singles out their manners as an indication of the problems: "It's very hard for me to be sitting at a table with somebody with no manners. [My stepchild] was pouring maple syrup on the pancakes this weekend, and she licked the drops off the bottle. . . . The worst part for me is their lack of manners. There is no mother, there is only a babysitter who watches TV." Although to a certain extent Sabine recognizes that her values about how to mother are different from the mother's, she believes that her standards are correct and the mother's are deficient.

Even stepmothers who marry widowers may feel in competition with the mother. This contest is even more unequal, however. The dead mother is almost always idealized and the stepmother can never match up. Sometimes the stepmother lives in the original family house, surrounded by another woman's possessions. In these circumstances, it is a challenge not to feel overshadowed. One stepmother who married a widower became annoyed when acquaintances and friends of the dead mother would draw parallels between the two wives. They would say: "You and Ann are a lot alike. She used to decorate the house beautifully at Christmas too." While their comments were probably intended as compliments and as encouragement for the stepmother, she felt thrust into a contest with a dead woman, a contest, of course, she could never win.

Stepmothers who want to be mothers or cast themselves in a mother role are more likely to find fault with the mother—and to believe they are the better mother. It does not matter whether or not they are mothers themselves. Childless stepmothers are just as likely to compare themselves with the mother as are those with children. The competition is fuelled, not by being a mother, but by ideology, how much stepmothers ascribe to the motherhood imperative.[3]

Attempting to be the better mother is doomed, of course, because although a stepmother may consider herself superior to the mother, she can never become the "real" mother. For some stepmothers, the mother is like a spectre reminding them of what they can never have. One stepmother felt haunted by the idea of the mother when her stepchildren were young: "I would have liked those kids to be mine solely. And, on my worst days, I had a lot of resentment that they weren't mine. . . . I kept thinking that life would be fine if she wasn't there. She was always there as a shadow."

Many stepmothers also believe that the mothers are caught in the same dance of competition, that the rivalry is a two-way contest. I cannot substantiate their perception because I did not interview the mothers, but it makes sense that they might become drawn into this dynamic. Here is a new woman in their children's lives who is cooking, cleaning, buying birthday presents, and ferrying children around to various activities. In short, she is doing a lot of the things that a mother does. A mother may feel threatened by this quasi-mother, particularly if she thinks that the stepmother is trying to usurp her place.

Stepmothers see the ex's rivalry erupting in different forms. The mother may undermine the stepmother by badmouthing the stepmother in front of the children, for instance, referring to her as "bimbo," "bitch," or "slut." It can be difficult for a stepmother to counteract this poisonous buildup. Sheila, age thirty, met her partner, Michael, three years ago when she was a medical resident in the hospital where Michael is the medical director. When he left his marriage for her, there was a huge furor. Michael's friends and family were outraged and sided with Michael's ex-wife, Brenda. Sheila's family and friends were worried and warned her about getting involved with a man twenty-two years older than she.

Sheila dreaded meeting Michael's two sons, Daniel and Adrian, ages twelve and nine, because she knew that Brenda had loudly aired her opinion of Sheila as a gold digger, a marriage breaker, a scheming bitch. Sometimes Sheila could hear Brenda screaming invective at Michael over the telephone and would be painfully aware that her stepsons were listening in the background. "I was conscious when I met the boys that all of this stuff had been said about me, so I was wondering, 'Well, what do they think of me after all of this has been said to them? And how can I prove to them I'm not?'"

Sheila did not meet her stepchildren for a long time, since Brenda had threatened to cut off Michael's access to his children if Sheila were present too. Michael's connection with his sons was already shaky. Not wanting to jeopardize it further, he caved in to Brenda. Sheila was left alone at home on weekends while Michael went off with his children. If the children came over, she had to make herself scarce. Brenda's successful bullying made it clear who had the power. Although I did not interview Brenda, I imagine that her actions were borne out of a sense of helplessness. Her husband had walked out of his marriage for a much younger woman and she was left to pick up the pieces.

The mother may also undercut the stepmother's relationship with her stepchildren, for instance, by ordering her children not to listen to the stepmother, or as in Babs's situation, by referring to the stepmother as a babysitter. Not only do these belittling comments sabotage the stepmother's relationship with her stepchildren, they also throw the children into a quandary. The children may feel that showing any sign of liking their stepmother is being disloyal to their mother. Some mothers also snipe at the stepmother and her partner. Criticisms will filter back from the children about the stepmother's lifestyle, her taste, or her cooking abilities—"My mother says . . ." Being surrounded by these negative comments can also lead the children to become wary, suspicious, and even hostile toward their stepmothers. Some stepmothers notice the negativity intensifying if they become pregnant: "When [the stepchildren's mother] found out I was pregnant, she started stirring them up . . . telling them, 'He'll love that child more than you,' and that kind of thing. And stirring it up. At the very beginning, they were somewhat happy about the pregnancy, but then withdrew a little bit, because they were afraid that this child was going to get more attention."

Sometimes stepmothers believe that the mother will even allow the children to suffer in order to score points. Anything that the stepmother or her partner suggests will be automatically opposed. Remember Patricia's very negative relationship with her stepdaughter, Amy? Patricia feels Amy's mother played a big role in feeding the fire. Jeff (Patricia's partner) and his ex-wife, Connie, had had a spectacularly bitter divorce. Connie did not want the marriage to end and promised Jeff he would suffer, and they spent many years in the courts battling out their separation agreement. Even today, six years after the divorce, most conversations degenerate into a row. Patricia is acutely aware that Connie runs her down, because Amy gleefully reports her mother's comments— that Patricia stole Jeff away from Connie (even though they did not meet until after the marriage ended), that she drinks too much, that she is a sloppy housekeeper. No wonder Amy feels free to be as rude as she pleases to Patricia. After a couple of years of Amy's rejection, Patricia had almost begun to give up hope. Nevertheless, she continued to cast around for ways to reach Amy. Amy loved music so Patricia proposed music lessons. She offered to rent Amy a keyboard and she found a teacher. For the first time, Patricia caught a glimmer of enthusiasm. Connie quickly quashed the idea, however, mocking Patricia's choice of teacher and suggesting that Jeff was too cheap to buy Amy a real piano. The lessons never happened.

Obstacle 5: When Mothers Abdicate

Paradoxically, some stepmothers find themselves in the opposite situation. Rather than battling over who will be dominant, the mother seems to view the stepmother's arrival as her chance to opt out. These stepmothers believe the mother uses them as a replacement, as a "step-in mother," so that she can let go of her responsibilities. Betsy, the "compulsive organizer" we met in the previous chapter, could read the signs that Angela, the children's mother, wanted out, but she was still annoyed at how Angela engineered it. First, Angela announced she was taking a two-month work contract in another city so the three children would need to live temporarily with Mick and Betsy. When Angela gave up her apartment and moved the children's belongings to their father's house, Betsy suspected that Angela had more permanent plans. Mick brushed off her suspicions, insisting that Angela had always been very involved, almost overprotective, with her children and would not let them go. Angela kept extending the contract month by month. Finally she called Mick late one night and told him she was not coming back. Mick was left to break the news to the children. Being right was no comfort for Betsy, because of the devastating effect on the children. All three children missed their mother and were counting on her return. The news was a huge blow, particularly since she did not invite them to join her.

Betsy and Mick had been married for only a short time when Angela announced she was leaving. Betsy is certain that Angela would not have made the move without Betsy being there: "As soon as I came, I was her ticket out, because I think she knew that Mick couldn't handle it on his own. . . . Other people who knew her said to me, 'Oh yeah, you've given her a chance.'" Angela's ambiguous and protracted departure made Betsy's life considerably more difficult. She had to adjust almost overnight to life with three children. The children were distraught when their mother did not return. Rather than the distress being directed at Angela, they turned it on Betsy.

Other mothers slip away more gradually and less traumatically. Sometimes these women are caught up with their careers and are not that interested in caring for their children. Some hand the children over when they become difficult adolescents and tell their ex-partners that it is their turn now. Often it is the stepmother who picks up the slack, not the father. Although these women sometimes find the extra work burdensome, most are happy to have the mother off the scene. Their wish has come true—the ex-wife has disappeared.

Obstacle 6: She Thinks That Money Grows on Trees

Money is often stretched thinly in stepfamilies. Sometimes one salary is being divided across two households—for instance, when neither the stepmother nor her partner's ex-wife works outside the home. When stepmothers are working, often their salaries make a significant difference to the financial health of the situation. In an extreme example, one of the stepmothers I interviewed was supporting three households on her salary when her ex-husband, her partner, and her partner's ex-wife all lost their jobs at the same time.

Stepmothers' frustrations about money often focus on their partner's ex-wife. While most stepmothers support their partner's desire to contribute to his children's well-being, they may resent that money is going to the children's mother, particularly if the relationship is hostile or troubled. The stepmother may find it irritating that her salary is helping to support the mother's household when the mother is undermining the stepmother's relationships with her stepchildren. Even though Angela had handed over all responsibility for her children to Mick and Betsy, she did not expect that she should provide any financial assistance. Moreover, she demanded that Mick pay for the children's expenses while they were visiting with her. In keeping with his nonconfrontational stance, Mick acceded to Angela. Betsy and Mick pooled their salaries, and since Betsy earned more than Mick, she felt that she was actually underwriting Angela's new independent life. Far from being grateful for Betsy's efforts, Angela often criticized Betsy's spending habits. When Betsy would not give her teenaged stepdaughter Olivia $80 for a pair of jeans, for instance, Angela told Olivia that Betsy was a cheapskate. Betsy was livid, not the least because one reason for Betsy's careful approach to money was Angela's refusal to contribute anything to her children's upkeep.

Conversely, some stepmothers criticize the mother's spending. They believe that their stepchildren are disadvantaged because the mother spends money frivolously or siphons off child support to buy things for herself. It is frustrating for stepmothers to see their money being used in ways that they disapprove of. Occasionally stepchildren will arrive for a visit with a long list of items to be purchased, such as winter coats and boots, even when the child support payments were designed to cover these expenses. This situation creates a bind for the stepmother and her partner: if they refuse to buy them, they risk denying the children things that they need and also appearing cheap, but if they do buy them, they feel they are paying twice.

Stepmothers also fume over what they feel are inequitable

financial arrangements. It grates to see their stepchildren's mother have a better standard of living than they do, particularly if the stepmother's salary helps to sustain the mother's lifestyle. Why should the mother be able to afford a two-week cruise when the stepmother and her partner have to make do with a camping holiday! Similarly, stepmothers will seethe when support payments are not reduced after the children move out of their mother's house and into their father's. Because the payments are mandated by law, the mother may still receive the same amount of money in child support, although her expenses have been reduced.

Molly, now age thirty-three, has been with her partner, Bruce, for the last five years. When Molly met Bruce, his two children, Stephanie and Owen, then six and two, lived with their mother. Just after Molly and Bruce were married, Bruce's ex-wife, Pamela, asked Bruce to take Owen full-time because she could not work and take care of two young children on her own. Molly assumed that Bruce's child support payments would be halved, but Pamela insisted on holding to the original agreement. Even when Bruce was laid off from his job in the construction industry, Pamela refused to consider a reduction. Molly said, "When my husband lost his job about two years ago, we still paid the amount that we were supposed to. Then we hit rock bottom. We had to sell our house and move. We tried to talk to her about it, and say, 'Look, we are broke. This is what we can afford to give you.' She said, 'See you in court.' So we got a lawyer and went for custody of Owen."

Molly was pregnant when all this was going on, and she and Bruce now have a two-year-old son, Max. She had hoped to stay home, but this has not been possible: "I'm so angry, because I have to work part-time to make up the difference. If we didn't have to pay her, I don't think I'd have to work." Their financial situation has improved since the courts reduced Pamela's support payments and Bruce found another job, but Molly feels Pamela still has the advantage: "She's living in a free-standing, two-storey house, with a garage, and she's got a very nice car. We're in a semi-detached, two-bedroom home for the four of us. When Bruce left her, he left everything because the two kids were there. He came out of it with nothing, and we had to start from scratch."

Although Molly can understand why Pamela may not care about her or Bruce or Max, Pamela's cavalier attitude to her own son astonishes her: "I tried to talk to [Pamela] about it, and I said, 'Owen needs things, he needs clothes, he needs a tutor because he's not doing well at school.' I explained that I wanted to keep him in after-school activities, and if she was continually going to financially drain us, Owen was going to suffer. . . . I don't know if she thinks money grows on trees or if we're rolling in dough, but I wonder sometimes if she has any empathy for her kid."

Given all these obstacles, it is perhaps unsurprising that stepmothers frequently list the mother as their biggest stress. Since their contact with the mother is often limited or sporadic, it is often difficult to resolve conflicts and miscommunications. A couple of the stepmothers I interviewed lamented that, under different circumstances, they might have become friends with their partner's ex-wife, but the dynamics of the situation prevented this: "Maybe if [I and his ex-wife] met as strangers we might quite like each other. It's unfortunate, because almost they're set up as confrontational relationships. You're not expected to like each other, or understand each other, or be friends, and yet you could be." Although a minority of stepmothers develop good relationships with the mother, and I discuss them later, the stepmother-ex-wife relationship often seems fated to be adversarial.

Chapter 5

Walking on Eggshells:
Relationships with Stepchildren

Although stepchildren occupy a huge amount of stepmothers' time, thinking, energy, and concern, only a minority of stepmothers I talked with regarded their interactions with stepchildren as the most onerous part of stepmotherhood. Many had reasonably good relationships with stepchildren and identified at least one positive aspect. Only a small group felt there was nothing redeemable.[1]

Although stepmothers may get along with stepchildren, there are plenty of struggles and difficulties. Even when the relationship is harmonious, it usually has strict limits and boundaries. Stepmothers tread very carefully with stepchildren. They often feel tentative and constrained in their interactions. No matter how close they feel to their stepchildren, rarely does this match their intimacy with biological children. Among the hundreds of stepmothers I talked to over the course of my research and writing this book, only one ever said she felt the same toward both her stepchildren and her children.

Somebody Who Doesn't, Somebody Who Isn't

Stepmothers often struggle with how to define their role. Although trying to be a mother to their stepchildren is problematic, at least it offers them a clear and familiar model. When they step outside this framework, stepmothers are often at a loss. One stepmother confessed, "I have absolutely no idea [what a stepmother is]. Somebody who doesn't, somebody who isn't. I've got a lot of things that a good stepmother wouldn't do: somebody who isn't cruel and isn't what they say in all the fairy tales. I don't feel like you can mother your stepchild, that's kind of presumptuous. You're talking about a child, so it's not really like a friendship."

Stepmothers often hunt around for a term that might capture their relationship with their stepchildren. Rarely do they find the perfect label. "Stepmother" is often anathema because of its association with wickedness. "Mother" has many thorns. "Friend" is not really accurate. Some stepmothers reach out for kin terms such as "aunt," "sister," or "cousin." They are usually forced to qualify these too—they are like an aunt but feel closer to their stepchildren or like a sister but without the easy laughter. Not having a clear model can be troubling: "I haven't the foggiest idea [who I am as a stepmother]. And that's what makes it so difficult. I'm not the mum, I don't feel like the stepmum, I don't feel like the friend, I don't feel like the babysitter. I couldn't put a label on it." Some stepmothers resort to saying what they are not—"do *not* expect anything," "do *not* try to replace the mother," "do *not* interfere with their partner's relationship with his children," "do *not* impose themselves on the situation," "do *not* interfere generally." All this ambiguity leaves stepmothers unsure about how to act, what to say, how to respond.

Grateful for Peace

What do stepmothers mean when they say they have a good relationship with their stepchildren? Some are satisfied with pleasant, friendly, but distant, interactions. They do not expect to have a close, intimate alliance. As long as there is no conflict or hostility, they are content. Others see themselves as friends to their stepchildren. These women focus on the fun they have, whether it is helping with school projects, taking the children swimming, or just horsing around. For childless stepmothers, stepchildren can become an opportunity to revisit their childhood. Some are surprised to discover that being a stepmother can be pleasurable.

Despite her trepidations about her stepchildren's reactions to her, Sheila rated her first encounter with her stepchildren as a success. Sheila did not meet her stepsons, Daniel and Adrian, until eight months after she and Michael started living together since Michael's ex-wife, Brenda, had forbidden Sheila to associate with them. The longer Sheila waited to meet them, the more apprehensive she became. Michael did not want to confront his ex-wife head on. His solution was that he would take his sons away camping for the May long weekend and Sheila could just happen to "drop in." Sheila was leery about his proposal. She wanted Michael to prepare the boys for her appearance, but he refused. Thinking that perhaps this might be her only opportunity to meet them, she finally agreed to his plan.

On her drive to the campground, she imagined an interminable rainy weekend, trapped inside a tent with two resentful children. It unfolded quite differently: "I got bonus points because I like camping, while their mother detests camping. She will not go camping with them and will not do anything outdoors with them. They're big in the Boy Scouts thing. So that was good. I brought games and just activities and things that we could do together, and things that I remembered from camping as a kid that I liked to do. And that night I got a hug from both of them. Oh my God! I was really, really emotional about that." Like Sheila, stepmothers often feel gratified, even grateful, if their stepchildren are friendly. Stepmothers often give the credit for a successful relationship to their stepchildren, saying that their stepchildren welcomed them or that it was easy to respond positively because their stepchildren were so engaging. Although they feel a lot of satisfaction when the relationship runs smoothly, relatively few refer to their own efforts in making the relationships work.

Stepmothers who have good relationships with stepchildren often feel fortunate. Perhaps negative stereotypes about step-mother-stepchild relationships lead them to have modest expectations. Some women describe themselves as lucky that their stepchildren have not accused them of being wicked. Even step-mothers whose relationships with stepchildren are pretty terrible will point to stepmothers in worse predicaments, as though to sal-vage a small scrap of comfort. I have already described Patricia's stepdaughter, Amy, whose rudeness knew few bounds. Amy lit-tered her dirty clothes, dishes, and garbage all over the house. When Patricia asked her to clean up her mess, Amy would brush her stepmother's complaints aside, claiming she was too busy, as she lounged in front of the television. She also insulted Patricia directly, making slighting comments about Patricia's age and her dowdy taste in clothes. Even in this bleak situation, Patricia was able to dig up a more miserable stepmother: "I do know of other cases," she said, "that are much worse. One with an eighteen-year-old girl where the second wife is only twenty-six and the husband is forty-four. She is absolutely atrocious, stealing the wife's clothes and goodness knows what and making terrible scenes all the time. So I kept thinking to myself, 'Well, at least Amy isn't like that. She's bad-tempered and selfish and messy and rude, but she's not steal-ing clothes and lying.'"

Taking Their Cue

Stepmothers' assessment of the quality of their relationships with stepchildren is largely in response to their stepchildren's reactions to them. Although stepmothers may talk about feeling more in sync with one child than another, or liking one more than an-other, this usually relates less to how they think and feel and more to how the child acts toward them. We can see this clearly when they have a good relationship with one stepchild but a difficult one with another. The stepchild's response is usually the distin-guishing factor. One child is friendly and enjoys spending time with the stepmother. The other is uncommunicative and uninter-ested. While it is perhaps understandable that stepmothers would be drawn toward the children who like them, this means that they take their cue from their stepchildren, rather than setting the agenda themselves.

Many stepmothers would like to have greater intimacy with their stepchildren than their stepchildren will tolerate. Initially, they look forward to a close, physically affectionate relationship with their stepchildren, but back off when they recognize this is unwelcome. They learn to curb their impulse to touch their stepchildren or engage them in an open conversation. Only infrequently do their stepchildren want more from them than they are willing to give. It can be disheartening when relationships with stepchildren are more distant than the stepmothers had initially hoped for.

One-Way Relationships

When stepmothers characterize their relationships with stepchildren as friendships, this usually does not mean the mutual give-and-take that we generally associate with friendship. Their relationship with stepchildren is usually one-way more than reciprocal. They are available for their stepchildren, but do not expect the same in return. They rarely confide in their stepchildren or go to them for support. The term "friendship" is meant to capture an interaction that is non-parental and positive. While most stepmothers accept this asymmetry from the beginning, a few discover—sometimes painfully—that they cannot depend on their stepchild as they would on a friend.

Abigail has been a stepmother for twenty years and has always felt very close to her stepdaughter, Sonia, who was only five when Abigail came into her life. As a woman without children of her own, Abigail was delighted to have a child on whom she could lavish attention, and she encouraged Sonia's talent in art and music. Even after Sonia moved out, Abigail and Sonia continued to spend a lot of time together, going to concerts and art shows or travelling on their own. When Abigail's partner lost his job two years ago and they had to sell their house, Abigail told Sonia how hard it was for her to lose her house. Sonia, perhaps thinking that Abigail was criticizing Sonia's father, reacted explosively: "She told me to go to hell—it was just the most devastating experience. Because not only had I just lost everything, but I had suddenly lost my stepdaughter virtually. And she didn't speak to me for months while this was going on. It was just awful. I was calling her looking for sympathy which I shouldn't have done. . . . I know now that I can't treat her as that sort of peer company. So I don't talk about anything personal."

As a result of Abigail's persistence, two years later, she and Sonia have regained their old friendly footing and recently took a trip to New York City together. Abigail has never dared broach the incident with Sonia. Their relationship feels too fragile. While her connection with Sonia is one of the most important in her life, it has strict boundaries. Most stepmothers do not discover the limits with their stepchildren, because they never test them. They may describe the relationship as a friendship, but they are generally friends *to* their stepchildren and rarely friends *with* them.

Stepping Cautiously

Stepmothers often tread very carefully in order not to overstep the limits of their relationships with stepchildren. Since they are unsure of their role, it is often difficult, however, to identify what these boundaries might be. Over and over stepmothers characterize their relationships with stepchildren as walking on eggshells, tiptoeing, treading on thin ice, holding back: "It's not like I don't love the child, but I notice there is always a certain amount of tension in the house. And that to me is the hardest thing to deal with, like you're always sort of walking on eggshells."[2] They often constrain themselves. If they are upset, irritated, or angry, they will hold this in or express it in such a roundabout manner that the message is obscured. Partly this is because they do not want to appear wicked, but also because it is hard to know what is permissible.

Even affectionate impulses feel risky. Stepmothers hold back from touching, hugging, or even praising their stepchildren in case their gestures are misinterpreted. Relationships with stepchildren are seen as fragile, tenuous, easily severed. This is the case not just with difficult or strained relationships. Even when stepmothers are close to their stepchildren, they keep themselves in check in order not to upset the balance and take the chance that their stepchildren might turn on them. One stepmother is very fond of her teenaged stepdaughter and believes her affection is reciprocated, but she is wary of testing this: "I think I'm really afraid of being rejected . . . so I'm probably holding myself back. [I'm afraid] she would say, 'You're not my mother, leave me alone' or something like that. I probably don't touch her as much, or put my hand on her shoulder even. I just keep my distance." Their fear of taking the wrong step is often more troubling than any actual interactions with their stepchildren.

The Lightning Rod

Although most stepmothers identify some positive dimensions with their stepchildren, a significant minority are locked into troubled and unhappy patterns. Their stepchildren refuse to talk to them or are rude, obstructionist, defiant, and hostile. I have already described Patricia's and Deborah's struggles with stepchildren. No matter what tack they take, they are unable to moderate their stepchildren's antagonism. These women often begin to despair that they cannot make the relationship work. After four years, Patricia has run out of steam: "There are no solutions. How do you cope with this? How do you make it better? I thought if I just keep on trying to be nice and trying to do a reasonable amount surely, surely it would get better, but it didn't. So I don't know any answers, I think it's terribly, terribly difficult."

The first few years can be rocky with stepchildren, particularly if they are angry about their father's remarriage. Good relationships with stepchildren usually develop over time. Stepmothers often understand and accept their stepchildren's initial resistance. It can be difficult to maintain this equanimity, however, if, despite the stepmother's best efforts, her stepchildren remain intransigent. Faced with no other alternative, stepmothers often end up withdrawing. Patricia, for example, has given up expecting Amy will ever come around and no longer makes any effort to reach her. At the same time, she wonders what she did wrong. This is typical. While stepmothers usually do not take credit for successful relationships, they frequently blame themselves when they do not work.

Some stepmothers also believe they become a convenient target for their stepchildren's distress over their parents' divorce or death. Their stepchildren direct their anger at them because it is safer than aiming it at their biological parents. Divorce and remarriage can create an atmosphere of insecurity, and the children may fear jeopardizing their relationships with parents. Stepparents are more expendable. Sometimes stepmothers are blamed for the breakup of the first marriage, even if they were not around at the time. An absent mother will be idealized, while the stepmother will be hated: "I don't know why I have had to be the fall guy when their own mother is never there. When I sewed for them, and cooked for them, and cleaned for them, drove them here and drove them there." Since their relationship with stepchildren is often so tenuous, stepmothers rarely confront their stepchildren and have to live with being the lightning rod for misdirected hostility.

Martha, the "wicked" stepmother, is convinced that her stepchildren's unresolved grief over their mother's death was partly projected onto her. When, initially, Martha tried to talk to them about their mother, she was met with stony faces. She now realizes that raising the subject intensified their mistrust of her. Seven years after their mother's death, the three children, now aged sixteen, fourteen, and twelve, have still never mentioned her. Wilf and his first wife had decided to protect the children from the severity of her cancer and never told the children she was dying. The children were sent off to their grandparents' when their mother was very ill and thus missed their chance to say goodbye. Based on her own work experience with families of AIDS patients, Martha believes the children, particularly the older two, are angry about this and have channeled their rage toward her.

Martha's personality is also the opposite of their mother's. Martha is extravagant and flamboyant. Their mother was reserved and quiet. Martha also believes that people should air their differences. Living with three children who, like their mother, keep everything bottled up is a strain for her. The three children were clearly not happy about their father's remarriage, but they never directly expressed their hostility, letting it leak out through sullen looks and monosyllabic responses to her inquiries. Martha has become trapped into this same pattern: "I felt that I couldn't be honest with my feelings and I guess I wanted more feeling and honesty from them in their feelings, but it felt like it never came. It felt like they were full of anger, but it never got expressed, and so we never got past it. And so it felt like there was anger in the house all the time."

Divided Loyalties

As mentioned in the previous chapter, stepmothers often believe their stepchildren are torn between their allegiance to their mother and permitting themselves to like their stepmother. If the stepchildren enjoy being with their stepmother, they may feel they are betraying their mother. They may react by spurning the stepmother's offers or by driving home the message that their mother is superior in every way to the stepmother. While stepmothers may respect their stepchildren's loyalty to their mother, it is disheartening to face this wall. In order not to fan the flames, stepmothers generally avoid criticizing the mother in front of the children—even if this means choking back anger. It is infuriating if the mother has no such compunctions. Some mothers make it plain—whether directly or indirectly—that their children should not be friendly to their stepmother.

In the last chapter, I described how Betsy became a full-time stepmother when the mother, Angela, went off on a "temporary work contract" and never returned. Although her two older children, Alasdair and Olivia, rebelled against Betsy's new household regime, her youngest stepson, Simon, had welcomed it. He was naturally orderly, and the chaos of Mick's house had been hard for him: "Simon is a fastidious young man, so he thought [Betsy's household overhaul] was a great idea. One of the first times I met him, he was vacuuming a two-foot square of the carpet. And I said, 'Simon, what are you doing?' And he said, 'I need some place to sit down, I can't stand it any more.'" Simon and Betsy have a similar take on life, and he was Betsy's greatest ally in the stepfamily, for which she was grateful.

The summer after Angela left, the three children visited her for a month. When Simon returned from his mother's, he would not talk or even look at Betsy. Betsy was devastated. Eventually she realized that Angela had been filling her children's heads with criticisms of Betsy: "We got along so well before he went to see her. It's funny because a lot of our friends that know her said, 'She's brain-washed him against you.' And I kept saying, 'No, why would she do that? She doesn't want them to live with her, so why would she want her kids to be unhappy at home?'"

Betsy never dared ask Simon what his mother had said, nor did he volunteer anything. Betsy says, "I didn't know how to deal with it. I was afraid and I was nervous, I was scared. I didn't know what to do. . . . He'd come home from school and I'd go, 'Hi, Simon, how are you?' Sometimes I'd get absolutely nothing, most of the time I'd just get 'Uhn' and then he'd walk to his bedroom and close his door." With time Betsy and Simon have recovered some of their former companionableness, but a new distance exists. Betsy cannot forgive Angela for trying to spoil Betsy's relationship with her stepchildren after she waltzed off and left Mick and Betsy to deal with the aftermath.

Spoiled Rotten

Betsy's stepchildren's behaviour presented another challenge. While she was charmed by their lively energy, she was less impressed with their rudeness and lack of discipline. One of the first times Betsy had dinner at Mick's house, Alasdair swore at his father and called him a wimp. More than hearing this, what horrified her was Mick's lack of reaction. Instead of reprimanding Alasdair, he carried on talking as though this was acceptable behaviour. Betsy realized later that she should have seen this as a sign of what was to come: "The kids were basically spoiled rotten. They had no responsibilities whatsoever. They could drop their clothes, their books, their dishes, apple cores, anything, anywhere. And they never had to do any dishes, anything to help."

Betsy took it on herself to whip this household into shape. Meals had been haphazard and uninspired, so Betsy, who loved to cook, took over in the kitchen. In addition to her campaign to re-organize the house, she proposed that all three children have weekly chores and that their allowance be dependent on completion of their responsibilities. She also encouraged Mick not to tolerate his children's rudeness. While the children appreciated her cooking, the older two in particular rebelled: "All of a sudden, their lives were changed upside down. They had this wonderful lazy life where they had no responsibilities, no obligations, and got whatever they wanted, whenever they wanted it. And if they didn't get it, they'd scream and yell and cry until they got it." When Alasdair and Olivia tried to wear Betsy down with the same bullying techniques they used successfully with their father, they found her less tractable. Although it hurt when Olivia called her a bitch or claimed that Betsy had ruined her life, Betsy held fast, in large part because she could not stand the mess.

Stepmothers do not usually consider their stepchildren bad children, but badly brought up. Betsy felt her stepchildren did not act properly because they had not been taught. Only a minority of stepmothers characterize their stepchildren as selfish, unpleasant, or manipulative by nature. They generally hold the parents (and sometimes the grandparents) accountable, believing they have been overindulgent, lax, or unavailable. Unfortunately, stepmothers have to live with the consequences. It is difficult to know how to react. If they ignore the rudeness and lack of manners because they fear disrupting their relationships with their stepchildren, they may become fed up and withdraw. But if, like Betsy, they try to challenge the behaviour, they risk alienating their stepchildren.

Having No Power

One issue dominates stepmothers' discourse about stepchildren—feelings of powerlessness. Almost all stepmothers experience this, whether it manifests as having no influence over their stepchildren, having no authority in the stepfamily, or being pushed to the periphery.[3] They had expected to have a voice in the family, but feel overlooked or marginalized. Some fear to make the smallest request of their stepchildren in case the children refuse and they do not have the clout to insist the children follow through. Four situations heighten stepmothers' feelings of powerlessness.

1. Being Out of the Loop

Stepmothers often feel invalidated when decisions that directly affect them are made without their input. In the last chapter, I described Hillary's struggles with her partner's ex-wife, Marika, who changed the children's visiting schedule without consulting Stefan and Hillary. Hillary feels that Stefan's children have also adopted a variation on this dynamic. If they want something, they go to their father when Hillary is out of the house. Stefan will usually say yes without discussing it with Hillary, even though Hillary and Stefan share expenses equally. Last year her stepson Peter's bicycle was stolen after he left it lying unlocked in the front yard. Stefan bought him a new one the next week. Hillary was furious, not just because Stefan had not told her first but because of the message he was giving his son. She lambasted Stefan, but bit her tongue around Peter because she did not want to be the wicked stepmother. It rankled, however: "The hardest thing is not having equal say or equal power. The hardest thing is not being equal."

Some stepmothers feel they are the lowest person on the totem pole. Even their in-laws, who do not live with them, may have more authority. As researchers have documented, grandparents often play a pivotal role after divorce. They may take an active, almost a quasi-parental, role in their grandchildren's lives. Particularly if the father is a widower or has full custody, his parents may play a major part in their grandchildren's lives.[4] When their sons remarry, grandparents may be reluctant to relinquish their role. Some stepmothers welcome their in-laws' support. Others find it hard to establish themselves with their in-laws peering over their shoulder or offering unsolicited advice. After one new stepmother packed her stepchildren's clothes for camp, she discovered her mother-in-law rifling through the bags, taking things out and adding others. Not at all abashed, her mother-in-law told the stepmother the children needed more socks and pants. Although the stepmother recognized that her mother-in-law's interference reflected her concern about her grandchildren, she was annoyed.

2. Locked Outside the Magic Circle

Stepmothers often feel initially excluded from the tight little unit formed by their partner and his children. They are the outsiders in this family. One stepmother characterized it as a "magic circle" that she could not penetrate. New stepmothers are often onlookers, rather than participants in the new family. As has been documented in the research on families after divorce, parents and children often form a strong bond and develop traditions and habits as a single-parent family. It may be difficult for this close family to open up for the newcomer. Children may also see their parents' remarriage as a loss and become jealous.[5]

Susannah describes her husband, Marty, and his two children as a nucleus. Marty's first wife died when his two children were eleven and twelve. When Susannah met Marty five years later, the three of them were inseparable. Susannah, then age twenty-three, was fourteen years younger than Marty. She worked as legal secretary in the firm where Marty was a lawyer. From casual conversations at work, she knew that he was lonely and she longed to help him.

Once she and Marty married, however, she discovered it was not going to be easy to find her way in. Marty and his children seemed so contented together that it felt like she was interfering when she tried to join in with them. The hour before dinner each night was the worst. Some of Susannah's happiest childhood memories were of hanging around the kitchen after school with her two sisters, chatting and helping their mother prepare the meal. She fantasized that the same tradition would play out in the new family, but it was the opposite. Susannah would rush home from work in order to start cooking. When Marty and the two children returned home, she would be in the kitchen. Marty would pop in to say hello as he headed to the family room but the two children would pass by without a greeting. All three would watch TV until Susannah called to say dinner was on the table. As she listened to them chat and laugh together, she would feel lonely, "and I used to say it all the time, 'Why doesn't somebody come and visit me?'" But they didn't. It was as though she did not exist. She told Marty how isolated she felt, but "he couldn't see it at all, he didn't think there was anything unusual about it." Susannah said his response was "'Well, it's just that we like to sit and watch TV together before dinner.' I said, 'Yeah, but that was when you had the housekeeper.' I said, 'But I'm not the housekeeper, I'm your wife!' " Marty never grasped why Susannah was upset. Until both children left home, this pattern continued. Unlike Susannah, many stepmothers break into the magic circle, and their feelings of being an outsider fade. Others always feel stuck on the outside looking in.

3. I Wasn't There for Their First Step, the Family Vacations, the . . .

Lacking a shared history with stepchildren can also stir up feelings of helplessness. As her partner and his children reminisce about family activities, holidays, and vacations that predate the stepmother's arrival, the stepmother will have nothing to contribute. Often these stories feel like additional signs that she is not a member of this club. Even when she recognizes her stepchildren are using these events to heighten her outsider status, she may still feel hurt or jealous.

Stepmothers also have to live with the past through their stepchildren's habits and personalities, which are often formed to a great extent by the time the stepmother arrives. The stepmother may confront behaviours and attitudes that she does not like or condone, but over which she has little influence. Particularly if she had hoped to rescue her stepchildren, a stepmother may feel an enormous sense of futility when she cannot fix a troubled situation. Often she believes that, if she had taken care of her stepchildren since birth, she could have set them on a better path. All she can do now is lament the waste. At the same time, she has to live with the consequences of problems she did not create.

I have described Julie's struggles with having responsibility without authority. Recently her stepdaughter, Rachel, now age twelve, was caught smoking. Julie was the only one to become agitated. Rachel's mother, Melanie, smokes herself, while Julie's partner, Gordon, shrugged it off as adolescent rebellion. His attitude was that the more adults react, the more Rachel will persist. Julie is virulently opposed to smoking and is already indoctrinating her two young children. She is frustrated—with Rachel for smoking, with Melanie for being so careless, with Gordon for being so lackadaisical, and with her own powerlessness: "I didn't want her to do that, I didn't want her to be stupid enough to do that. Gordon couldn't understand why I was so mad. I remember thinking to myself, 'If I had her from day one, she'd know better.' If you don't have a child until they're older, there are some things that you just can't have an influence over, you just can't make happen."

Stepmothers whose partners are not supportive or who brush aside stepmothers' distress often feel the most powerless. If their stepchildren ignore them, this is understandable, if hurtful. If their partners do not take them seriously, it is a big blow.

4. An Alien in My Own House

For some stepmothers, living in their new stepfamily is like moving to a foreign country where they do not understand the language or customs. No matter what they do, they cannot seem to get it right. One stepmother has married into a family where her partner and his adult children are passionate gardeners and cooks. Winter and spring they study seed catalogues, deciding what they will plant that year, summer they are busy with their huge gardens, while fall is an orgy of canning and jam making. Coming from the defrost-and-microwave school of cooking, the stepmother was initially at a loss about how to fit in. She did not particularly enjoy cooking, nor was she even that interested in food, but she wanted to belong. On top of this, her eldest stepdaughter was very competitive. If the stepmother baked a cake, her stepdaughter would either belittle it or create some magnificent confection that dwarfed the stepmother's. Though she understood her stepdaughter's need to stake her prior claim, her inability to find a footing in this family made her feel like an awkward foreigner.

Sometimes the living space becomes alien territory for step-mothers. Rather than a place where they can unwind and relax, their new environment produces stress. For Hillary, it was a huge adjustment sharing a house with Stefan and his two children, Peter and Emily, particularly since they were crammed into a small space. After the divorce, Stefan's ex-wife kept the house and he took an apartment. When Hillary and Stefan married, every-one moved into Hillary's "little cottage-type house, which was perfect for me as a single professional but for four people it was just bursting." All of sudden, she had no place of her own. The bathroom was strewn with the children's clothes and towels, the living room with their clothes and toys, and even her bedroom was public space as Peter would crawl into bed with them in the mornings.

Hillary worked long days as an English as a Second Language teacher. Although her job was to teach English to new immi-grants, she often took on far more—finding a doctor for her stu-dents, helping them look for housing, or acting as a translator at parent-teacher meetings. While she loved her work, she was often wiped out by the end of the day. Her house had been a haven, a place to unwind. Now, as she walked through the door, "three people would come rushing at me and, wow, it's six-thirty, I worked hard all day, give, give, give. And Stefan would say, 'Oh they just want to give you something.' But it didn't feel like they were giving me something, it felt like they wanted something from me." She hated that she was constantly nagging the children to pick up after themselves. In order to get a little quiet time, she found herself staying later and later at the office.

Other stepmothers move into the house where their partner has lived with his ex-wife. These stepmothers are confronted with daily evidence of their partner's history that they are not a part of. Sometimes, the stepmother's efforts to put her own stamp on the house or to integrate her own possessions into the existing ones are met with resistance. A tension, which is not always resolvable, can arise between a stepmother's need to establish her own space and her stepchildren's need to live with their past.

The more impotent some stepmothers feel, the more they attempt to exert control. This strategy usually backfires. Since their wishes are already being disregarded, being more demanding does not usually translate into greater success. In Delia Ephron's funny and perceptive book, *Funny Sauce,* about her experiences as a stepmother, she describes trying to get her stepchildren to leave an empty fountain in which they were playing. When they refused, she insisted more vehemently. They dug in their heels, and the battle of wills was on. Ephron, of course, lost. As she reflected back on why she got caught up in this struggle, she realized that, although she was saying "Get out," what she meant was "Let me in."[6]

When stepmothers do ask for something for themselves or try to gain a modicum of control, they sometimes feel they are being unreasonable and unbending, that they *should* adapt. One stepmother described herself as "neurotic and anally retentive" because she wanted her stepson to adhere to the visitation schedule. This woman's two teenaged stepchildren lived with her and her partner from Monday to Friday and stayed with their mother on the weekends. The stepmother looked forward to the two-day break as a time to unwind and do things with her partner. Recently, her stepson had chosen to stay at his father's on the weekends because his friends lived in that neighbourhood. If the stepmother insisted that he go to his mother's, she felt mean and selfish, thinking she should "go with the flow." If her stepson stayed the full week, she felt resentful. There was no way to win.

Biological versus Step-Relationships

The ambivalent nature of stepmothers' relationships with stepchildren becomes even more evident when set against stepmothers' relationships with their own children.[7] Stepmothers often characterize four ways that these two kinds of relationships are opposites.

1. Ease versus Constraint

Whereas stepmothers may tiptoe or walk on eggshells around stepchildren, they feel easy and relaxed with biological children. The constraint they feel with stepchildren is absent with their own children. While they may second-guess and agonize over how to act with stepchildren, they react spontaneously with their own.

Although some stepmothers fear their stepchildren will regard them as wicked, they do not worry about being a wicked mother. Sometimes this creates a double standard. Stepmothers will bend over backwards with stepchildren, but will let fly if annoyed at their children. One stepmother described how she will yell at her children that their messy rooms look like a barn, but, with her stepchildren, she will say "something very gently like 'Do me a favour. You know, could you please, could you, sort of make your bed? Do whatever you want to the room, but just, I hate unmade beds.'" Reluctant to play the heavy with stepchildren, they sometimes will be stricter with their own children. In an ironic reversal of the Cinderella story, their children sometimes complain that their mothers are harder on them than on their stepsiblings.

2. Unconditional versus Contingent

None of the stepmothers with whom I spoke ever said they loved their stepchildren unconditionally. With their own children, unconditional love is a given. It is not that stepmothers do not love their stepchildren, because many do. The unconditional part is trickier. Even the most harmonious stepmother-stepchild relationship contains some ambivalence. Some stepmothers feel guilty about their differing feelings for step- and biological children. Others are less conflicted. While they might not openly admit it, many acknowledged to me that their relationships with their own children feel limitless. If their child needed something, nothing would prevent them from fulfilling it. With stepchildren, it is more a choice. One stepmother confessed: "As a mother, you're not aware of having to be dedicated. You just are. There's no question about it. But with stepchildren, you are in the position of 'Good God. I chose this! Do I want it?'"

3. Mutual versus One-Way

Relationships with biological children—in contrast to those with stepchildren—are reciprocal. There is mutual affection and mutual exchange. Their children generally let their mother know what is on their mind and vice versa. Of course, there can be conflict, and their own children are not always appreciative. In these situations, though, the mother feels she can usually mend or at least address the issues with her own children. With stepchildren it feels too risky to do this.

In Chapter 1, Martha described how her daughter, Sarah, is much more defiant and rude than are her stepchildren. As Sarah has become a teenager, the rebellion and high-handedness have increased. Although Martha gets infuriated with Sarah, she also forgives her: "We went shopping, and she always gets in a snit when we shop, because they want everything at that age. So she was really quite bratty. By the time we got home, I'm really ready to be home and put this kid to bed or say goodnight. And then she says, 'I'm sorry for the way I behaved tonight.' Well, your heart kind of melts."

With her stepchildren, there is no opportunity to repair. Martha recognizes that she contributes to the awkwardness of her relationship with her stepchildren. Just as her stepchildren are not forthcoming with her, she is not open with them. While she will blow up at Sarah and tell her she is a brat, if she is angry with her stepchildren, she will just retreat to her room: "It's much harder to be honest [with my stepchildren], and that is one of the things that really bothered me initially. I believe in being honest about feelings and it was hard for me to be honest with my feelings, because I felt that my feelings would be so brutal to them."

4. Authority versus Impotence

A mother's right to set the agenda with her children is unquestioned. A stepmother, by contrast, can be overruled. A mother's authority is unassailable, while a stepmother is vulnerable to criticism. Julie has noticed that, although her partner and in-laws openly challenge Julie's decisions regarding her stepdaughter, Rachel, they do not question her actions with her son and daughter. Julie has equal responsibility for all three children, but legitimacy only with her biological children.

Although most stepmothers identify positive elements in their interactions with stepchildren and only a minority feel there is overt hostility between them and their stepchildren, relationships with stepchildren are not straightforward. Most stepmothers are perpetually testing the water, trying to ascertain if they can safely venture in deeper. Stepmothers generally expect a lot less from stepchildren than from family, friends, and their own children. They also tend to receive a lot less and to feel grateful for the crumbs that come their way. As I discuss in the next chapter, their partners are often critical in determining whether the stepmother finds a place in the stepfamily. While some men are supportive, others let the stepmother flounder. This lack of support can be devastating, even harder to deal with than their complicated relationships with stepchildren.

Chapter 6

Unsupportive Partners, Awkward Fathers

Stepmothers are far more critical of their partners than they are of their stepchildren. While they do not count on their stepchildren to be welcoming and open, they do expect their partners to stand behind them. Maura was furious at her partner, Dylan, because he brushed off her problems with her ten-year-old stepdaughter, Phoebe: "[The hardest thing about being a stepmother] is just wrangling with Dylan. You can take jibes from these kids. Well, fine. But to have to convince him that there was any hurt at all or what the substance of that was—it's too much."

Stepmothers often feel let down by partners.[1] As I discussed in Chapter 2, many initially assume that their partners will share their views about the stepfamily and that they will work as a team. It is disappointing when their partners do not seem to understand their difficulties or do not rescue them when they are floundering. Many stepmothers also are critical of their partners' fathering, and this dissatisfaction can seep into the couple's relationship.

The Unsupportive Partner

Particularly at the beginning, stepmothers often feel their partners are unaware of, or insensitive to, their struggles. When they tell their partners how overwhelmed they feel, some men dismiss or trivialize their concerns and do not seem to grasp the stepmothers' need for support. Maura's fury at Dylan built up over time. From the start, her stepdaughter, Phoebe, was very possessive of her father and seized every opportunity to mark her territory. Each morning, she would barge into the couple's bedroom and jump into bed beside her father, squeezing Maura over to the edge. No matter how many times she was asked to knock first, she persisted. If Maura was talking to Dylan, Phoebe would plunk herself on her father's lap, blocking Dylan's view of Maura. While Maura could understand Phoebe's attachment to her father, she felt under siege. She started waking up earlier and earlier, bracing herself for the inevitable moment when her stepdaughter would burst in. Dylan was no help. He thought his daughter was charming and spontaneous. When Maura tried to explain her discomfort over Phoebe sharing their bed, he shrugged it aside, saying that she would understand when she became a mother. Maura was outraged at his smug assumption that she was the one with the problem.

The final straw was when Phoebe "criticized me for eating my spaghetti with a spoon and fork and she said, 'It's quite obvious that she wasn't brought up in our household, right, Dad?' I thought it was the height of cheek when she's sitting in our house-hold eating spaghetti I had made!" Dylan did not rebuke his daughter. Since there were guests there that night, Maura held her anger in until they had left. When she cornered her partner, his explanation was that his daughter "feels a lot of pain toward her mother for historic reasons, plus she's angry about the breakup. She's not able to blast her mother for it, because her mother comes right back with sarcasm." Maura felt, although Dylan's rationale might be correct, he should make some attempt to understand her feelings and not let Phoebe use her as a "safe punching bag."

It can also be devastating for a stepmother to discover that her partner has a secret coalition with his children. The stepmother will assume that she and her partner have agreed on the house rules and then find out that her partner has negotiated a separate deal with his children. When Betsy—the stepmother with a mis-sion—moved in, her partner, Mick, had an open-pocket policy with his children. Whenever the three children asked for money, he handed it over. Betsy felt the children were taking advantage of their father. She and Mick also had opposing philosophies regarding finances. Betsy liked to live within a budget and had established a retirement savings plan. Mick, by contrast, was happy to "live paycheque to paycheque. He'd never thought about his future." Since they had a joint account, Betsy believed she should have some input into how money was dispersed. As part of her program to overhaul Mick's and her three stepchildren's lives, Betsy insisted that the children's allowances be contingent on completing chores. Her stepchildren protested. Mick agreed with Betsy, however, so she assumed they would settle in. Her two stepsons adapted fairly quickly, but her stepdaughter, Olivia, was more intractable. Olivia was adept at winding her father around her finger. She would not finish her chores but would wheedle her allowance out of Mick. Betsy confronted Mick, who conceded that Olivia should abide by the same rules as her brothers. So when Betsy stumbled on a covert transaction between Mick and Olivia, she blew up: "I found [Mick and Olivia] whispering outside the room I was in. That was it. I said, 'If you guys are going to whisper behind my back, I'm out of here. I can't live in an environment where my husband has stooped to the level that he's whispering behind my back.'" Mick's position was that if he wanted to give money to his daughter, it was his right. Betsy conceded the validity of this, but she felt he should have been straightforward, instead of setting her up as an ogre.

As in Betsy's situation, disagreements with partners about money often mirror stepmothers' general dissatisfaction with their partners. Money becomes a symbol of their unhappiness. Betsy was not really distressed over the $20 that Mick was slipping his daughter now and again but because of what his action represented—her exclusion from their relationship, Mick's inability to be firm with his children, and his lack of recognition of Betsy's contribution to the household. Stepmothers' biggest complaint about partners and money is when their partners spend money without consulting them. Particularly if the stepmother is putting money into the household, she wants some say about how it is disbursed. Some stepmothers also criticize their partners for spending money unwisely. Their partners may buy expensive treats for their children that they cannot really afford or, like Mick, give in to all their children's demands.

When Bernice married Martin, she assumed they would be equal partners. Martin, however, had been a widower for eight years and was accustomed to acting as a single parent. He rarely informed Bernice about his decisions regarding his two teenaged children, Amelia and Ryan, and regularly bought them expensive presents. Bernice would discover these purchases only when the Visa bill arrived. If she confronted Martin, he would wave away her objections saying it gave him pleasure to spoil them. Bernice worked full-time and shared the household expenses. Martin's high-handed behaviour infuriated her. She also felt it gave Amelia and Ryan licence to dismiss her as irrelevant.

One of the most humiliating situations for stepmothers is when their partners contradict them publicly. For many stepmothers, it takes courage to request their stepchildren do anything. It is distressing if their partners do not back them up. Discipline is often a focus of contention. Some men do not want the stepmother to correct their children. If they take the responsibility for their children, this decision presents less of a problem. If, however, the stepmother is in charge of the household and her stepchildren but does not have any power, she is put in an impossible situation.

Such an arrangement almost ended one stepmother's marriage. Maria, age thirty-nine, has been a stepmother for six years. From the outset, her husband, Matthew, age forty-seven, made it clear that he did not want Maria disciplining his two children, Chris and Jonathan, who were then twelve and eight. He thought that each parent—Maria had a son, Paolo, age fourteen, from a previous marriage—should be in charge of his or her own children. Maria thought they should present a united front and work as a team with all three children. Maria had been a single parent for ten years and her previous husband had been a "deadbeat" father: "No support, financially or emotionally, nothing. He wasn't there for Paolo. He lives [in this city], but he's never picked him up once." Maria welcomed sharing the responsibility for parenting. She encouraged Matthew to discipline her son, but Matthew was adamant about the division.

Friction began two years later when Chris moved in after his mother could no longer control him. This shift coincided with a promotion for Matthew. Matthew, a high-level civil servant in the federal government, had always worked ten- to twelve-hour days, but now he was also out of town two or three days a week. Maria was left to cope on her own: "Matthew travelled. Not only did he travel, he used to be at work at 7:30, so I would have to make sure Chris was ready for school. And Matthew didn't get home till late at night, and I used to have to not only do Chris's laundry, get his supper, but try to get his homework underway." Chris had heard his father on the subject of who was in charge of whom, so he was not inclined to listen to his stepmother: "Every night was a vicious fight for him to do his homework, he wouldn't come in on time, he was very disobedient and disrespectful, and Matthew would not let me handle any of the situations."

Chris was failing in high school, skipping classes, and generally being defiant. Since Matthew was often away, Maria was left to field calls from the school about Chris. Her son, Paolo, was at the same school and on the honour roll. Maria, a schoolteacher herself, knew the principal well and was embarrassed when he called to tell her they had suspended Chris. Even though she had no influence over Chris, she felt his bad behaviour reflected poorly on her. She was also the one at home when the police phoned after Chris had been caught shoplifting.

Maria and Matthew's fights intensified over Matthew's refusal to let Maria take charge. Maria also felt Chris fanned the flames: "He's very smart, a very smart boy, and he would play us against each other, and then we'd be fighting. So I saw all this, and I said, 'Matthew, this is what's happening here: if we don't get together as parents, as a team, Chris is going to be lost.'" Matthew's rules were much more lax than Maria's. While Paolo was not allowed out on school nights, Chris came and went as he pleased. Maria insisted that Paolo finish his homework before watching television. Chris had no such restriction. Paolo complained to his mother that it was unfair that Chris had so much more freedom even though Paolo was older. Maria agreed with Paolo, but felt that Matthew was doing Chris a disservice. One reason Maria had married Matthew was to provide a father for Paolo, but she now worried about the effect of the tensions on her son.

It came to a head one evening: "I just blew. I had enough of it because I wasn't allowed to discipline Chris. I told Chris to do something and Matthew told him that he didn't have to in front of me. And I thought, 'You don't do this to a child.' I mean, if he had called me into the basement and said something to me, that's one thing, but not in front of the child." Feeling mortified, Maria left with Paolo and moved to her parents'. Eventually Maria and Matthew reconciled, but Maria feels that her marriage has been seriously damaged.

Chris's behaviour did not improve. He left home at seventeen, having dropped out of high school in Grade 10. He rarely contacts his father. Although it is a relief to have Chris gone, Maria has many regrets: "I said to Matthew, 'I'd rather take him on my own. If you'd leave me alone, I really think I could do something for him.' . . . I think I've got a half-decent feel for kids. I think somebody needs to take them under their wings and just love them to death. And it would be twenty-four-hours-a-day love. That's what I think he needs." As it is, Chris is adrift, Maria and Matthew's marriage is strained, and Maria feels a profound sense of disillusionment.

Stepmothers also feel disappointed when their partners do not help them become part of the stepfamily. They are outsiders at the beginning and often need their partners to invite them into the magic circle. Even if they tell their partners how lonely they feel, their partners may either make light of the stepmother's desperation or expect the stepmother to find her own space in the stepfamily. As might be expected, stepmothers often feel resentful if their partners leave them to find their own way.

A frequent complaint of stepmothers is that their partners are terrible at attending to, and balancing, everyone's needs. Usually, in families, women assume this role of mediating between family members and making sure that everyone is happy. In stepfamilies, as we have seen, stepmothers often do not have the authority and their partners are the only ones who can take on this task. Yet many stepmothers believe their partners do a poor job here. While some men neglect the stepmother because they are so involved with their children, others let everyone sink or swim—the children as well as the stepmother. There can be total chaos, and these men are either oblivious or incapable of dealing with the problems. Some stepmothers become frustrated, because, like Maria, they believe that, if they were given the chance, they could straighten out the mess. Instead, they have to live with the effects.

When their partners are unsupportive, stepmothers may feel like second-class citizens in the family. Sometimes they see themselves as third in line, trailing their partner's work as well as his children. The sense of being second-best, a nobody, as stepmothers variously describe themselves, is particularly acute for some stepmothers whose stepchildren are there part-time. While the children are there, stepmothers become invisible while their partner focuses completely on the children. A stepmother may support her partner's desire to be with his children, but she will also want him to recognize her needs. Lacking support from her partner, she may question why she is staying in this situation.

The Incapable Father

Many stepmothers criticize their partners' performance as fathers.[2] They do not consider their partners abusive, overtly mean, or bullying. Nor do they view them as neglectful fathers. Only a handful of the men in this study had minimal or no contact with their children. This makes this group somewhat atypical. Many studies on the effects of divorce have found that a sizable number of fathers drift out of their children's lives after the divorce, either seeing their children rarely or losing contact completely.[3] We can therefore assume that the partners of the stepmothers in my study might be more—rather than less—committed to their children than many fathers after divorce. Yet these women often disapproved of their partner as a father. Although they felt that their partner loved his children and wanted to be a good father, they often believed he lacked some crucial skills and insights.

It is ironic that stepmothers become disappointed in their partners as fathers, because many are initially drawn to these men's dedication to their children. Watching their partners play and interact with their children offers them insight into a more vulnerable and emotional side than they might see otherwise.[4] A man caring for children is enormously attractive for some stepmothers: "I was impressed that he was raising two little girls. There's just a bunch of your heart that goes out to a man. If you watch men with children in shopping malls, women are talking to them constantly, because your heart goes out to a man who's nurturing children." Some stepmothers are so swept away with emotion, they neglect to notice whether their partners are any good at being a father. Some comment, with a wry amusement, that they might have been less enthusiastic if they had taken a closer look at his parenting skills.

The Chaotic Father

Stepmothers' biggest complaint about their partners as fathers is that they do not establish clear routines and rules. Even if their partners do set a structure in place, they are often poor at following through. Rarely do stepmothers criticize their partners for being overly rigid and strict. Rather they view them as disorganized and too apt to let things slide. Some chalk this up to guilt—that, because of the divorce, these men are reluctant to discipline or set limits with their children. These fathers tend to overcompensate and spoil their children in an attempt to right the balance.[5] Stepmothers believe that caving in does not help their children in the long run. Other stepmothers interpret their partners' slackness as ineptitude. Their partners' apparent lack of ability spurs some stepmothers to rescue not only their stepchildren, but their partners too.

Mick's passivity with his children irritated Betsy. Rather than making them pitch in around the house, he let the mess pile up. Although she admired Mick's willingness to play and engage with his children, she was less impressed with his permissive attitude to his children's sloppiness and rudeness: "He just didn't deal with a lot of problems in the house. He just said, 'I don't know.' And that would be it. And he'd ignore it until it came up again and then he'd say, 'I don't know.' . . . He'd far rather ignore it until it's solved or goes away or has passed. That's his major coping skill."

One reason Betsy demanded so much from her stepchildren was that she felt Mick asked so little. She was compensating for his unwillingness to discipline his children. Although Betsy knows that she tends to take charge—as an engineer, she is often the manager of projects where she is the only woman—she feels Mick has taken advantage of this. He can be the good guy, while she has to be the heavy.

Awkward Fathers

Many stepmothers describe their partners as "awkward" fathers. Their partners seem uneasy, hesitant, unsure about how to approach their children, and they rely on the stepmother to plan weekend activities, buy the children's presents, or organize the meals. Just as stepmothers feel like they walk on eggshells around their stepchildren, they often think their partners are tiptoeing around too, because they don't know what to do. One can imagine the strained atmosphere that these two dynamics create.

Fathers who have their children with them part-time seem particularly diffident. Perhaps because they spend less time with their children, they may be more out of touch. These men sometimes lean on the stepmother for guidance about what to do with their children. If they have drifted away from their children, the stepmother may be the one to urge these fathers to reconnect. With particularly incapable or uninterested fathers, stepmothers may become solely in charge.

Some stepmothers feel their partners are unaware of signs that their children need them, that they are "emotionally" awkward. One stepmother commented, "I don't know if men don't have a maternal instinct. I never really believed in maternal instinct, but he's not particularly affectionate with them. I don't know if that's a male thing. He kisses them goodnight and all of that. But if they get upset and they're crying, they come to me." Even if they do pick up on their children's distress, some men either pass it off or impatiently counsel the child to "snap out of it." Stepmothers may expend an enormous amount of energy encouraging their partners to become more emotionally in tune with their children. These endeavours are not always successful. Stepchildren may come to them for comfort—rather than to their fathers—because the reception is more empathetic. In some stepfamilies, the stepmother becomes the mediator between her partner and his children—listening to her stepchildren's upsets and then counselling her partner about how to respond.

Once Sheila discovered on her camping trip that her stepsons were delighted to have her around, she plunged into stepmother life, taking them to the movies or museums, playing cards, and generally horsing around. Perhaps because she is closer in age to Michael's children than to Michael, she feels she relates better to them than he does. Although Michael loves his two sons and is proud of them, he has always been distant: "Even if Michael was [still in his marriage] anyway, it would be no different. He would be no closer to his children than he is now, because he has no idea what to do with the children when they see him. He doesn't talk to his boys about issues that matter today. He's not a good communicator with them, and the boys are so interested in television and Nintendo, they don't care whether their father is there."

Sheila feels that Michael has made her an intermediary: "This getting closer to the boys is something Michael's not happy about. He doesn't really want to get close to his boys and he uses me now as a buffer between them, so they don't ask him embarrassing questions." The boys will often talk to her, rather than to their father. While they might tell their father about an accomplishment at school, they confide their problems with friends to Sheila. She has started coaching Michael in how to interact with them: "I'll say, 'I think you ought to think about talking to them about this, or think about this or that.' If he doesn't react right then, he'll often think about it and then next day, he'll say, 'You know, I've been thinking about what you said, and I think it's a very good idea and in fact I'm going to go about it this way.'" While she is gratified that Michael values her advice, she is astonished he is so clueless: "Michael has been a father for twelve years, he ought to know how the game is played. And I'm just flabbergasted that he doesn't." Here she is, a young woman without her own children, yet she has more insight than the father does.

At the beginning, Sheila was delighted to assume responsibility, because she genuinely liked the boys and it offered her a foothold in the family. By the time she talked to me, this role was beginning to chafe. She had begun encouraging Michael to become more engaged. Instead of her planning the weekend, she will hand the newspaper over to him. Michael is an accomplished cook so she has suggested that he teach his boys. Knowing that the boys and Michael will rely on her to organize the kitchen, she will disappear until dinnertime.

Because Sheila is so close to her stepsons, she is much happier than many stepmothers. At the same time, she thinks her job would be a lot easier if she were a stepfather: "It's doubly difficult for a stepmother because the fathers have so much to learn. The role of a stepfather would be so much easier because the mother has got it all down pat." She believes that stepmothers have twice the number of challenges that stepfathers do because not only do they have to learn how to be a stepmother themselves but they must teach their partners how to be engaged fathers. By contrast, she hypothesizes that women already know how to be engaged mothers and thus stepfathers have a lot less work to do.

More and More Unequal

When partners are incapable, many stepmothers become capable. As mentioned earlier, stepmothers are usually responsible for most of the housework and are the main organizers—deciding about household routines, planning meals, and orchestrating family events. Some decide that it is better that they have this role so they can ensure everything runs smoothly: "I'm the mother and choreographer here. That's how I feel it should be, up to a point. You can't shove people together, but you can provide an environment. If you provide an environment, people will fall into place."

Fathers are more actively involved in the care of their children than they are in the household. Here, too, however, stepmothers either do more or share it equally with partners. It is an unusual father who does most of the child care. The division of labour generally splits along traditional gender lines, with men not taking the lead even though they are the biological parent.[6]

Rarely do stepmothers and their partners discuss at the outset how the housework and child care will be divided. They seem to slip "naturally" into their roles. Over time, stepmothers tend to take on more and more of the household, while their partners do less and less. Often before the stepmother arrives on the scene, the father is fairly active but pulls back as the stepmother steps in. Among the women with whom I talked, it was rare for fathers to maintain the same level of work after the remarriage. When one stepmother met her partner, he had been a widower for two years. During this time, he had cared for his three children on his own: "He washed the clothes, he vacuumed the house, he went to the supermarket and got the groceries, and he did tell me for the first year after his first wife died, he cooked meals. . . . He made sure that there was all kinds of food in the house for the kids. When he got married to me, just like that he said, 'It's all yours. I don't want to do it any more.' And he won't even go to the supermarket!"

While most men are not this blatant, the effect is the same—the majority of stepmothers end up with the majority of the household work. Stepmothers generally do not object to this. Although the stepmother quoted above was taken aback by the rapidity of her partner's abdication, she accepted it. She was already caring for her three children so three more children did not seem that onerous, although she now ran a household of eight people, compared to four before her remarriage. Some stepmothers offer excuses for their partners' lacklustre involvement. As one stepmother said, "He really cares about his kids and he tried to do the best for them. The thing is, his business takes up so much of his time, he can't be around as much as he'd like." These women often work themselves and find time to do everything their partners cannot, yet remain surprisingly uncritical of their partners. The stepmother with the new family of eight works full-time as a bank teller and then heads home to cook and clean and do laundry.

Although she would like her partner to be more supportive, she does not question his right to opt out. A handful of stepmothers even discourage their partner's involvement in the house. Being in charge gives them a way to claim a space in the stepfamily.

Other stepmothers resent the extra work, however, not anticipating the extra household demands. As I will discuss in the next chapter, childless stepmothers often react most strongly. They have moved from a single life where they can please themselves to a family life of cooking, cleaning, ferrying children to dentist appointments and hockey games, and sorting mountains of mismatched socks. A partner's casual assumption that they will assume, or even share, the household work can be irksome. They got into this stepfamily to be with their partners, not to be housekeeper and babysitter.[7]

Even those stepmothers who willingly take charge become annoyed if their work is taken for granted. They want recognition from their partners. If unhappy and unappreciative stepchildren are added to the mix, stepmothers often feel justifiably overburdened.

The Relationship Suffers

Given all the stresses of stepfamily life, it is perhaps not unexpected that the couple relationship often becomes strained.[8] The crucial element for stepmothers is their partner's attitude. If their partner is supportive, they can withstand a lot of acting out from stepchildren. The couple relationship can even be strengthened by the two of them working in tandem to deal with a difficult child. One stepmother believed the drama of living with her teenaged stepdaughter brought her closer to her partner: "It made us more intimate. It pushed us into a decision-making situation that I think developed a bond with each other. We had lots of crises with Kayla [my stepdaughter] disappearing and coming in drunk, trying to pick a fist fight with us when she was fourteen. It was awful, traumatic, and I think that in the end it made us stronger."

If, however, a partner dismisses the stepmother's struggles, shuts her out of the family, or makes unilateral decisions, the stepmother often becomes angry or withdraws from the relationship. I have already described Patricia's terrible relationship with her step-daughter, Amy, who treated her stepmother with contempt. One evening at dinner Amy was mocking her English teacher (Patricia's profession). Her final salvo was that the teacher was "almost as old and useless as you, Patricia." Patricia was stunned, not just at Amy's rudeness, but at Jeff's lack of reaction. After dinner, Patricia confronted him. "He said, 'Oh, but she was embarrassed afterwards.' I mean, he was trying to cover up for her! Well, maybe she was, maybe she wasn't. I don't know. But she has said that sort of thing at other times." This passivity was typical of Jeff. In his first marriage, his ex-wife had made all the child-care decisions and Jeff was fairly peripheral. After Amy moved in with Patricia and him, he continued to be a hands-off father. Although Patricia was hurt by Jeff's failure to back her up, she did not confront him directly, because she worried that he would feel caught between her and Amy.

Arguing over stepchildren can create wear and tear in a couple's relationship. Some conflicts arise over major problems—children being expelled from school, stealing, acting out, drugs—but they can also be over relatively minor issues. Deborah, the stepmother whose children thought she was their mother, believes her and John's constant battling over Emma damaged their marriage. Deborah has already described how John usually took Emma's side. Even asking Emma to pick her towel up off the floor could escalate into a screaming match with John: "[The fighting about Emma] strained the relationship with my husband. There were times when he'd be very upset and he'd say, 'If I couldn't look after her and be nice to her, then you know, that was it, our marriage was no good.' He was ready to call it off many times." Deborah finds it depressing that John does not acknowledge how she has cared for his children over the last twenty years. Despite the antagonism between Emma and Deborah, Emma, now twenty-two, is more grateful: "Things were always tense but at the same time, when [John and I] were arguing, she would say, 'Why do you put up with all that? If you were to separate I would stay with you.'" Although Emma's desire to live with Deborah, rather than her father, made Deborah feel that she "must have done something right," it also highlighted John's lack of appreciation for Deborah's efforts with his children. She and John now live pretty much separate lives. Her allegiance is to her son, Steven, now age fourteen. Since she believes divorce is harmful for children, she has hung onto her marriage.

The complicated dynamics of stepfamilies also usually translate into less time for the couple. Even when stepmothers like their stepchildren and their partners are supportive, the couple relationship can get lost. Three key transitions pose the greatest challenges for the couple—the first few years of the stepfamily, the time when stepchildren arrive and depart for their regular stays, and when stepchildren move in full-time. The turmoil at the beginning of the stepfamily may overwhelm the couple relationship. Some stepmothers feel put upon by all the new demands on their time and energy, and this may translate into dissatisfaction with their partners.

Stepchildren's comings and goings can stress the couple relationship. When stepchildren first arrive, they often demand their father's total attention. Particularly if the children are just there on weekends or more sporadically, their fathers may want to focus entirely on them. Before the children head back to their mother's, the same dynamic may ensue. Although stepmothers may rationally understand this, it is hard not to feel shunted aside. Sometimes stepmothers feel they get the worst of both worlds: while the children are with them, they are invisible. When the children leave, their partner may pour his energy back into work. One stepmother really likes her two stepdaughters, who are with the stepmother and her partner every weekend. At the same time, she finds the inexorableness of the schedule wearing: "I'm human. I sometimes really do resent kids showing up here. They come with clothes that are dirty or need to be fixed, and then they're, 'I want to eat this, I don't want to eat that. Wash this for me.' I just sometimes resent it. Then if I get snappy, it puts a strain on the relationship." This woman does not have children and is pleased to have two young girls in her life. Her partner is also one of the rare fathers who does most of the domestic work. At the same time, stepfamily life can be too intense: "It's one of those things where I think, 'Okay, there's other things I'd rather do.' And sometimes I'm not that good at expressing what I want and it comes across like, 'All of you, get out of my face.' "

Having stepchildren move in full-time usually creates another challenge for the couple. Even if the stepmother supports the decision—and almost all the women with whom I talked did— there is less time available for the couple. If the children are young, evenings are swallowed up with baths and bedtime routines. Older children may go to sleep at the same time as the stepmother and her partner. One stepmother had supported her adolescent step-son's desire to move in with his father. Nevertheless, she found it hard that she and her partner no longer had any evening to them-selves: "I did resent losing my freedom at night. Instead of the two of us watching TV, there were three of us."

Even if a couple protects their privacy, they may be too worn out to enjoy it. Their sex life is one place this shows up. Some step-mothers feel inhibited by the presence of stepchildren, never sure when their stepchildren may walk through the door or overhear them. Others will not hug or touch their partners in front of their stepchildren because they sense the children's discomfort. Some are so unhappy with their partners that they pull back and their inter-est in sex wanes. Sometimes, it is their partner who withdraws. One stepmother was frustrated because she and her partner had no sex life while her stepchildren were with them: "We're moving now toward being able to have sex on weekends when the kids are around. For a long time, that was an issue. There would be no cud-dling, no intimacy, no sex. There would be no time to just sit and chat with one another. It was either that he was totally preoccupied with them, or that he had exhausted himself physically and emo-tionally paying attention to them until they went to sleep."

Of course, there is also less time and energy to work out prob-lems that arise. Some stepmothers realize that their relationship has become frayed. One couple found themselves squabbling con-stantly over his two boys. The stepmother disapproved of how her partner "caved in" to all his sons' requests while he thought she was too rigid and stern. While the children were with them, the couple were too distracted to resolve their differences. The unpleasantness began to spill over to their time on their own. Both had already gone through divorces and did not want to repeat that: "When [the stepchildren] were there part-time, it was causing problems with Jean-Jacques and me. Neither of us wanted to see that. We don't want to go through another broken relationship." They began to refocus on their relationship. The children were required to knock before they entered their bedroom, not just barge in. The couple started going to movies again and took their in-laws up on their offer to babysit the children for a weekend.

For some, however, the accumulated stresses and the neglect of their relationship can cause irreparable damage. In these situations, stepmothers usually feel so betrayed and disappointed by their partners that they question whether they want to make the effort. Maria reacted to her partner Matthew's steadfast refusal to grant her any authority with her stepson Chris by pulling away. Even though Chris has gone and the house is calm, Maria still feels bruised. Maria contemplated leaving for good, but does not want a second divorce. She has many regrets about her marriage, how-ever: "I would never do it again, never. Absolutely never. The price is too high. . . . I was absolutely fatigued to death. I would never, ever marry again and have stepchildren."

· · ·

As you may have noticed, stepmothers' criticisms of their partners are often gender-based. They dismiss them as "typical males," point to their lack of "maternal instinct," or suggest that their failures of empathy and support stem from their being male. By contrast, when stepmothers praise their partners, they often cite qualities usually associated with mothers, like nurturing or caring or domestic, or they refer to their partners as maternal. Paulette, who felt hurt by her stepchildren's rejection of attempts to nurture them, describes why she thinks her partner, Richard, is a wonderful father: "He's like a mother. He's very caring, very loving. Nothing is too much trouble for him to do for them. He puts a lot of effort into disciplining and training, talking to them. He's not imposing or irrational. If he has to discipline them, he thinks it all through and then he will talk to them very rationally about something they did and why it wasn't acceptable. To me, he's very motherly." To be a good father in a stepfamily is to be a good mother!

In non-divorced families, women often assume the emotional work of listening and responding, of mediating, connecting, and attending to everyone's happiness. The stepmother's outsider position may not allow her to do this. It may be that stepfamilies with a stepmother and a biological father demand more of men than non-divorced nuclear families. As the biological parent, they must take on the so-called maternal work. As stepmothers like Sheila point out, the dilemma is that many men have not acquired these skills. The challenge for couples in stepfamilies may be to switch places—stepmothers have to resist acting like mothers, while fathers have to become more maternal.

Chapter 7

The Childless Stepmother:
Will It Ever Be My Turn?

Stepmotherhood can be traumatic for childless stepmothers. They face the same issues as stepmothers with stepchildren, but often also have extra stressors. The increased commotion and demands on their time and energy can be overwhelming at first. Cultural attitudes toward childless women can undercut their legitimacy within the stepfamily. Most anguish, however, surrounds the decision of whether to have children.[1]

A Monumental Amount of Work

While stepmothers with children from previous relationships are already adapted to life with children, childless stepmothers are often unprepared for the huge shifts in their lives. They are accustomed to living as they please. Now, they are hard-pressed to find a quiet moment for themselves, everyone else's schedules seem to take precedence over theirs, and the household chores seem never-ending. Some feel they have become transformed into snappish, irritable nags.

Peggy considers herself a happy stepmother. She and her partner, Simon, share many of the same values, and she really likes his two children, Mara, age ten, and Jacob, age seven. Every now and again, though, she regrets how much she has traded away. Before Simon, Peggy's life was very free. She loves travel, and her work as a consultant permitted her to live in Europe for extended periods.

She was willing to give up her peripatetic life for Simon, but had counted on occasional trips with him. Simon's joint custody arrangement has complicated their plans. Money is also tight. Simon's ex-wife has chosen to stay home with her children, so he is supporting two households. Peggy had saved enough for a two-week trip to Costa Rica for herself and Simon. When Simon suggested she put it toward a new van, she was furious at his casual assumption that she should contribute and told him off: "I don't even think I need a car in the city. I take the subway to work. We're getting this car because you have kids. How can you possibly suggest I use my money! In fact, you should be paying even more than half because of that!" Peggy detests cars and, before Simon, did not own one. Now, instead of travelling the world, she spends a big chunk of her life in a car, ferrying Jacob and Mara to friends' houses, swimming lessons, and soccer games.

Then there is the never-ending housework. While Simon is a wonderfully attentive father, organization is not his strong point: "I feel like I'm already putting in an awful lot of time. I make the lunches, I do the shopping. I do laundry like I've never done before. I'm doing what feels like a monumental amount of work and I often resent the fact that not only do I have to do it, but I have to initiate it. I wouldn't mind so much if I felt he took the lead more often. I feel like he's slipping into a comfortable role." Peggy recognizes that Simon cannot grasp how radically her life has been transformed. He is so enamoured of his children that he assumes she will be too. Peggy agrees the children are charming, but wishes he could appreciate her perspective: "He wants to deny that they are such a big burden to me because he doesn't want to think that he's asking me to do so much. And it's partly he just loves his kids like mad. To him they're just so wonderful, why wouldn't you want to drive them everywhere? . . . He's not quite there yet in terms of seeing where I'm at. He still doesn't quite understand how I feel."

While stepmothers in general feel like aliens in their own

homes, childless stepmothers often feel this more acutely. They are used to a quiet, orderly space. Now their stepchildren are scattering their clothes and school books all over the floor, rifling through the stepmother's belongings, or charging into the bathroom while the stepmother is in the shower. Not surprisingly, many feel under siege.

Some childless stepmothers recognize that their frustration results in part from trying to bend the situation to their will. Unlike stepmothers who already have children, childless stepmothers may be less familiar with what is reasonable to expect from children. They may assume that they will have the same kinds of relationships with their stepchildren as they do with their peers. Some attempt to transfer their work strategies to their stepfamily and usually discover—to their dismay—that the stepfamily is less tractable than the workplace. Their lack of success can be particularly galling if they are used to managing their lives. Hillary believed that, if she explained the house rules rationally to her stepchildren, they would fall into line: "I expected them to be little adults. Yes, they're physically small, but I expected I should be able to deal with them the way I deal with an adult. And it quickly became very clear to me that that was pretty stupid."

Half a Person

Childless women in our culture are often considered incomplete, deficient, not fulfilling their "feminine" nature. Women who are physically unable to have children are pitied. Those who elect not to have children are branded as selfish, a judgement that's somewhat paradoxical since, by having children, a woman passes on her own genes and cares for her own children. Childless women sometimes feel discounted, because they have missed out on an *essential* experience for women.[2] Childless stepmothers are thus doubly saddled with negative stereotypes—that of the wicked stepmother and of the childless woman. Their opinions will be brushed aside, first because they are not their stepchildren's mother and second because they do not have their own children. Even if a stepmother cares full-time for her stepchildren and spends more time with them than the biological parents do, her insights about the children may be given less weight. Bearing a child confers a legitimacy that caring for children does not. One childless stepmother was irritated with friends and colleagues who questioned her abilities to be a stepmother because she did not have children: "Lots of people's reaction was 'But you don't know anything about children.' Which nobody says to somebody when they decide to have a child, right? But the fact that I was now taking on some responsibility for these kids was seen as a bad thing."

Some childless stepmothers feel their partners use their childlessness as ammunition to discredit their opinions. (Interestingly, stepchildren never used this ploy. It is hard to know why they do not. It may be because children tend to view adults as authorities, so it is less relevant whether their stepmother is also a mother.) One childless stepmother has teenaged stepchildren who live half the time with her and their father. Frustrated with her partner's unwillingness to set limits, she proposed establishing house rules. He brushed her aside: "Kenneth says, 'You say all of that because you don't have a child.' And that's another thing I get: I don't know because I'm not a mother. And I get a lot of that." His casual dismissal made her feel "completely incomplete and completely incompetent."

His comments also made her "feel like a teenager." This speaks to another stereotype about childless women, that they never really grow up because they have not assumed the responsibilities of motherhood. They are regarded as children because they have not borne a child. This stepmother has run into the same attitude with her in-laws. If the stepmother ventures an opinion about child-rearing at a family gathering, she senses lots of eye rolling: "Sometimes the whole family will be sitting together and they all have children and they'll talk about children and I'll come up with something and I feel like everybody is looking at me and saying, 'Well, wait 'til you have your own.'"

Some stepmothers note they become legitimate or are accepted into their in-laws' family only after they produce biological children. One stepmother had a close relationship with her stepdaughter, but her in-laws were distant. Her two sisters-in-law were close friends with her partner's ex-wife and were consequently cool to the stepmother. Her parents-in-law were sceptical of her attachment to her stepdaughter, questioning why a single woman would marry a man with a child. Only after the stepmother's twin girls were born did everyone thaw: "I was doing everything for [my stepdaughter] just like her own mother would. But to society, I was nobody because I wasn't her mother. It was really difficult in the beginning, being accepted by his family—being believed to be sincere. . . . They're great now. I've produced two perfect children, so I've been accepted into the family."

Some childless stepmothers internalize this notion of inferiority, discounting their contribution because they lack the biological connection. The fact that they love and care for their stepchildren is not enough. They do not question their feelings for their stepchildren, but view the relationship as being of less consequence because there is not the biological tie. One stepmother is devoted to her eight-year-old stepson. She is the one to pick him up from school, take him to his soccer practice, and bake the cookies for the school fair, yet she feels incomplete: "I feel like I'm not a real mother, because I don't have colic stories, I don't have the postnatal depression stories, I don't have the stories about them saying the cute little things. . . . When the stories come up, that's the time when I feel bereft."

Will I, Won't I?

The most excruciating conflict for some childless stepmothers is whether to have children. This is an enormous decision for most women, whether or not they are stepmothers. For stepmothers, the extra complication is that they already have children in their lives. Thus, choosing to have a child is an assertion that they want their *own* child. The impetus to start again is less compelling for their partners since they already are fathers. Childless stepmothers are usually more eager to have children than are their partners, and they may encounter resistance and heel dragging from their partners.[3]

The decision whether to have a child is uncomplicated for some childless stepmothers. Childlessness may be a temporary state, because they plan to have children and their partners support their desire. A few stepmothers are content to remain childless. They have always been ambivalent about becoming a mother and their stepchildren fulfil their faint maternal impulses. One stepmother married in her late forties. She had never yearned for children and was surprised by how much fun she had with her teenaged step-son, who spent summers with the stepmother and her partner. This contact was sufficient, however: "I haven't ever really wanted children. And this was a nice way for me to have a pseudo-child, you know. A little bit of a child without the work."

Other childless stepmothers want children, but are physically unable. Their stepchildren can become serendipitous, a chance for them to have children in their lives. Siobhan, age forty-six, is one of the happiest stepmothers I interviewed. Early in her marriage she discovered she could not have children. Larry's two sons, Sam and Derek, have been a huge bonus: "Having [stepchildren] really enriched my life, and I'm really grateful to them for that. I wouldn't have had children in any sense without them, and I think they've been marvellous." Although Siobhan was tempted to mother her stepsons, she avoided this pitfall. Her way around this trap was to recognize that she could be connected and loving with her stepsons without being their mother. As a young woman, Siobhan had imagined she would have lots of children. If someone had told her then that she would never have children, she would have been very upset. After thirteen years as a stepmother, her attitude has shifted: "Well, I think probably being a physical mother, biological mother, became less important. When I was a single woman in between relationships facing the fact that I might never have another relationship and never become a parent, I expected it might really bother me when I got to the end of my childbearing years. . . . Then, of course, I did acquire these two children. . . . I realized that there are many ways you can nurture."

Even if their partners agree to more children, the timing and number of children may not be straightforward. Some couples in stepfamilies delay having children for financial reasons. The expense of maintaining two households is so great that they cannot contemplate starting another family. Other stepmothers elect to wait until the stepfamily is calmer and their stepchildren are more settled. One stepmother and her partner postponed their second family for seven years: "I had a little trepidation, and that's why we delayed having children of our own, because I think we really needed to feel that the kids felt secure. They didn't have to worry. They could feel secure in my relationship with them. And they were somewhat independent themselves. All those kinds of issues because I think the separation-divorce process was tough on their self-esteem."

Other stepmothers scale back on the number of children they want, either because their partners are reluctant, because of financial considerations, or because they already feel overwhelmed by the logistics of caring for their stepchildren. One woman who has two teenaged stepchildren and a new baby daughter has already adjusted her expectations: "I might like more children someday, but I don't think it's going to happen. He's had three and I don't know if he wants four. And it's been more expensive."[4] Stepmothers with children from previous relationships are also sometimes torn about whether to have more children. Juggling two sets of children already, they fear another child might tip an already delicate balance. At the same time, they may feel a loss that they will not have children with their new partner.

Some childless stepmothers start out wanting to have children, but change their minds. Having now had the responsibility of children, they are reluctant to start again. As their stepchildren grow up, they have greater freedom. Their experience has been so stressful that they are reluctant to plunge in again. At least with stepchildren, there is usually free time while the children are at their mother's. A new baby would require twenty-four-hour care. Their maternal reserves have become depleted.

Gina had always assumed she would have children. When she met her partner, Barry, she was twenty-five. One of her conditions for marriage was that Barry be willing to have another child. He agreed. At the time they met, Barry's daughter, Bethany, was five and his son, Liam, was two. Barry had joint custody. Gina had not reckoned with how draining it would be to live half-time with two young children. Barry assumed that he and Gina would share the child care and housework equally. He headed off early each morning to play squash before work, and Gina was left to herd her stepchildren to daycare and school. The children resented their father's absence and fought against Gina's efforts to dress and feed them. Gina has a demanding job in the newsroom of a television station. Before Barry, she had prided herself on her unflappability. Now she arrived late and frazzled at the office and spent much of the day playing catch-up. At home, there were major rows. Gina was furious with Barry for his off-loading of responsibility. Bethany and Gina had screaming matches. In retrospect, Gina believes that some of their battles were avoidable, that, lacking confidence and experience, she used a heavier hand than she needed to. Over her seven years as a stepmother, her urge for children has waned: "I think his kids ruined it for me. To some degree, I think they were awful. I went through a horrendous time with Bethany. . . . I got the old 'I hate you. You're not my real mum,' and that was hard. I just went through so much in the early years with those kids that it made me think, 'Why do I ever want to go through this again. Why would I actually make a choice to go through this?'"

Gina now gets along well with both Bethany and Liam and regards herself as a third parent, along with the two biological parents. The house is on an even keel. Gina and Barry enjoy their time alone while the children are at their mother's. Both are currently dragging their feet on the child question, though: "I always thought I would have at least one kid. . . . And then the years just went on and on. Now I'm thirty-two, he's forty. The older he gets, the less he wants to have another kid. We really have a good life now. We have every other weekend without children. The kids are older now. We're out of the boots and snowpants and tying shoes [stage]. That stage in their lives was very hard." Her only lingering doubts have been planted by her family. They are pressuring her to reconsider, telling her, "You'll be a much more complete person with your own child. Bethany and Liam are great, but you should have your own. You'll love them better and differently." Note how her family subscribes to the idea that women without children are deficient. Gina's reaction to them is mixed. On the one hand, she wonders if she will regret missing this apparently essential female experience. On the other, she feels that it is unfair to Bethany and Liam to regard them as second rate because she does not share a biological link with them.

Childless stepmothers whose partners unilaterally decide they will not have more children suffer the most.[5] Some stepmothers know before they become stepmothers that their partners are opposed to having more children. Others find out afterwards. When their partner announces he does not want a second family, some childless stepmothers believe they can win him over: "He told me on our second date he'd had a vasectomy and he didn't think he wanted to have any more children. But who believes it, right?" Others initially convince themselves that they can live without having children. Over time, their desire for children may become stronger, particularly if their relationships with stepchildren remain distant or troubled. As her childbearing years start to shrink, one stepmother has more and more doubts: "When you're twenty-eight years old and madly in love with somebody, it isn't necessarily the same way that you feel when you're thirty-three knowing that you're not going to have [a baby]." One reason that this conflict may be so pronounced in remarriages is that the age difference between men and women is greater in second marriages than it is in first marriages, so that the stepmother and her partner may be at different stages in their lives.[6] About a third of the women I interviewed were more than seven years younger than their partners. Their partners felt they had already had their family, while the stepmothers were ready to start theirs.

Natalie has struggled for many years with Greg's refusal to have children. On their first date, he bluntly told her that he did not want more children. When they met, he had three teenaged children and did not want to plunge in again with diapers and interrupted sleep. Natalie was only twenty-four when they met, and Greg was in his mid-forties. He did not want children underfoot when he was in his sixties. Natalie initially believed she could win Greg over to her side, that love would conquer all: "I knew [that Greg did not want more children] but I believed that I could convince Greg to do anything I wanted. And that he would change. When I realized that was not the case, I was really angry and hurt."

Her stepchildren, particularly her stepdaughter, Lisa, who was the eldest and used to being in charge of the family, made it obvious that they did not want her in their family. Natalie felt she endured a lot of aggravation with Greg's children as they struggled through the turmoil of adolescence. Both boys were rude to their father and, by extension, to Natalie. The middle child, Fergus, had a turbulent time at school and repeated Grade 9. Natalie believed that the least Greg could do to compensate for her forbearance with his children was to have a baby with her. She kept trying to persuade him, but he was resolute.

Finally Natalie accepted defeat. This decision triggered enormous sadness and grief. She realized that she was mourning both the loss of this anticipated baby and the dream that it would connect her to this family: "I've always thought in the back of my mind that having my own child would help cement some of this stuff for me, some of the things about values and really feeling part of the family. Maybe might even help the stepkids to see us as truly a family. And so that's not there. So I'm trying to sort it out without that." Eventually she sought therapy to help her. Unlike other stepmothers in her situation, Natalie did not think of leaving Greg. Their relationship had always been very strong, and Natalie thought that it would sustain her.

Natalie has now been a stepmother for six years and has pretty much reconciled herself to never having children. Her resolve wavers sometimes, however. Two years ago she became distressed when her sister's baby was born. Last year, Greg had a mild heart attack. He promised Natalie to lose weight and cut back at work, but within three months he returned to his old habits. Natalie was furious and stunned by the intensity of her rage toward him. After considerable thought and talking it out with friends, she realized she believed that, since she had given up the chance to have a baby, the least he could do was to keep himself healthy. She expected him to recognize the extent of her sacrifice by making a few sacrifices of his own. Although she and Greg worked out that conflict, Natalie believes that the baby issue will never go away entirely. She hopes that, as she becomes more connected with Greg's children—perhaps through the grandchildren—she will feel at peace. At the same time, she suspects that it will be a life-long process: "I'm trying to sort [my feelings about not having a baby] out. That's difficult and I still haven't completely done that. But I'm very aware of it."

If partners change their minds about having a baby, stepmothers become even more distressed. Before the couple starts living together, these men are willing to have children. Then, after the stepfamily is underway, they renege on their promise. Although I did not interview the men, one can understand why these men might waver. Raising a child is a huge undertaking. If the first few years of the stepfamily are shaky, the men may not want to start another family and risk having this relationship split up too. From the stepmothers' perspective, however, their partner's reversal is crushing. All the women I talked to in this situation were committed stepmothers, and they felt a huge sense of betrayal when their partners backed out. Some relationships were almost destroyed. In the study, I met only the women who had decided to stay. I suspect that others leave their relationships over this issue.

I have talked about Betsy on a number of occasions. Although she was frustrated in her mission to transform Mick and his three children's lives, this undertaking was dwarfed by the conflict over whether to have children. Betsy was forthright with Mick from the outset that, although she liked his children, she wanted her own child too. Because Mick already had three children, she was willing to settle for one, but he was enthusiastic about having two: "Then he announced he'd changed his mind. That he didn't want any more kids. And I was just devastated because I didn't know what to do. Do I walk out on the marriage now? I was absolutely devastated. Because now, not only was I in love with Mick, but I was in love with Alasdair, Olivia, and Simon. If I walked away, I was walking away from the three of them. And I wasn't worried about Mick, it was the kids I was worried about."

In contrast to Natalie, Betsy felt more of a commitment to the children than to their father. All the children had suffered after their mother moved to another city without telling them that she would be staying there permanently. After a lot of wariness and suspicion, Betsy felt that they were starting to trust her. If she left, she would be another woman failing them. So she stayed, but Betsy's desire to become pregnant created "major hell" in their relationship. Betsy was furious. She felt Mick had betrayed her trust. They had many, many raging arguments: "He kept saying the same thing. 'I appreciate the fact that you need to have a baby. I think you'll be a wonderful mother. I think you should have a baby. I just don't want to have one.' . . . I said to him, 'I understand where you're at, that you don't want to go to camp, you don't want to be a cub leader, you don't want to go to school plays. But I've got the energy for both of us. . . . So, if you don't want to do that kind of thing, you don't need to. It doesn't mean your child will feel unloved.' And he just said, 'No, I can't do it. Can't do it.'"

Betsy had always been able to handle high levels of stress, but now she became a wreck. She could not sleep, stopped eating, and developed terrible tension headaches. Whenever she saw a baby on the street, she was overcome with sadness. She had to leave the baby shower for her best friend because she was afraid she would burst into tears in front of everyone. She tried to convince herself to walk out of her marriage: "I wanted to leave a thousand times. My heart and soul and brains and guts said, 'Get the hell out of here, lady. You're a fool.' . . . I racked my brains out about it over and over again and I knew I should leave. I just said, 'This is crazy. You're young, you're intelligent, you have a good job, you can go out there and start out there and start over and find somebody else who wants to have kids.' But I couldn't leave him. I love Mick dearly but it was probably more the kids than him. . . . I can't imagine my life without them."

After a year of wrangling, Betsy is worn out. She has not left, but has not relinquished her desire for a baby. About a month ago, she told Mick that she will no longer use birth control, that if he does not want a baby, then it is his responsibility. She still hopes he will change his mind, but she cannot continue to fight. Unlike Natalie, who has more or less accepted that she will not have children, Betsy sees this period more as a moratorium, a temporary truce in the ongoing battle.

Although both Natalie and Betsy decided to stay, their partners' refusal to have children shook their confidence in the relationship and in their partners. Other stepmothers who are caught in this dilemma feel very let down by their partners. They feel their partners are delighted to hand over the care of their children but are not so willing to extend themselves in return. In the end, this issue rarely has a happy resolution. My interviews with these women were perhaps the most painful of all the discussions I had with stepmothers. Although not all childless stepmothers face such a terrible conflict, being childless often creates extra complications for the stepmothers. Being denied the opportunity to choose whether to have children is a stark symbol of stepmothers' powerlessness.

PART TWO

Becoming a Stepmother:
Five Models

In the previous section, I focused on the seven biggest stressors for stepmothers. During the interview process, I became aware that the stepmothers understood and defined their roles in diverse ways, and that these conceptualizations influenced how they reacted to their stepchildren, partners, and the stepchildren's mothers, as well as how they perceived themselves. Five main models of stepmothering emerged from my analysis.[1] The first is what I call a Nuclear model. Here stepmothers attempt to mould the stepfamily into a nuclear family. The second is a Biological model. Stepmothers who fit within this perspective value biological or blood connections over other kinds of relationships. The third is the Retreat model. This model encompasses those stepmothers who feel unconnected and isolated in the stepfamily. With the fourth, the Couple model, stepmothers' main priority is their relationship with their partners, and the relationship with their stepchildren is less central. The fifth is an Extended model. Stepmothers who fit within this model imagine the stepfamily as an extended family that is inclusive, rather than exclusive.

Whether a stepmother leans more toward one model than another depends both on the stepmother's ideals about what a family *should* be, and on external pressures—what her stepchildren, partners, or others expect from her. These models are not fixed, however. Stepmothers frequently shift from one to another over time. For instance, a stepmother may start within the framework of the Biological model, believing that she needs to protect her children, and gradually move toward an Extended model as she recognizes the advantages of having many new family members in her life. Or conversely, a stepmother may aspire to an Extended model but her partner's and stepchildren's negative responses may cause her to pull back into a Retreat model.

I offer these five models as a kind of guide for stepmothers to help them recognize how they may be organizing their experiences. While some are happier solutions than others, each represents an attempt for stepmothers to reconcile their ideals with the reality of their situation.

Chapter 8

The Nuclear Model: We're Not *Really* a Stepfamily

Some stepmothers are convinced that the ideal form for a stepfamily is the nuclear family. They aspire to be a non-divorced, nuclear family. "Nuclear family" generally means a mother, a father, and their biologically related children, all of whom live in the same household. More extended relations, such as grandparents, aunts, uncles, and cousins, are not included as part of this nuclear family. In our society, our primary criteria for kinship—how we decide to whom we are related—are blood and residence. We tend to call people "family" if we are biologically related to them and/or if we live with them.[1] Stepmothers who fit into a Nuclear model latch on to the second piece. They consider their family the people with whom they live. Since almost all of them are residential stepmothers—their stepchildren live with them more than half the time—they include their stepchildren as part of their family.[2] By contrast, they regard relationships outside the household, such as those with ex-spouses and in-laws, with mistrust and often seek to sever these connections. Although there are some advantages to refashioning the stepfamily as a nuclear family, as you will see, few stepfamilies can squeeze comfortably into a nuclear box.

Erasing the Step

Stepmothers who adhere to the Nuclear model go to great lengths to look and act like a nuclear family. They are delighted if they are mistaken for their stepchildren's mother and often expend tremendous effort to ensure this happens. Some enroll their step-children in after-school activities in another neighbourhood where the biological mother is not known so people will assume they are the mother. They encourage their stepchildren to call them Mum, and to refer to their half-siblings and stepsiblings as brothers and sisters. One stepmother even dyed her hair to match her stepdaughter's in order to accentuate the similarity: "Rebekah just refers to me as her mum. It's easier, because we've been living together for five years. We look alike. I know it sounds crazy, but it's true. I picked her up at a birthday party a while ago, and this lady came to the door. She says, 'Oh, you must be Rebekah's mum. You look just like her, I'll go get her.' And I thought, 'Oh, that's so cool!'"

These women consider the "step" connection inferior, almost shameful. If they can bury it, they will. For some, their aversion to the label stems from its association with wickedness. The step-mother quoted above has an eight-year-old stepdaughter who lives full-time in the household and two preschool children who were born in this marriage. She has not told her son and daughter that Rebekah is her stepdaughter, so they assume that Rebekah is their full sister "because I would like to be Rebekah's mother. I don't really want to be her stepmother. It would be nice to pretend that we'd been together forever. . . . [My biological children] don't know I'm a stepmother. I don't know what they'd think if I told them. I wouldn't tell. [They'd] probably think I was going to cut them up and bake them."

Another reason to erase the stepfamily is that the stepmother believes the nuclear family is the ideal environment for children. Whenever the stepmother compares stepfamilies and nuclear families, the former always falls short. As one stepmother put it, "A step-mother is not as good or as important as a real mother." This kind of thinking has been called the deficit-comparison approach.[3] The stepfamily is considered second-rate or deficient in relation to the nuclear family. It's not just stepmothers who engage in this stigmatizing. Researchers in the United States, Canada, Europe, Israel, and

Australia have found many people routinely stereotype stepfamilies negatively. Studies have found that stepchildren are regarded as neglected, unhappy, and unloved. Even professionals, such as teachers, counsellors, nurses, and social workers, people whom you might imagine would know better, fall into this kind of thinking.[4] Nuclear stepmothers' negative attitudes toward stepfamilies thus just mirror societal attitudes about stepfamilies.

In earlier chapters, I have described how Deborah and John decided not to tell John's children that Deborah was not their mother. Since Emma and Luke were only infants when Deborah entered their lives and the family moved shortly after to another community, it was easy to disguise themselves as a nuclear family. Emma and Luke were teenagers before they learned the truth. Deborah's relationship with Emma was already tense before the secret was leaked. Now Emma accused Deborah—but not her father—of tricking them. Deborah and John's motivation was not deception, however. Rather they believed a nuclear family would be healthier for the children. Since Deborah was prepared to act like a mother, why not have her pretend to be one too? "We just figured that it might be best for them. Why tell them, or what's the need to tell other people? It's nobody's business and, for all practical purposes, I was their mother."

I'd Die for Them

Family is paramount for Nuclear stepmothers. They say things like "Family comes first," or "Family is who you can count on." Often they had wanted to be part of a family, and the stepfamily offered a ready-made opportunity. They often place the family ahead of their relationship with their partner and consider the couple relationship less critical than the overall well-being of the family. Some feel more attached to their stepchildren than to their partners and are initially attracted to their partners *because* they are fathers. Tina, whom we last met in Chapter 3, was already beguiled by her future stepdaughter, Caterina, before she fell in love with Jake: "To be quite honest, it was because of Caterina that I agreed to date him in the first place." Family life is paramount for Tina. She and Jake rarely have an evening to themselves, and she is content with this arrangement, believing it is best for Caterina and her infant daughter, Hannah.

Nuclear stepmothers maintain their strong commitment to their stepchildren. Compared with other stepmothers, they do not see their stepchildren as interfering or stirring up tensions in the marital relationship. Often it is the opposite. They feel their stepchildren enhance and enrich the couple relationship. If their relationships with partners hit a rocky patch, their bond with stepchildren often sustains them. One stepmother described her stepchildren as the glue holding her together with her partner: "I read an article in a magazine a couple of months ago about loving your children more than your husband. It sounds very awful in the headline, but as she said inside, there are certain aspects of your love for your children that your husband can't know. Your husband isn't defenceless. Your husband can fend for himself, can go. Your kids can't. I'd die for my husband, but I'd die for [my stepdaughter] in a different way."

In deciding what kind of stepmother they would like to be, these stepmothers look to their childhood. Most grew up in non-divorced families, so that this is their ideal. They model themselves after their own mothers and want their stepchildren to experience the same kind of milieu they enjoyed. Tina comes from a close, stable family. Her mother stayed at home and devoted herself to her four children. Although her father worked full-time, Tina always felt that family came first for him too. Tina wanted Caterina to have the same loving, safe environment: "My own family experience was such that, although I wasn't prepared to be a stepmother, I was prepared to show Caterina a home. Because my home life was always very secure, my mother was always there, my parents were always there, they were always very supportive, so I knew how to do that for Caterina."

Earlier we saw how some stepmothers set out to rescue their stepchildren. These Nuclear stepmothers are the most apt to cast themselves as rescuers. Perhaps because they believe the nuclear family is superior, these women often think their stepchildren have been wounded by the divorce, that they need the stepmother to wipe away their unhappiness. Tina was convinced Caterina had suffered under the joint custody regime where she alternated between her mother's and father's houses on a daily basis. At age three, Caterina lagged far behind where Tina thought she should be. Her speech was delayed, she could not dress herself, and she still wet her pants. Believing that Caterina needed full-time parenting, Tina quit her job. Two years later, she feels vindicated: "What I see as a success is that she's ready for school. She can print the letters of the alphabet, she knows her numbers, she can colour. I taught her to colour. All those things that I see every day, things that she's able to do, just weren't there two years ago." Tina also does not regret interrupting her university studies in early childhood education because she feels she has put them to use in teaching Caterina.

Stepmothers who embrace the Nuclear model are eager to be mothers to their stepchildren, and they interpret this role quite conventionally. Like Tina, they often quit their jobs to stay home and care for their stepchildren. Their partners, who are the biological parents, generally do not alter their work schedules at all. Compared with other stepmothers, these Nuclear stepmothers take on the most responsibility for the household and child care. Often they become the primary parent, replacing both the father and the mother.[5]

Their partners usually wholeheartedly endorse the stepmothers' desire to mother their children. These men may be content with this arrangement because it liberates them from domestic work. From the stepmothers' descriptions, their partners appear to be fairly disengaged, what is generally considered to be a traditional father. Before Tina met Jake, he had shouldered half, often more than half, of the responsibility for Caterina. Tina now does everything. In addition to the cooking and cleaning, she is home with Caterina and Hannah all day. Jake's role has shifted enormously: "He doesn't get as frustrated with [Caterina] because no longer is he getting up in the morning, getting her dressed, driving her to daycare, coming home from work, picking her up from daycare, getting supper. He's just much more relaxed because he gets a break. . . . And because I'm the one who looks after the home things, he has that much more time to play with her. And of course, Daddy's the fun one and I'm not. I'm the one who does all the teaching things."

Tina's observation that "Daddy's the fun one and I'm not" is not a criticism of Jake. She is satisfied with the division of labour and believes that Jake is a better father, in her conventional definition, now that he is relieved of housework and child care. Although, as discussed in Chapter 6, some stepmothers become frustrated with partners handing over their parental duties, Nuclear stepmothers do not. They welcome the domestic responsibilities since this is a further validation of their mother role.

If their stepchildren return their affection, they feel an intense gratification. Any indications that their stepchildren regard them as mothers are treasured: "I found out in the past couple of years, she liked it when I said she was my daughter. . . . It means that she likes me and that she's happy in this situation and that's wonderful." Conversely, they feel crushed if their stepchildren reject them or are ambivalent. This may be because they invest so much energy in caring for these children.

Cutting Ties

Nuclear stepmothers focus on strengthening relationships within the household and tend to distrust connections outside their little family. Often they try to limit or sever them. Most would prefer if their stepchildren had no contact with their mothers, and some curtail their in-laws' involvement with their grandchildren. As described in Chapter 6, after divorce, some grandparents assume a quasi-parental role with their grandchildren. Rather than viewing their in-laws as allies—as additional people to help raise the children—stepmothers who fit into a Nuclear model usually want to reduce their in-laws' influence in the new stepfamily. After his divorce, Andrew, Bettina's partner, had "relied quite heavily on his parents." They often babysat the children, and Andrew spent most weekends at his parents' house. Bettina thought this "was quite a big mistake, because grandparents, the ones I know, don't raise children the way that children need to be raised." After Andrew and Bettina married, his parents continued to drop by the house and offered Bettina advice about her stepchildren. Bettina resented this. Bettina was thirty when she met Andrew, age thirty-nine, and ready for a change. She cut back her job as an actuary to half-time and embarked with great enthusiasm on caring for her two stepchildren, Eva, age eight, and Mackenzie, age six. Bettina felt that Andrew's parents were too lax with their grandchildren, that the children were crying out for more structure and regularity in their lives. Bettina intended to establish a new regime: "I truly didn't think it was [my mother-in-law's] responsibility to look after these children. When I moved in, I hired sitters. And I sat her down and I said, 'I know that you've done this with Andrew for a long time, and I think perhaps some people would say he even took advantage of you, and I can't do that. And there's a lot of babysitters on this street and I'm going to hire sitters. So if you want to see your grandchildren, you call me and tell me what is convenient for you. You can have them whenever you want, but I'm not going to ask you any more to take them.' And that was construed as me keeping the children away from them. . . . That hasn't been resolved; they have never phoned once to speak to their grandchildren since we moved to the new house." Although Bettina regrets the coolness that has developed, she prefers the more distant relationship: "We're too busy raising children, doing all our stuff to fit them in to our schedule."

These stepmothers also cut off family relationships if relatives do not share their vision of the stepfamily, that is, do not regard this reconstituted nuclear family as the "real" family. Bettina, for instance, also cooled her relationship with her sister, because "I'm disappointed that my sister hasn't been taking a more active role. . . . I wish she would be more like an aunt." Another Nuclear stepmother and her partner have eliminated his whole family: "Why should I bother trying to cultivate any kind of relationship with [my in-laws] if they're still hanging on to [his ex-wife]? That's my general attitude, like what's the point? If you want to visit with her, visit with her, make your choice. . . . There's still a very active relationship between them and the ex. That just doesn't sit well with me. I don't want a picture of us hanging on the wall of [my in-laws'] house and [the ex-wife] seeing it. . . . I can't cultivate a relationship with [my partner's] brother or his wife either because everything I say goes right back to [his ex-wife]." This stepmother believes the ex-wife should be "history—get rid of her." The fact that her in-laws continue to talk to her stepchildren's mother makes her feel that they do not recognize her position in the family.

Flies in the Ointment

Nuclear stepfamilies have many strengths—the stepmothers love their stepchildren, they are delighted to take over the housework and child care, their partners generally applaud their efforts, and, for the most part, their stepchildren respond fairly positively. The catch is that they are *not* a nuclear, non-divorced family. No matter how hard these stepmothers strive to achieve this ideal, they cannot. Another family existed before, and this fact cannot be entirely erased.

The "biggest fly in the ointment," as one Nuclear stepmother put it, is the biological mother. She is the most obvious symbol of the previous family. While, as I have described, many stepmothers become irritated with the ex, stepmothers within the Nuclear model are generally scathing about their partner's ex-wives.[6] Most are highly critical of her competence as a mother. When they compare her actions with theirs, the former always fare badly. Tina feels Caterina's mother, Beth, has put her career ahead of her daughter's well-being. While Tina left her job to be with Caterina, Beth now works longer hours and will go away on business for three or four days at a time. Caterina used to live half-time with each parent. Now she is with her father and Tina at least three-quarters of the time, and sometimes more if Beth is out of town. Just as Jake interacts less with his daughter since Tina's arrival, so too does Beth. While Tina welcomes her increased involvement with Caterina, and on many levels would prefer Beth to disappear, she is contemptuous about Beth's performance as a mother: "One of the reasons she doesn't want to look after Caterina is because she wants to work. Whereas we made the choice that Caterina was more important. . . . We felt that Caterina had a much better chance for success in every way if I stayed home. So to us, Caterina was more important than money."

Tina believes Beth only considers herself: "She's not willing to put her life on hold, or to put anything on hold for Caterina's sake. She does what she wants to do—if she wants to leave the country for six months, she'll take off for six months." At the same time, Beth's casual attitude to mothering also suits Tina because she has far more time with Caterina. Tina's comments reflect the clashing ideologies that contemporary Western mothers have to contend with. On the one hand, they are supposed to be completely available for their children and, on the other, women are now expected to contribute economically and be successful in the work world. This creates a situation where they are damned if they do and damned if they don't. Mothers who choose to stay home with their children often feel that their work is not valued, while mothers who work outside the home feel branded as irresponsible. Tina and Beth fall at opposite ends of this spectrum.

Tina also disapproves of the values Beth is passing on to Caterina. Beth lavishes presents on Caterina, which Tina and Jake cannot afford because Tina is no longer working. Beth buys Caterina sophisticated clothes and allows Caterina to try on her makeup, which Tina feels is inappropriate for a five-year-old. It is fun and games at Beth's house: "Nobody's checking to see how much junk food or candy she's eating or how much TV she's watching. Nobody is saying, 'Okay, you've watched three shows, that's enough.'" Tina feels frustrated because Caterina comes home with her schedule thrown out of whack and Tina has to play the heavy. "When she's home with us, we put limits on the kinds of shows she watches, how much she watches. If she has a candy bar, she has to wait to eat it until after lunch." Tina tries hard not to criticize Beth in front of Caterina, but worries that Caterina is being confused by the conflicting messages she receives at the two houses.

The ex-wife is a huge impediment for Nuclear stepmothers. Many believe that life would be perfect if the biological mother just disappeared. No matter how much work the stepmother may do, the biological mother has the ultimate power. Even though this tension exists for many stepmothers, Nuclear stepmothers feel it most keenly because they would like to be the mother. They tread carefully with their stepchildren. In contrast to other stepmothers, this is not because the relationship feels fragile, but because they believe the biological mother is scrutinizing them, waiting to pounce when the stepmother slips up. This heightened vigilance makes it harder to be relaxed with their stepchildren. Tina is extra-scrupulous with Caterina. If Caterina appears sick, she will immediately carry her off to the doctor, while she might wait a little longer with her daughter, Hannah: "Basically [I] cover my tracks, because ultimately, I guess I feel that someone's going to have to answer to her mother as well for what I'm doing."

Although Nuclear stepmothers can intellectually understand that their stepchildren are attached to their mothers, it is painful if their stepchildren pull away or prefer their mothers. They do the work and caring of a mother but do not receive the recognition or love in return. It is distressing if their affection is not reciprocated. In contrast to most Nuclear stepmothers, Parminder became a full-time stepmother less by choice than by default. Her partner, Jimmy, had been transferred to another city with his work, and she had to leave her job as a nurse when they moved. Her nine-year-old stepson, Alex, was close to his dad and elected to move with them. Parminder was landed in a new community with no job, no friends, no connections, and an uncommunicative stepson.

Parminder had not planned to be a full-time stepmother, but she took it on vigorously. She believed Alex needed a stable home with a stay-at-home mother. Alex was a nervous child who did not make friends easily. Starting a new school was excruciating for him. Parminder's heart went out to him as he trudged mournfully into school each morning. He loved sports so she signed him up for soccer and hockey and attended all his games. Despite her efforts to reach him, he was unresponsive.

Jimmy, preoccupied with his new job, was relieved to have Parminder assume all the domestic responsibilities. So were her in-laws. They shared Parminder's conviction that children need a mother at home and had criticized their former daughter-in-law for working full-time when their grandson was little. Even Alex's mother supported this arrangement. The holdout was Alex. Without ever directly rejecting his stepmother, he made it obvious that his loyalties lay with his parents. He allowed Parminder to buy his clothes, do his laundry, cook his meals, help him with homework, drive him to soccer games, and take him to the doctor, but he barely tolerated her presence and rarely volunteered any information or initiated conversation. If she touched him, he would wince. One "episode that really, really bothered" Parminder was when Alex "had to do this family tree thing—the important people in his life. . . . And I wasn't on it. I just started crying because I feel like I'm doing so much and I'm not even part of this."

Alex's loyalty to his mother was particularly galling because Parminder considered her an unreliable mother. The mother rarely cooked, her house was a disaster, and her work as a journalist was so preoccupying that she would often not arrive home until late at night. Yet Alex idolized his mother. Parminder had dedicated all her time to her stepson and received no appreciation: "It's this sense that I'm being used. . . . I don't get the loyalty that his mother gets and yet I have to do all the shit work." Because she believes Alex needs her care, Parminder has continued to act as a mother. She is increasingly resentful, however. Clearly, her stepson does not want her to be his mother and she is ambivalent herself, but her beliefs about maternal behaviour have locked her into a miserable situation.

Other Nuclear stepmothers get caught in this trap. Believing that they *should* mother, they persist, whether it works or not. This creates a dilemma. They are providing a mother's care and attention without the reciprocal affection and love most mothers enjoy. It is hard to love children who do not like you, yet Nuclear stepmothers demand this of themselves. They become martyrs, giving everything with no expectation of anything in return.

Perhaps the greatest challenge for the Nuclear stepmothers is not others' reactions, but their own. They believe that they should love their stepchildren unconditionally and without ambivalence. While other stepmothers are susceptible to this notion, these women feel it most acutely. They excoriate themselves if they do not love their stepchildren fully. While an outsider might understand how Parminder would have mixed feelings for a stepson who is so unyielding, she cannot forgive herself. Nuclear stepmothers also feel ashamed if they react differently to their stepchildren than to their biological children. As we saw in Chapter 3, it would be hard to find a more committed stepmother than Tina, yet she felt intense shame when she realized that her connection to her new baby daughter, Hannah, was more intense than that to her stepdaughter. It is not that Tina does not love Caterina.

She does. She considers herself Caterina's mother. Therefore, in her view, she must feel the same way toward the two girls: "I don't want to feel differently about them." Despite all her accomplishments with Caterina, she feels like a fraud. She is also anxious that Caterina, or even Jake, will discover her guilty secret. Even though Caterina shows no signs of feeling neglected or overlooked, Tina finds herself reassuring Caterina: "I try to reinforce the fact that even though I spend more time with Hannah right now, it's not because I love her more, it's because Hannah needs me to spend more time with her."

Rather than questioning whether the nuclear family is the best model for the stepfamily, most Nuclear stepmothers blame themselves if they cannot achieve it. It is their fault if they do not love their stepchildren as they do their biological children, if their stepchildren do not love them as a mother, or the stepfamily does not coalesce into a nuclear family. The onus is on the stepmother to make the situation work. For some, the belief that love should conquer all saps their confidence and abilities. Given the impossibility of ever attaining their goal of becoming a nuclear family, surprisingly few of these women even wondered whether the nuclear family was feasible for their stepfamily.

Deborah is one stepmother who now doubts the wisdom of trying to create a nuclear stepfamily: "In retrospect I wouldn't try to do that again. I wouldn't try to be their mother because I wasn't. No matter what you, do you can't change that fact." One might think that Deborah would have had the best shot at forging a nuclear family. Not only was the biological mother dead but her stepchildren had believed Deborah was their mother. Unlike most stepmothers, she could freely step into the position of mother. As we saw, even before her stepchildren discovered that she was not their mother, she found the illusion difficult to sustain. She and her stepdaughter, Emma, were constantly at war. Both Emma and Deborah's partner, John, accused her of favouring her son, Steven, over Emma. There was a certain truth to this. In comparison with her troubled relationship with Emma, her relationship with Steven was uncomplicated—he was not running to his father complaining about Deborah, nor was his father overseeing Deborah's behaviour with him. It was easy for Deborah to feel unambivalent about him. This made her feel guilty. She also wonders if, in her eagerness to be a mother, she jumped in too quickly and imposed an overly demanding regime on her two young stepchildren: "Overnight I became their mother. Actually from the day we got married, except for a week when we went on our honeymoon, they were there with us. . . . So, it was hard for them, and I guess I was young and I tried to discipline them a little bit more and they rebelled."

Deborah started out thinking "that I could be a good mother to them, I could give them the love and affection and caring." Her views have shifted radically. "Biologically, they are different people. When they aren't yours, they are so different. Also depending upon where they've lived, what they've inherited, how they're brought up, it's so different from what you might have done." Deborah now has abandoned the Nuclear model. As she related in Chapter 6, her relationship with John has been damaged by their fighting over his children, and she feels estranged from him. Deborah describes her current situation as two families living in the same household: Deborah and her son, Steven, are one family, and John and his two children, the other. Ironically her relationships with Emma and Luke, now twenty-two and twenty, have improved since she no longer considers herself their mother. Deborah's day-to-day responsibilities have remained constant and she still is in charge of the household. What has shifted is the obligation to feel a certain way. She accepts that she and Emma "do not get along" and may never become close. While she would never voice this thought to her husband, it is a comfort to acknowledge it to herself. I asked Deborah what advice she would offer a new stepmother: "I would never tell anyone to marry someone who has kids. If they decided to, then [I would] tell them, 'Don't think you'll ever be their mother, because you can never be.'"

The Nuclear model depends on the illusion that no family existed before. Yet the reality of the stepfamily is that strong connections pre-date in the stepfamily, and these are not erased by the formation of a new family. Even if the biological mother is dead, she is there as a psychic presence, not only for her children but for the stepmother as well. Even if stepchildren are young at the start, as were Deborah's and Tina's, they still have a history over which the stepmother has no control. All the Nuclear stepmothers with whom I spoke were committed to their stepchildren and expended tremendous energy in trying to make the stepfamily work. Their dilemma was that, no matter how much effort they poured into the stepfamily, they could never transform it into a perfect nuclear family. They were trying to fit a hexagonal peg into a round hole.

Chapter 9

The Biological Model: What's Mine Is Mine and What's Yours Is Yours

In contrast to Nuclear stepmothers, who use residence as their criterion for kinship, this group of stepmothers focuses on the other side of the kinship equation—the biological or blood connection. For them, kin are those people with whom they share a biological link—primarily their children and secondarily their family of origin. I refer to this as the Biological model because these stepmothers consider the biological link the critical element in determining kinship. All Biological stepmothers have children of their own, whether from a previous relationship or their current one. They regard the stepfamily as two families co-existing in the same household. The stepmother makes up one family with her children, and her partner and his children form the other. Some stepmothers include their partners in their family as well. They see their partner straddling two families: one with the stepmother and her children and the other with his children.[1]

Two Christmas Trees

At the outset, a Biological model often makes sense because there really are two families in the household. Recognizing that the stepfamily is initially two families permits its members to ease in slowly. Relationships and traditions need time to develop, and the Biological model allows for this. In contrast to the myth of the instant stepfamily described in Chapter 2, stepfamilies often take a long time to find their identity. Researchers and clinicians estimate that a stepfamily may need anywhere from four to twelve years to reconstitute itself as a family.[2]

When Marnie, age forty-seven, and her partner, Paul, age fifty-five, met seven years ago, each had three children from previous marriages. The six children ranged in age from eleven to twenty. Both Marnie and Paul had been widowed and had been single parents for a long time—Marnie for twelve years and Paul for five. Marnie had been lonely and was eager to have someone to share the parenting, as was Paul. The children's reactions were more mixed. They were used to having their parents to themselves and balked at having to share their mother or father. Although Paul's daughter told Marnie she was glad to have another woman around the house, Paul's eldest son was less happy because he had been bumped into second place by Marnie's daughter, who was two years older than he was. Paul and Marnie wished they could have bought a house with separate bedrooms for each child, but this was not financially feasible. Paul had seasonal work in the fishery and Marnie worked as a sales clerk. Some of the children grumbled about sharing bedrooms with their stepsiblings. The first few months were very unsettled as everyone tried to establish his or her place in the new configuration.

Their first big test came at Christmas. Both families hauled out huge boxes of Christmas decorations. Both groups of children wanted their family's treasures on the tree. There was no way the tree could accommodate everything. Tempers started to fray, and Marnie could sense their first Christmas unravelling. Her solution was to race out and buy another tree: "First couple of years after we got married, we had two Christmas trees, one in the living room and one down in the rec room. Once they got older you could say to them, 'It's really a big hassle,' but the first couple of years there was so much decoration and everybody wanted everything on it. I mean, my kids wanted this because we always had that on our tree, and the other ones wanted this because they had it on their tree." The two Christmas trees allowed each family to celebrate their own history. Similarly, Marnie was careful to include traditional Christmas foods from both families when she prepared Christmas dinner.

After a few years, Marnie gauged that the family was ready for a joint tree and recommended that they consolidate the decorations. None of the children objected, which she interpreted as a sign that they were ready to cede ground. If she had insisted on a shared tree from the start, hard feelings might have sprung up and impeded their integration as a family. The Biological model is a natural first stepping stone for many stepfamilies, particularly if both adults have children from previous relationships. Later on, many stepfamilies segue into another model. Marnie and Paul's family now fits more within the Extended model (see Chapter 12).

Some never make the transition to another model. In my study, I found that families who do not connect over the longer term generally have more conflict. In this chapter, I describe some Biological stepfamilies that have become two armed camps battling it out in the same household.

Protecting Your Own

Biological stepmothers are adamant that they should not become mothers to their stepchildren. They believe their stepchildren's mother—the biological mother—should be the primary parent. That is, because she has the biological connection, she should be responsible for her own children. Similarly, they expect to take care of their own children themselves. Their children are their priority and they say things like "I would do anything for my children," "My children mean more than anything else to me."

Some Biological stepmothers with children from previous relationships hope their new partners will become fathers to these children. Like the Nuclear stepmothers, they are attracted to their partner for his outstanding qualities as a father. In their case, they want him to become a father to their children. One stepmother commented, "What I found most appealing about him was the fact that he was a wonderful father, and he truly loved his children. I watch him with my children and I can't help but love him for the way he is with my children." At the same time, their partner's commitment to his own children can stir up less pleasant feelings of envy and jealousy. For instance, the woman quoted above lives full-time with her two biological children, and her stepchildren are with them on the weekends. Although she is not proud of her feelings, sometimes she resents her stepchildren's arrival: "I see him with my children all week long. Then there's a little jealousy there when [the stepchildren] come in. It's like now my kids have to share him. Even though 'him' is 'theirs.'" These Biological stepmothers wish to re-create a nuclear family, but in this instance they want it to include them, their partners, their biological children, but not their stepchildren.

When their stepchildren's life is primarily with their mother and their involvement with the stepmother's household is more peripheral, Biological stepmothers are happiest. Often their stepchildren want only a fairly detached relationship with their stepmother, because they are so close to their mother. This suits these stepmothers fine. The stepfamily is two quite separate families. In the stepmother's eyes, their stepchildren are more like visitors than family members.

Margot has two stepdaughters, Chloe, age fourteen, and Norah, age eleven, who live with their mother and stay with their father every second weekend. Their mother remarried seven years ago and the girls are close to their stepfather, who does not have his own children. Margot and her partner, Keith, have two little children, Jeremy, age four, and Alice, age one. Margot knows that her stepdaughters' main allegiance is to their mother. Margot's relationship with them is not hostile, but neither is it particularly warm. She will chat with them about TV shows or school activities, but she does not invite confidences, nor do they offer them.

Although Keith is a dedicated father, he has not pushed Margot to be more involved. On the weekends, he will often head out with all four children, leaving Margot to catch up on housework or take a break. As a working mother (she is an elementary school teacher) with two small children, Margot already feels overburdened, so she is happy with this arrangement. Although she would never say this to Keith, she would not welcome her stepchildren moving in: "I don't think I want teenagers to come and live with us. It may sound nasty or whatever, but I don't want them. . . . I think it sounds nasty because they're his daughters, his family, and I should be more kind about it." Given the current dynamics it is unlikely that Chloe or Norah would choose to switch households, so Margot's desire for the arm's-length relationship with her stepchildren to continue will probably never be tested.

I did not interview Margot's stepchildren, so we cannot know if they are satisfied with this arrangement. Perhaps they would like greater intimacy with their stepmother or feel shut out of their father's new family. From Margot's perspective, however, this pleasant but distant connection with her stepdaughters is ideal. Since her stepchildren are well looked after by their mother and stepfather, she does not feel compelled to do more for them. Here there are two families in two households.

While stepmothers in general almost always feel more at ease with their biological children than their stepchildren, Biological stepmothers draw a sharper line between the two groups. Their relationships with their own children seem effortless compared to those with their stepchildren. While they would automatically "do anything" for their own children, their response to their stepchildren is more constrained, more equivocal. One stepmother told me, "I feel much safer to be angry at my kids, or to tell my kids that I don't like something. I also feel much more open to tell them I love them, to touch them, to be affectionate with them. I like my kids. I like my kids as people. If I met them socially, I'd like them. I like their values. I like what they've done with their lives."

Like Margot, some Biological stepmothers are comfortable with this distinction. They refer to the history they share with their biological children, which extends from carrying these children through pregnancy, to giving birth, to birthdays, family events, and repeated routines of daily life that have woven mother and child together. By contrast, their stepchildren have their own history, in which the stepmother has no part.

Guilt: If I Was Really Good . . .

Most Biological stepmothers, however, are not comfortable with having differing feelings toward the two sets of children. While they do not want to be mothers to their stepchildren, like the Nuclear stepmothers, they usually believe in the superiority of the two-parent, nuclear family and the "essential" nature of a mother's love. Their inability to love their stepchildren can create conflict. Before she had children of her own, one stepmother was content to have a fairly superficial, albeit pleasant, relationship with her stepson, but once she experienced the intensity of her connection with her two young children, she felt ashamed: "A mother's love, a mother's nurturing, is to me, I think, very special and unique, now that I've experienced it with my own children. And I feel guilty that I haven't been able to give that to [my stepson]." Of all the stepmothers, Biological stepmothers are the most likely to suffer from guilt.[3]

If others push the stepmother to become a mother to her stepchildren, the conflict is amplified. One stepmother admitted, "I feel guilty for being angry at a child, and for not loving him as much as [my partner] does and then angry about feeling guilty." The children's mother also plays a significant role here. If, as in Margot's situation, the mother is doing her job "properly"—that is, if she is an involved, devoted mother—and the stepmother is not required to step in, the stepmother's guilt is relieved. If the mother is absent or disinterested, Biological stepmothers feel more torn and guilty for not responding to a need.

Kay, age thirty-nine, is a classic example of a Biological step-mother who feels tremendous guilt. When she first met Craig, also age thirty-nine, three years ago, she was impressed with his patience and steadiness with his children. Craig represented a huge contrast to Kay's first husband, Bob, who had always been a lackadaisical and hands-off father. During their marriage, Bob had left all the child-care decisions to Kay and, since their separation five years earlier, he had become increasingly less involved. The two children, Julia and Sam (now ages twelve and ten), spent two days a week with him, but he was often distracted and caught up in his work. Recognizing how hurt and disappointed her two children had been by their father, Kay believed they would blossom with Craig as a new father. She imagined the four of them as a close-knit family: "Craig was a natural dad and he gave my kids a lot of attention and I saw him as a role model of a father that they didn't have with their own dad."

Craig was willing to do this, but wanted Kay to take a similar role with his two children, Jason, now age thirteen, and Brittany, now eleven. The problem was that Kay found them pushy, whiny, and demanding. Brittany was a particular trial: "She was so needy. She couldn't let her father out of her sight. She was negative attention seeking all over the place, would do anything just to be talked to." There were constant crises. Craig was frequently called by Brittany's school because Brittany was not following through on schoolwork, was rude to her teacher, and aggressive with other students. At home, she fought incessantly with her brother and would fly into rages when frustrated. She was jealous of Kay's daughter, Julia, who had a big circle of friends and excelled at sports. On a number of occasions Kay caught Brittany rifling through Julia's room and items would sometimes disappear. Brittany also had a lot of anxieties, and Craig often spent two hours in the evenings helping her calm down enough to fall asleep. Jason was less wearing but also had academic problems that required many hours of help with homework. He would compete for attention with Kay's children, particularly with Sam, who was three years younger than Jason. Kay tried to bury her aversion to the two children: "I knew going in that there was part of me that wasn't comfortable with this. . . . I wanted my two children, but I didn't necessarily want his, but then we wanted each other and they were a package deal. So I tried to tell myself that maybe it would change."

At first things were tolerable, because Craig's children lived with their mother and stayed over on weekends. During Jason and Brittany's visits, Kay would occupy herself and count the hours until they left. The uneasy compromise fell apart when Craig's ex-wife, Andrea, asked him to take the children full-time. Throughout Craig's first marriage, Andrea had had several serious episodes of depression, some culminating in hospital admissions. Kay had sensed that things were deteriorating at Andrea's. Andrea looked drawn and shaky, and Jason had mentioned that his mother was sometimes still in bed when he came home from school. Even though Kay dreaded the change, there was no question of saying no.

While Kay was willing to take responsibility for the everyday details of her stepchildren's lives—clothes shopping, doctors' appointments, socks paired neatly in their drawers, lunches packed for school—she shied away from emotional involvement. Her stepchildren wanted more than clean laundry: "Both Jason and Brittany wanted to call me Mum. They kept telling me how much they loved me and this kind of stuff. I felt really uncomfortable with it. I wasn't their mum, I would never be their mum, and I didn't want that." She asked Craig to ask them to stop calling her mum, but felt very guilty about turning them away: "[Brittany] said things like 'I wish Kay was my real mum.' It makes me feel awful, of course. . . . It eats me up that she feels that way and I don't do anything about it."

Craig was also unhappy with Kay's reaction because he wanted Kay to become a mother to his children. Just as Kay admired Craig as a father, he admired Kay's dedication to her children. He hoped she would give his children the same attention. Like Kay, he viewed the stepfamily as a chance to compensate. He believed that Andrea's depressions had deprived Jason and Brittany of maternal attention, which they craved from Kay. He acknowledged to Kay that his children had problems but he counted on Kay to help them. Kay's unwillingness to step in caused rows between Kay and Craig. While Kay recognized it was unfair to expect Craig to parent her children when she would not reciprocate, she could not force herself to love them. If anything, over time, she found herself recoiling from them even more.

Her inability to love Jason and Brittany has created inner turmoil for Kay. In all other parts of her life, Kay is the first one to jump in and rescue others. On top of her full-time work as a community aid worker, she volunteers at a local homeless shelter. She is known as a giver. When Kay and Craig announced that they were marrying, everyone applauded. "People would say, 'Nobody else would do this except you. You're the only person I could even imagine in all the people I know, who would take on somebody else's children like this. You've got so much patience and so much tolerance and you're such a nurturer.' People would come out of the woodwork and call me a saint!" Of course, this praise makes her feel like a hypocrite. Kay is ashamed of herself: "If I was really a good, caring, nurturing person, like everybody thinks I am, I wouldn't allow [my stepdaughter] to have those worries and fears and I would do something about it." Mixed in with her guilt is anger, anger at her stepchildren for wanting a response she cannot manufacture. This anger—at apparently innocent children who are just craving affection—redoubles the self-recriminations. Becoming a stepmother has undermined Kay's sense of herself as a basically kind person: "I don't like who I've become. . . . I don't like the feelings that I have. I feel pushed away from my other self, the nice caring part."

Balanced against her internal struggle is Kay's commitment to her children. Even Craig agrees his children demand a great deal. Kay worries that if she attempts to rescue them, she would have nothing left for her two children. She already feels that "my kids are being compromised by being in this situation, because I don't have the energy. And I think some of the anger I am feeling toward the [stepchildren] is sort of permeating my reaction to them." Both Julia and Sam have commented on how crabby she has become since Jason and Brittany moved in.

Kay also resents that she and her children have little time alone. Her children visit their father every weekend while Jason and Brittany rarely see their mother: "It's one of my biggest issues around the stepmother stuff, because I don't have my own as much as I want, but yet his are around all the time." She and Craig had a big blowup over this recently after her children returned home from a weekend with their father: "I hadn't seen them for two days while they were at their dad's. I came in the house, and they were sitting at the dinner table. They jumped up and they came running over and giving me big hugs and kisses and everything else. Then I got chewed out by my husband for not saying hello properly to his two kids. So, I'm thinking, 'Wait a second, I can't win! I want to see mine and I want to be with mine the way I want.'"

Kay wants more separate time with her children. Craig is advocating for more family activities, not fewer. Part of their conflict is that Craig and Kay have disparate notions of family. Craig includes all six of them in one family, casting himself and Kay as the parents (the Nuclear model). Kay, by contrast, sees her family as herself and her children, with Craig somewhat attached (the Biological model).

If Kay buys an extra treat for Julia or Sam, even something as minor as a Popsicle, she hides it from Craig and ends up feeling sneaky and underhanded. Craig insists that all four children receive identical treatment. Kay clashes with him over this. She feels that, particularly living in the stepfamily, her children need to know they have a special connection with her, that they have already made a lot of adjustments and need extra assurances from her. Kay's sister Betty has invited them to her cottage for a week. Kay would love to go just with her children: "Craig definitely has the feeling that it would *not* be a good thing to do, just me and my two go off to the cottage, but I actually believe that the little family within the big family still needs time on its own."

In the Kitchen

Even though they do not want to be mothers, Biological stepmothers often take on the traditional work of mothers, organizing the household and assuming responsibility for many of the chores—cleaning, cooking, laundry, and shopping.[4] Most willingly assume the extra work, considering it their domain. Kay is mixed. In contrast to her first marriage, where Bob dumped everything on her, Craig is highly competent: "He's always been inclined that way anyway because he had to compensate for an essentially depressed wife who did nothing in the house. Never changed a diaper. He'd come home from work and the kids were still in the same diaper that they'd been in when he left for work in the morning. And so he's always cooked, cleaned, and run the house. It was no big thing to him." Although Kay expected she would enjoy sharing the household work, she found herself reluctant to relinquish her primary role: "I sometimes have more trouble with him taking on some of the more maternal, more female roles, than he does. He's quite used to it, and I'm not used to a man doing laundry and cooking and stuff like that." Kay has realized that she is a "control freak and like[s] having things the way I want more than he does. . . . I said, 'Look, this is going to be an issue for me. Is it okay with you if I lay down some of the rules?' And he was quite comfortable with that."

Kay wants to be in charge of the house. The down side is that she has surrendered her free time. Before her remarriage, when her children were at their father's, she would immerse herself in work, socialize with friends, or lounge around by herself. Now she is cooking and cleaning for Craig's children. Her ambivalence about this is another source of guilt: "When my kids aren't there, I have these other kids that are there, that I have to put something out for. Yet I have no motherly instinct to want to do that. So that really eats me up, because as I said, it's not feelings that I feel proud of. It took me a while to even openly admit that I have them."

Craig has noticed that Kay prefers to opt out when her children are away. This has become another sore point: "About four weeks ago he got really angry with me about the fact that I had left the table. My kids weren't at the dinner table, they were at their dad's house. I had made the dinner and I cleaned the dishes. Then I chose to take my dessert away from the table and sit in another room and do some reading for work. And he came to find me in the other room and blew his top about the fact that I had not asked permission to leave the table when everybody else was still sitting there eating." Kay, feeling that she had already done enough and deserved a little quiet time, reacted explosively: "I really, really got angry, and I actually ended up hitting him. I haven't done that before and that really scared me." Recognizing that their marriage was running into serious trouble, Kay and Craig called a therapist and have started couple counselling.

While they might not be in the kitchen, the partners of Biological stepmothers are often actively involved as fathers. (This is another contrast to the situation of the Nuclear stepmothers.) Most either share the child care equally with the stepmother or take the lead role with their children. One might expect that, since Biological stepmothers do not want to be mothers to their stepchildren, they would be pleased by their partners' commitment to his children. A number view it as a mixed blessing, however. Compared with other stepmothers, Biological stepmothers are generally more critical of their partners' parenting skills.[5] Usually they consider their partners far too lenient. The stepmothers believe their partners' laxity does more harm than good. Although Kay admires Craig's engagement with his children, she thinks he caters far too much to both Jason and Brittany. While Kay requires her children to help with dishes and keep their rooms tidy, Craig will often let his children escape from chores and does the work himself. If, at bedtime, Brittany calls out for one more glass of water, one more back rub, he will run back upstairs to her room, no matter how exhausted he is. Kay believes he is trying to compensate for Andrea's absence. From Kay's perspective, his constant accommodating has backfired, because Jason and Brittany are not learning how to consider others or to take responsibility for themselves. By insisting on stricter rules, some Biological stepmothers feel that they have become the heavy. Their children may complain because they must do chores while their stepsiblings get off scot-free. In some stepfamilies, the situation deteriorates so there are two separate sets of rules in the same household, the stepmothers' always being the more stringent. Having two standards only widens the gulf between the two families.

Compared with the other four models, Biological stepmothers describe the most discord with their partners over stepchildren.[6] Sometimes it is disagreements with partners that lead them to the Biological model. Initially, they imagined that they and their partners would co-parent but the fighting and the fundamental differences in approaches to parenting create a schism. Their relationships with their stepchildren are also often troubled, which places another wedge between the couple. Stepmothers in this situation often react by pulling back and protecting their little family. Instead of the two families growing together, they split farther apart.

Meredith, now age fifty, and Ted, now age fifty-four, were married seven years ago. Meredith had two daughters from her first marriage, Bridget, age fourteen, and Jenny, thirteen, and Ted had two sons, Bryce, age fourteen, and Adam, eleven. Meredith worried that, with four teenagers, the household could become a circus, unless she "took charge of the house. I felt like I wanted to do that. I suspect I was proving what a wonderful life this was, and how efficient I was. I've read about stepmothers being overachievers. I think certainly I fit into that category." While her first priority was her own children—"I wanted to protect my kids, and I wanted to run things so things would stay the same for them"—at the same time she "was working really hard to make it nice for everybody." She started out optimistically. She could see that Bryce and Adam, were closed off, but "there was something quite appealing about each of them, and I thought that would grow more positively. I thought they would love me, so instead of having two kids who I loved, I would have four!"

Meredith loves to cook, so food seemed like a natural means to draw everyone together. The catch was that she "was making these wonderful meals and Ted's kids weren't eating them." For the first year she knocked herself out making meals that her stepsons did not eat. Recognizing that their resistance was only making her angry, she switched tactics. She quizzed her stepsons about their favourite foods, filled the refrigerator, and stood back. This approach backfired too: "They'd go to the fridge and they'd stand and look. And then they'd close it, and then they'd look in the freezer. Then they'd sort of sigh that there was nothing to eat, and then they'd leave." When Meredith expressed her frustration to Ted, he just shrugged and suggested that they would eat when they were hungry. Although she recognized that he was right, she wanted more sympathy from him, an acknowledgement of her efforts to accommodate his children.

Ted and his ex-wife had gone through a bitter breakup. Ten years later, they barely exchange a civil word. Meredith knew her stepsons were caught in the middle, that their mother interpreted any positive signs toward Meredith as disloyalty. It helped her to recognize that rejecting her food was a means of placating their mother. At the same time, it was hurtful to be so consistently rebuffed. While the two boys were never overtly nasty to Meredith, they were never friendly. If Meredith asked them a question, they would grudgingly respond but never initiated a conversation. After many attempts to engage them, Meredith gradually withdrew. Now, if she happens to be in the same room as one of her stepsons, they go about their business separately, like strangers in a waiting room.

Meredith believes that Ted's approach to his children has exacerbated the situation: "I felt that he tolerated behaviour that was really unacceptable socially, and was making the kids very unlikeable to a lot of people, and it wasn't necessary for it to be like that." Meredith and Ted clash over what is acceptable behaviour from their children. No matter how rude his sons are to him, Ted never chastises them. Even when, on a couple of occasions, they hit him, he still did not react. Meredith has had to grit her teeth to keep from exploding at both the boys and Ted.

Meredith and Ted had agreed, at the beginning, that each parent should discipline his or her own children and not direct the other's children. They also decided that the children should have simple household chores, like clearing the table, stacking and unstacking the dishwasher, and shovelling the walk. Meredith's children did their chores. Ted's did not. When Meredith would bring this to Ted's attention, they would end up in a fight: "If I would ask him to get the kids to clean up their room, he'd say, 'Well, I mentioned it to them, and they're just not doing it.' And I'd say, 'Well, ask them again.' And he'd say, 'Why are you always bugging me; why are you always riding me?' I said, "Because you don't want me to ride them, so if I don't ride them, I'm going to ride you.'"

Meredith's children started to complain: "Then they started to get really annoyed because his kids weren't doing anything, and they were saying, 'Hey, how come?' So I finally started saying, 'Well, if they don't have to do it, you don't have to do it either.'" Most of the housework has now devolved to Meredith.

These unresolved tensions have permeated her relationship with Ted. Meredith feels that their marriage has been worn down by the constant battling over the children. Meredith used to urge Ted to go away with her for a weekend on their own. She has gradually stopped suggesting this. Recently when Ted suggested the two of them go out for dinner alone, she put him off. At the end of our interview, she mentioned that she had been thinking of leaving her marriage.

From her initial dream of one big happy family, there are two separate families in the same household, Meredith and her two children and Ted and his two children: "It's funny when you talk about families, because I see Ted as my next of kin . . . but he's not part of my family. My parents, my brother, my kids, those people are my family." Unlike Kay, she does not feel guilty, because she cannot imagine anything else she could have tried. She does regret the acrimony between her and Ted, just as she regrets the gulf between her and her stepsons. For Meredith, the Biological model represents failure. When I asked her what has been hardest for her as a stepmother, she started to weep: "Not having it work. It should've worked! Because I'm capable, because I'm smart. Ted's smart. We're nice people. We have enough money, we're not hungry. We have a big house with lots of supportive family and supportive friends. It should've worked!"

The Biological model is often a good transitional solution for stepfamilies in the first few years. It also may work well if the children's life is primarily with their mother and they are with their father part-time. When there are two families in one household, however, friction usually mounts if they do not find some way to connect. In Meredith's case, the stepfamily has become two armed camps. Kay worries that her situation is moving in that direction. The insistence on the primacy of biological connections can be an obstacle to the family's integration. Of course, biological parents and their biological children usually share closer bonds than stepparents and stepchildren. This is understandable. Since most relationships in stepfamilies do not have a biological basis, however, stepmothers box themselves in if they place too heavy an emphasis on blood ties. By overvaluing the biological connection, they may miss out on the rich variety of potential ways to relate to others in the stepfamily.

Chapter 10

The Retreat Model: I Had to Opt Out

Mired in unresolvable situations, some stepmothers withdraw from the stepfamily. Although they are physically present, they are emotionally and mentally absent. This is not a step that these women take lightly, but because they have to find some way to mitigate their pain and unhappiness. I have called this the Retreat model because these stepmothers see themselves as isolated and alone within the stepfamily. Although relatively few of the women with whom I talked became caught in this position, their stories were striking, because of their misery. In this chapter I describe how they end up in this unhappy position.[1]

Stepping Back and Assessing

Many—if not most—stepmothers retreat, to some degree, from their initial expectations about their role. Often this stepping back is positive, a recognition that they have attempted too much too soon. Stepmothers often start off with high hopes that they later realize were unrealistic. Sometimes they jump in too far too fast and withdraw. Either they feel overwhelmed by how much they have undertaken, or they recognize they are demanding too much. Others pull back from their stepchildren when they become aware their stepchildren do not want the same kind of closeness the stepmothers had anticipated. Stepmothers who wish to be mothers sometimes abandon this course as they pick up their stepchildren's resentment or resistance. For others, the withdrawal is self-protective. If their stepchildren are hostile, rebuffing the stepmother's attempts to reach them, or if their partners are unresponsive and unsupportive, or their in-laws slight them, stepmothers may feel hurt, neglected, and unappreciated. Disengaging is a way to protect themselves. It also allows them some distance in which they can heal their wounds. After having had time to reflect, and perhaps gain support and insight, stepmothers may re-enter the stepfamily and rebuild their relationships. More cautious, and perhaps wiser, their expectations are less ambitious.

When Leah first met Tamas twenty-five years ago, he was struggling to care on his own for his two children, Mark, age six, and Kathleen, who was only eighteen months old. Tamas's first wife, Sonia, had died giving birth to Kathleen, who was born with a digestive condition that required many operations and hospital stays. Leah worked as a dietician in the children's hospital and first encountered Tamas through consultations about Kathleen. At twenty-six, she was in no hurry to get married. She loved her work and her freedom as a single woman. She felt great compassion for Tamas, however. He was gentle and patient with Kathleen, yet obviously out of his depth trying to manage Kathleen's illness, caring for a six-year-old and keeping up with his work as a manager in a department store. Leah jumped into stepmothering with both feet. She and Tamas agreed that the children needed a full-time parent at home, so she quit her job. Although she did this willingly, she missed the activity and social contact. Whenever she broached the idea of working part-time, however, Tamas discouraged it, saying that he earned enough to support everyone. Although these were his children, Tamas did not expect that he should alter his work schedule.

Leah initially was an enthusiastic proponent of the Nuclear Family model. Believing "that love would conquer all," she used her own mother as her guide and dedicated herself to rescuing Kathleen and Mark. Dealing with Kathleen's health—which was almost a full-time job—became her responsibility. Mark was an anxious, tentative child. Life had been unsettled since his mother's death, and Leah felt he needed a lot of nurturing. He was a picky eater, preferring to live on bread and pasta. As a dietician, Leah wanted him to eat more healthfully. She discovered a ploy: "I found out early that he liked chocolate chip cookies, so I made more chocolate chip cookies the first year we were married than I made in the next twenty-four years. I would put the cookies out on the counter and then we'd sit down to eat. I'd say, 'You have to eat what's in front of you, or no dessert.' And then he'd look over and see it was chocolate chip cookies and then he'd eat his vegetables and meat."

For the first eight years, everything went swimmingly. The children were prospering, Tamas was delighted to have Leah take over, and although she missed her work, it was satisfying for Leah to recognize positive changes in the household. Things began to sour, however, when her stepchildren headed into adolescence. Mark became increasingly hostile toward Leah, ignoring her or rolling his eyes if she tried to talk to him. If Leah tried to hug him, it was "like putting my arms around a telephone post." The tensions came to a head one evening when Mark was sixteen and Kathleen eleven. Leah had asked Kathleen to finish her homework and Mark blew up: "He said I had no right to act like a mother to her because I wasn't her mother." When Tamas supported Leah, Mark "got mad at his father and he said, 'Well, everything was fine with us until you married that bitch.'" He stormed out of the house and went to stay with his friend. Leah was stunned. She knew Mark was unhappy, but had been unaware that his rage had built to such an extent or what she had done to provoke it.

With urging from his father, Mark apologized to Leah. Their relationship remained tense, however. Except for the most banal exchanges, Leah kept her distance. She was unsure how to effect a rapprochement and also afraid of instigating another attack. After six months of this, she sat him down. "I said, 'I'm trying to do what's best. It might not be what's best, but it's the only way I know to act. And we know that I'm not your mother. Maybe you shouldn't call me 'Mum' any more. Maybe you'll feel better calling me 'Leah.'" This suggestion represented a major concession for Leah. From the time she was married, both children called her "Mum." She had thought of herself as the children's mother, imagining she could replace their mother. Mark did not respond to her comments at the time, but subsequently he did switch to calling her by her name.

After Mark reached his twenties, his and Leah's relationship started to ease. Mark had moved away and visited infrequently, but was polite when he did come home. Mark is now thirty-one, is married, and has children. Leah still treads gingerly and thinks twice before she makes any comments to him. Although Leah was initially devastated by Mark's outburst, she has since accepted the constraints in their relationship: "I was sorry he felt the way he felt, but there really wasn't anything I could do about it." Since Mark has become a father, his relationship with Leah has relaxed. His two children call her "Granny," and Mark is delighted to have Leah as a grandmother for his children. Recently, he told his children the story of the chocolate chip cookies. Leah was pleased. This was one of the few times Mark has acknowledged, albeit in an indirect way, what Leah tried to do for him. Reflecting on her twenty-five years as a stepmother, Leah advised new stepmothers to be cautious and educate themselves: "Talk to people who are stepmothers. Before you marry a man with children, get to know the man well. Also get to know his children. . . . I think that you have to be a lot more careful than I was."

Worse Than a Servant

Stepmothers who fit within a Retreat model find themselves in a more dire situation than stepmothers like Leah where a partial retreat can lead to a détente with stepchildren. For Retreat stepmothers, their withdrawal is complete, and there appears to be no possible way back. Like other stepmothers, these women start off with optimistic expectations. Most believe their partners and his children need rescuing and that they will be the agents of transforming misery into happiness.

These stepmothers' disillusionment is more brutal than most other stepmothers', because their stepchildren's reactions are entirely negative. All Retreat stepmothers have terrible relationships with their stepchildren. Occasionally one of their stepchildren is less hostile than the others, but the overall picture is bleak. Their stepchildren are usually rude, contemptuous, and dismissive. While some stepmothers, like Leah, find that changing their approach may alter their stepchildren's response, Retreat stepmothers face unwavering resistance.

Retreat stepmothers sometimes attribute their stepchildren's animosity to the stepchildren's mothers, who, they believe, whip up their children's resentment and anger. Often they feel their stepchildren have been thoroughly poisoned by their mother. One stepmother initially had a companionable relationship with her stepson. When his mother discovered that he had made a Mother's Day card for his stepmother, she ripped it up. The message was clear that he should not like his stepmother and, overnight, he became sullen and unresponsive.

I have already described Patricia's bitter relationship with her teenaged stepdaughter, Amy, who moved in precipitously after a blowup with her mother. When Patricia and Jeff moved to accommodate Jeff's new job, they had bought a tiny house, because Patricia's twin sons and Amy had elected to stay behind. Their decision had primarily been financial. The housing prices in the new community were three times higher than those in their previous community, and Patricia and Jeff were sending child support back to their former spouses. While the house was perfect for two people, it was too cramped for three. Patricia was studying at home, while taking courses to upgrade her qualifications. Having

Amy living there full-time was a major adjustment for Patricia. Jeff, caught up with his new job, worked long days at the office, so his life was less affected.

If Amy had been cooperative, the challenge of their living quarters could have been overcome. But she was not: "[I was] treated worse than any servant, and with unbelievable rudeness and unfriendliness. Nobody had ever been unpleasant to me much in my life before. There was surliness and rudeness and downright insults, plus total and absolute refusal to help. . . . She absolutely would not do anything. She left her plates all over the house, she'd just eat anywhere anytime and leave the stuff everywhere. We have a teeny house and the only way to exist in it is to keep it tidy. Both her father and I have told her that a lot of times, but she would come in and just spread everywhere."

Patricia believes that Jeff's ex-wife, Connie, fuelled Amy's behaviour. Connie had not wanted the divorce. Even though Jeff and Connie had split up on two previous occasions before Jeff met Patricia, she told everyone within earshot—including her daughter—that Patricia had destroyed her marriage. Connie had spread false stories about Patricia, claiming that Patricia had broken up other marriages and had had affairs with numerous men. Patricia did not contradict these stories to Amy, because she felt this would be telling Amy her mother was a liar, but Connie's fantasies added to Amy's distrust of Patricia.

While it was hard enough living with Amy during the school year, it became impossible during the summer. New to the community, Amy did not have many friends, nor was she interested in looking for work or volunteering. Mostly she hung around the house. Patricia started to dread being home while Amy was there: "I felt the house wasn't my own because she took it all over. . . . If I was sitting having lunch or reading the paper or listening to music, she would just come and put on the television without asking." Increasingly, Patricia vacated the house or sat on their terrace whenever Amy was around.

When a friend came to stay, she was shocked at how Patricia had been marginalized in her own house. She urged Patricia to push Jeff to curb Amy's behaviour, but Patricia was reluctant: "I thought about the conflict that Jeff would be in if I made too much fuss because he is obviously torn." In any case, Jeff was little help. Even though he did not like the mess, he was unwilling to be firm with Amy: "He would sort of say, 'Just calm down.' Sometimes with things like cleaning up, if he came in, he would do a bit himself. But I didn't think that was the answer." He was not very sympathetic to Patricia's plight since Amy was charming to him.

Without his backing, Patricia could do little. Living far away from family and friends, there was no one in whom to confide. Although she registered for courses at the university, she could not motivate herself to study. She, who had always been so energetic and focused, spent most of her time drifting around: "I had basically no support at all of any kind. [I coped with it] by getting depressed, I think, mainly. I didn't achieve anything. I took a vacation when I should have been working."

One day after Patricia tripped over Amy's dirty dishes on the living room floor and broke a glass on which she cut herself, she reached her limit. Amy refused to pick up the dishes, claiming, even as she was lying around on the sofa, that she was busy. Patricia lost her temper. She told Amy she was a spoiled brat and she, Patricia, was no longer going to cater to her. Amy rushed upstairs, called her mother, packed her bag, and two days later was back with her mother, in much the same way she had arrived. Although it was a huge relief to have Amy out of her house, her departure created friction in her relationship with Jeff: "I think he thought I was unreasonable, I'm not quite sure why. I think he felt very caught. I also gather, and I haven't ever gotten to the bottom of this, that she had long sessions with him complaining about me, and I know that some of the things that she said were not true. . . . The version she gave to Jeff was enormously altered and changed and I couldn't say to him, 'Look, your daughter is lying.'"

Patricia has not seen Amy since she left, and their few telephone exchanges have been tense. Recently Connie called Jeff to complain about Amy's rudeness and slovenly habits, claiming that Patricia and Jeff had "wrecked her." Patricia felt a small, private moment of vindication. Even though Patricia "would be quite pleased to never see [Amy] ever again" and cannot figure out what else she could have done, she has a lingering guilt, the feeling that somehow she is to blame. She runs the final scenario with Amy over and over in her mind, trying to figure out how she could have prevented it or if there could have been another, less drastic, outcome.

Like Patricia, Retreat stepmothers feel trapped in unsolvable situations. Patricia escaped only because her stepdaughter left in a huff. No matter what approach they use with their stepchildren, they face relentless hostility. Although most stepmothers feel powerless, these women have a more crushing experience.

Abandoned

Retreat stepmothers generally feel betrayed by their partners. Most consider their partners weak or disengaged fathers who are unwilling to correct and challenge their children. As in Patricia's situation, they are forced to live with the consequences of unruly and unruled children. It is even more wounding, of course, if their partners passively stand by when their stepchildren attack or insult the stepmother. Retreat stepmothers often describe a kind of coalition between their partners and their children from which they are excluded. Patricia knew that Amy complained to her father about Patricia behind Patricia's back, but she was helpless to counteract Amy's distortions since she was not privy to them.

Most Retreat stepmothers consider their stepchildren a destructive influence on their relationship with their partners. Sometimes they describe their stepchildren as "splitters." One stepmother felt that her stepson was trying to break up her relationship with her partner: "He was darn sure he was going to keep his dad. Because that's his lifeline. He just threw a terrible wedge between us, because he never gave [my partner] and me any time alone. He never left us alone. And he was always talking to his father, talk, talk, talk, talk, talk, to a point where I'd go and sit up in our bedroom and watch TV alone." Although this stepmother was annoyed with her stepson for his constant intrusions, her real anger was aimed at her partner for allowing his son to intrude on his time alone with her.

Feeling that their partners do not value them, Retreat stepmothers, like the stepmother quoted above, often end up pulling away, emotionally and physically, from their partners. The longer Amy lived with them, the more Patricia withdrew from Jeff. She was unwilling to confront him directly, but she became less interested in talking and being with him: "I felt less outgoing and actually it affected my sexual response, because I felt unhappy and put upon."

Patricia's retreat from Jeff was secondary to her struggles with Amy. Other Retreat stepmothers focus primarily on their disillusionment with their partners. Irina's story illustrates this predicament. When Irina met Peter three years ago, she was enthusiastic about becoming involved with someone with a small child. Irina, now forty-six, has three children in their early twenties who have all left home. Her ex-husband remarried ten years ago and all three children get along well with their stepmother. Irina anticipated that her relationship with her stepson, Eric, would be even closer and more affectionate than her children's with their stepmother, because Eric was only two and a half when she met him, while her children were teenagers when their father remarried. Irina also imagined that Peter would rely on her for advice about child-rearing. She had already been a mother for twenty-one years, while Peter, who is six years younger than she, was learning how to care for a small child on his own. Peter's marriage to Céline had split up six months earlier when Eric was barely two.

Peter and Céline were locked in a rancorous custody battle. She wanted Eric full-time, while Peter was pushing hard for shared custody. Irina saw Eric being yanked in two directions and believed she could be a neutral and calm presence in the little boy's life: "I'm a mum. I mean, that's what I do. And I jumped into it with both feet and one hundred percent. Not that I had any expectations at all of being his mother. I didn't want that. He has a mother, and I would do everything that I could to support his relationship with his mum. But I expected that there would be some joint parenting in our home."

Far from her welcoming her experience, Peter pushed her away: "It would be before dinner time and I'd say 'Eric, how about going to wash your hands for dinner?' And I was politely told that that was not my job. . . . I have twenty-five years of experience at being a mum and it made me feel that he had no respect for the job that I had done as a parent!" Despite Irina repeatedly asking for direction, Peter did not clarify how he wanted Irina to act with Eric. The ambiguity of her status made it difficult to develop a relationship with Eric. She believes that Eric was also bewildered about Irina's role in his life. Now, three years later, he barely speaks to her, appears almost terrified of her, as though he doesn't "understand who I am or why I'm there or what my position is."

Perhaps if Irina had respected Peter's abilities as a father, she could have accepted a peripheral role. But she does not: "I didn't really think that it was appropriate that a two-and-a-half-year-old be allowed to stay up until eleven o'clock on Saturday night watching movies. And it was made quite clear that I didn't have any influence on what time the child went to bed. . . . I really didn't think it was appropriate that, at five years old, the kid had his feet on the dinner table while everybody's eating. I think at five and a half a child should have more in their routine of things to eat than just peanut butter sandwiches and macaroni." Irina sees Eric as troubled, as a result of being bandied back and forth in his parents' war. Now in kindergarten, he has not fit in well at school.

He has problems making and keeping friends and plays only by himself. Even around people he knows well, like his cousins and grandparents, Eric relates only to his father. Peter's solution has been to offer Eric greater latitude. Irina believes Eric needs more structure and predictability.

Eric lives with them about half-time. While he is there, Peter's attention is focused on him, and Irina is pushed to the sidelines. Eric stays up as late as he wants, sometimes until midnight: "Then I get resentful because I'm not prepared to be part of Peter's relationship at two o'clock in the morning. When he's finished with everybody else, I'm next." And when Eric is at his mother's, Peter works long hours to compensate for the time he devotes to Eric. After their first "family" vacation, Irina refused to share her holidays with Eric again. They had gone to an ocean resort for a week. Peter catered exclusively to Eric's whims. During the day, he devoted himself to whatever Eric wanted to do. Irina's options were either to trail along behind them or sit by herself on the beach. Evenings were spent in noisy "child-friendly" restaurants where Eric liked the food. Irina feels that Peter's lack of support has forced her into vying with Eric for Peter's attention: "If we go out in the car, and there's the three of us, I have to run like hell to get in the front seat because the kid thinks that's where he sits. And, everything's, everything's a race. And it just feels awful, it feels awful. . . . I have set myself up to be in competition with a five-year-old. When I think of it, it seems bizarre."

Each month, Irina scans the calendar counting how many days Eric will be with them: "I hate it when this kid comes and I can't wait for him to leave. And that is not how I envisioned it." She castigates herself for reacting like this toward a small child and often feels like the wicked stepmother: "If I ever say to Eric, 'Go wash your hands' or 'Maybe you could sit at the table while we're eating' or 'Put your seatbelt on,' I feel like that's all horrible stuff. Although certainly stuff that I would say to my own children. . . . I've never had feelings like this before. . . . It's terrible, I wish harm on this kid. For me to say this, it just makes me sick to even think that I even wish in some way that this kid would go away."

Peter's failure to respond to her dilemma has, not surprisingly, engendered tremendous resentment and hostility toward him. She feels that he created this impasse between her and Eric, because he "would not explain to Eric who I was and that there is a place in Peter's life for lots of people, and not just his son. I think Peter was afraid that his son would be upset with him." She and Peter bicker constantly about Eric. A couple of months ago, Irina could not stand the tension any longer. She felt her only option was to drop out: "I put my foot down and said, 'Hey, I don't need this, I don't need to feel rejected. I don't need to feel frustrated. I don't need to feel like I need to keep my mouth shut.' And I've just kind of backed away from the whole thing and said, 'Okay, you want to be the parent, you got it one hundred percent.'" Peter manages a theatre and, on nights when he had to work, he had counted on Irina to be there. No longer. When Eric is there, Irina goes out, spending her evenings with her children or friends. Although she is less angry, Peter is annoyed at her decision to opt out and the rift between them has widened.

Given her unhappiness, it is hard to understand what keeps Irina there. She admits she has thought of leaving. Her family, who can see how stressed she is, has been urging her to leave: "My kids are like 'What do you need that for? You don't have to be last on somebody's list!'" Some days it feels like "too much effort, too much rejection, it's too difficult." There is so much anger and bitterness built up between her and Peter that it is hard to imagine how they can ever repair their relationship. Often she feels like a visitor in her own house. She and Peter bought and renovated this house together, investing a tremendous amount of time and money. It was a symbol of their future. Now it almost seems to mock her initial dreams.

What Have I Become?

Resenting—even hating—their stepchildren is distressing for these Retreat stepmothers. They had expected to have close and nurturing relationships with their stepchildren. Now they can barely stand to be in the same room with them. Their responses are at odds with who they have considered themselves to be. The stepmothers I interviewed are generally competent, successful women. Their inability to manage this situation makes them feel as though they have lost control. Some, like Irina, brand themselves as wicked stepmothers, but, overwhelmingly, Retreat stepmothers consider themselves failures. One stepmother confided, "I know how much he hates me, and he resents me, and I'm starting to feel the same way about him and I don't know how to handle it. I feel like it's just snowballing and it's getting worse and worse and worse all the time. . . . I just feel like a failure. I am a failure as a stepmother." Irina defines herself as a mother—"I am a mum. I mean, that's what I do"—and has very close relationships with her three children, her nieces and nephews, and many of her children's friends. This picture clashes with a woman scrambling to capture the front seat of a car from a small child. Patricia, as well, always regarded herself as someone who deals with life calmly and competently and gets along well with almost everyone. She easily juggled being a single working parent with teenaged twin boys and has maintained a cordial relationship with her ex-husband and her former in-laws. Now she feels defeated by a teenaged girl.

If these stepmothers had initially wanted their stepchildren to be peripheral, incidental, to their lives, their stepchildren's rejection would have been less wounding. It would have been unpleasant, but would not have struck so deeply. Retreat stepmothers generally invest a great deal of energy and thought into being a stepmother—they want to be good stepmothers. Their inability to achieve this goal often engenders feelings of hopelessness.

How do Retreat stepmothers cope? Their feelings are usually

too painful and intense to keep stifled. Their partners usually offer little support and, in fact, contribute to the stepmothers' unhappiness. These stepmothers are usually reluctant to confide in others, fearing that they will be regarded as aberrant. Surprisingly few force a "them-or-me" choice on their partners. The familiar image of Hansel and Gretel's wicked stepmother, who forced her husband to abandon his children in the forest, might lead one to expect that stepmothers either push their stepchildren out the door or demand their partners do it. On the contrary: none of the stepmothers with whom I spoke ever required that their stepchildren leave. And it is only the rare stepmother who tells her partner she does not want her stepchildren to move in full-time. Most believe their partner should take responsibility for his children and applaud his desire to become a more involved father, although they may later rue their initial enthusiasm and secretly hope for their stepchildren's departure.

While they stop short of insisting their stepchildren move out, stepmothers sometimes employ more subtle methods to restrict and reduce contact with toxic stepchildren. They lobby to change schedules so that the children visit less frequently, or they will absent themselves from the house when the children are there. If stepchildren leave after a blowup, the stepmother may lay down conditions for their return. Patricia has gathered from Amy's mother's complaints that she and Amy are at war again. Dreading that Amy might turn up on their doorstep again, she has told Jeff that, if Amy returns, she must abide by house rules and be at least civil to Patricia. In her heart, she would be "happy never to have to see Amy again," but does not feel she can forbid her to live with her father. These measures depend on their partner's cooperation, which, for Retreat stepmothers, is not always forthcoming. What could Patricia do if Amy moved back in, continued to be rude, and Jeff did not crack down? I wonder if one reason that some stepmothers hesitate to give their partners a "them-or-me" ultimatum is that they fear they will be the losers. If the stepmother's partner has not supported her thus far, can she be sure he will choose her?

When all these strategies are unsuccessful, Retreat stepmothers disengage emotionally and mentally from the stepfamily. They are there in body, but their energy is elsewhere. One stepmother described it as drying up, having nothing left to give. Another stepmother backed off because she felt too bruised by her stepchildren's continued hostility. Withdrawing is a way to spare themselves further hurt. It also helps them feel like they have regained a modicum of control. When they stop trying to reach their stepchildren or their partner, they avoid the risk of more rejection and the accompanying humiliation.

While withdrawing protects them, the Retreat stepmothers are now even more isolated. They often feel intensely lonely and alienated. As I listened to their stories, I had an image of them peering through the window of their house while their partner and his children chatted and laughed together inside, oblivious to the stepmothers' pain at being locked out. Stepping out may give relief, but it is not a happy solution. Their homes often feel like war zones. One Retreat stepmother described why she used to stay late at the office when her stepchildren lived with her and her partner: "I'd come home from work every day. This was the place where I wanted to come and feel warm and relaxed and recover from the outside world. And, God, you'd open the door and walk in and knives are out. I found that really hard."

Retreat stepmothers are the unhappiest group of stepmothers. Usually, they face almost all the elements that make stepmothering so hard. They start off with unrealistic expectations, often casting themselves as rescuers for their stepchildren. All have conflictual relationships with their stepchildren, which, they believe, are frequently stoked by the mother's bitterness. Their partners are generally unresponsive and unhelpful. And their angry, resentful reactions at being caught in this situation make them feel wicked, like failures for not living up to the impossible ideal of motherhood. One wonders why anyone would stay trapped in this place. Some Retreat stepmothers console themselves by imagining the day when their stepchildren will grow up and move out. Others, like Irina, contemplate leaving themselves. Although I interviewed only stepmothers who were still part of a stepfamily, I suspect that, for some, the Retreat model may be the final step on the path to separation. Unless they gain some relief—as Patricia did when her stepdaughter stomped out—it is difficult to imagine that anyone would linger here for long.

Chapter 11

The Couple Model: Friendship, Not Kinship

Stepmothers who fit within the Couple model focus their energy on the relationship with their partners and place their relationship at the centre of the stepfamily. In contrast to some other stepmothers, these women are attracted to a man who happens to have children. For a few, it barely registers that they are becoming stepmothers. In Chapter 2, you met Priscilla, who was so wildly in love with Terry that she did not pay attention to the fact that she was inheriting his two children, Natalie and Steven. Only after Steven referred to her as his stepmother did it sink in that she had this new identity. Although most Couple stepmothers are not so oblivious, the couple relationship comes first. Emphasizing the couple relationship does not mean that stepmother–stepchild relationships suffer. While some of these stepmothers have rocky times with their stepchildren, most enjoy their stepchildren and feel their affection is reciprocated by the children. They consider the mother role inappropriate for stepmothers and aspire to be friends to their stepchildren.[1]

A Strong Relationship

I have already described Hillary's frustrations with her partner's ex, Marika, who holds the reins while Hillary is relegated to the sidelines, even in her own house. Before meeting Stefan, she felt in control of her life. Sometimes now she feels her life has run away from her. What anchors her is her relationship with Stefan: "We have a very, very strong couple relationship. Stefan didn't get involved with me to be a parent to his kids, he got involved with me for himself. And I didn't get involved with him because I was going to rescue his kids from something. . . . We wanted to be a couple." Although Hillary and Stefan's relationship does get taxed, it also provides Hillary with a bulwark against the stresses of dealing with his ex-wife and children. Their commitment to each other means that they work at resolving problems. The time that the children are at their mother's gives Hillary and Stefan some breathing space: "As two people on our own without the kids, we don't have a hard time working things out and that probably gave us the strength to tolerate some of the other stuff." By the time the children return, Hillary usually feels she has recovered her equilibrium.

A strong relationship enables the couple to act in a united fashion. We have heard about stepmothers' hurt and feelings of betrayal when their partners do not support them. Couple stepmothers generally believe that they work as a team with their partners. It is important to them that the children recognize this as well, in part so the children will not try to pit one adult against the other. Of course dissension and arguments arise, but Couple stepmothers see it as essential that each adult's views be respected, particularly since stepmothers often feel they occupy a less powerful position in the stepfamily. Shortly after Priscilla and Terry married, his sixteen-year-old-son, Steven, decided to move in. Priscilla was optimistic about the change. She and Steven are only eight years apart in age and share a number of interests, including a passion for mountain biking. Priscilla quickly became irritated, however, with Steven's cavalier attitude to tidiness, his loud music, and the incessant ringing of the telephone—in short, typical teenage behaviour not too far back in Priscilla's past. Occasionally when particularly frustrated, she has laid down rules that she knows are unreasonable. She admires Terry for never confronting her in front of Steven: "If I do something that he feels is out of line, he bites his tongue until Steven isn't around. Which is good because I can't stand to be challenged. I don't like being embarrassed or humiliated. I'm like a cat in a corner when that happens. Then we can discuss it privately." After Priscilla has calmed down, she can acknowledge to Terry that threatening to cut Steven off the telephone for two months is too extreme.

Another bonus to a strong couple relationship is that their stepchildren—and sometimes their own children—are witnessing a healthy relationship. Since most stepfamilies are formed after divorce, many children in stepfamilies have experienced only their parents' relationship at its sourest. Now they can observe a happy couple. Some stepmothers see it as an almost moral responsibility to provide their stepchildren with a model of a strong relationship. When they have disagreements with their partners, they feel it critical that they resolve them. First, they hope the children will learn from their example how to do this when they are adults, and second, they want to reassure the children that this marriage will not dissolve. Knowing that Terry's previous marriage ended tumultuously, Priscilla was careful to explain to Steven her bickering with Terry was not serious: "I want him to see a good way to have a partnership with somebody. So it was important for me to do it right, in order for him to see how it was done. . . . I remember saying to Steven, 'Don't worry about your dad and me, we snap at each other, and get upset. We're just tired. It happens, everybody does it, it doesn't mean we don't love each other.' At the same time, he sees us being very affectionate and hugging and laughing and having fun." Believing that a strong couple relationship benefits both them and their stepchildren, Couple stepmothers feel confident that it is important to safeguard their relationship. They may carve out some private time for the couple or insist on occasional weekends away.

One Mother Is Enough

Couple stepmothers do not aspire to be mothers to their stepchildren. Since their stepchildren already have a mother, they believe a second one would be superfluous. Most consider their stepchildren's mother a reasonably good mother and do not see any need to step in. Even if the mothers are not perfect, these stepmothers believe that, on balance, it is better for the children to stay connected with their mother. They want the biological parents to parent and see their own role as supplementary. If their partners or their stepchildren attempt to push them into mothering, they usually resist. They do not want the mother to perceive the stepmother as trying to usurp her role, nor do they want their stepchildren to feel pulled between their mother and stepmother.

Peggy last appeared in Chapter 7, where she described how swamped—and sometimes resentful—she felt by the increased demands on her time and energy as a result of living with her two stepchildren. The children, Mara, age ten, and Jacob, age seven, live half-time with Peggy and her partner, Simon, and half-time with their mother, Lynn. Peggy considers both Lynn and Simon committed, loving parents. The children are close to their mother and father and initially were very suspicious of Peggy's place in their lives. Peggy decided to address this directly with them: "I don't ever want to be their mother, or expect them to look on me as their mother. I've said that to them very clearly. In fact, when I said that, and when I've reiterated it a couple of times, it does tend to kind of clear the air a bit." This leaves her with the dilemma of what to call herself: "I wish there was a language that was more appropriate. I think maybe it's just a matter of time. As more and more of us are in this situation, the language will somehow be found to describe it. Because I don't want society, the general public, out there to think that I'm claiming to be their mother unjustifiably. I don't want their mother to think that, and I don't want them to think that. . . . So

I call myself their dad's partner, or their dad's girlfriend, depending on who I'm talking to."

While Peggy is not acting as their mother, she has instituted significant changes in the household. As a single father, Simon was barely coping. Jacob, at age six, was frequently up until eleven on a school night, and both children's belongings were strewn throughout the house. While Simon agreed with Peggy's plan to regularize routines for bedtimes, meals, and television watching, all Mara and Jacob noted was that they had less freedom now that Peggy was there. When proposing changes, Peggy tried to distinguish between the household over which she felt she could have some say—for instance, the general tidiness and orderliness in the house—and the parental domain from which she has steered clear—for instance, when and whether the children do their homework.

Couple stepmothers generally avoid badmouthing their stepchildren's mother around their stepchildren. Even if they disagree with her actions, they try to stay out of it or wait until the children are out of earshot. Although Peggy thinks Lynn is basically a good mother, she thinks she is too indulgent. Lynn drives the children everywhere, while Peggy believes the children should walk, particularly if the distances are short. She would never say this in front of the children, so it irks her that Lynn does not have this inhibition: "We are so careful not to criticize Lynn in front of the kids. Not to judge her or speak badly about her. . . . I know that she talks about me, and criticizes me, and tells the kids things about me that imply that I'm not so great, or that I'm a problem." Avoiding conflict with the mother is another way of acknowledging their secondary role. Although the stepmother might believe that another approach might be better, she does not think it is her place to object. If their stepchildren make a negative comment about their mothers, Couple stepmothers will bite their tongues, even if they agree.

One stepmother was annoyed that her in-laws complained about her stepchildren's mother, often in front of the children:

"The problem was that [the in-laws] were saying things about [Jessica, the ex-wife] or asking me, 'How are the kids? How are the kids?' And I felt like, 'I don't want to get into Jessica bashing, because it's not productive. I don't know this woman. I've never met her. If you have an ongoing hatred, then you talk among yourselves, I don't want to be involved. It's upsetting to me.' " Although this stepmother thinks that the mother could be more involved with her children—taking them to the library, getting them involved in after-school activities, curbing their television watching—she has some sympathy for her: "I realize it's not easy being a single mother. . . . I think she tries to be a good mother." Wading in with her opinion would only fan the flames.

Couple stepmothers believe it is best if their partner and his ex-wife get along tolerably well. While they might not want a relationship with their partner's wife, they encourage their partner to be civil with his ex-wife. It is in the stepmother's interest if the father and mother co-parent, because then there is less pressure for the stepmother to take this role.

Some Couple stepmothers even become the conduit of communication between their partner and his ex-wife. Helen's partner, Ian, avoided his ex-wife, Charlene, whenever possible. If forced to talk with her, he would nod and pretend to go along with her suggestions. While Helen thought Charlene could be a little less protective of her children, she considered Charlene a pretty good mother and believed they had similar values about parenting. Because Ian and Charlene communicated so poorly, however, Helen felt that the children were successfully playing one parent off against the other. Helen deduced that her stepchildren were relaying stories to their mother that, if they were not misinformation, were at least misinterpretations of what had happened. Helen was flabbergasted, for instance, when Charlene called to complain after one of the children's weekend visits. Helen had stopped serving desserts after Christmas in order to lose the weight she had gained over the holidays, but her stepdaughter, Sarah, told her mother that

Helen refused to give Sarah any cookies because she thought Sarah was too fat. After fruitlessly urging Ian to sort out the misunderstanding, Helen decided to call Charlene directly: "I think she was a bit taken aback because she certainly wasn't expecting to hear from me. But we talked for about forty-five minutes and I sort of explained things to her. I started off with saying, 'Look, there seems to be a lot of problems going on and I'd really like to talk about it because I can understand if the kids are coming home and telling you things, that you're going to be concerned.'" Their conversation ended amicably: "We talked and cleared up a lot of things. The next time the kids were with us, I told them that their mother and I had talked and all this kind of stuff. And they were really taken aback. . . . We haven't had much in the way of conflict since then." Helen does not imagine that she will become friends with Charlene, nor does she particularly want this, but, since Ian will probably continue to avoid his ex-wife, it will likely be advantageous if she can occasionally check in with Charlene about the children.

Friendship, Not Kinship

If not mothers, then what role do Couple stepmothers play in the stepfamily? In contrast to Nuclear stepmothers, they do not count their stepchildren as part of their family, but at the same time, unlike the Biological or Retreat stepmothers, they usually are pleased to have their stepchildren in their lives. Their challenge is to create a space that is both non-parental and positive. Their ideal relationship is as a friendly adult to their stepchildren, someone who is interested in the children and likes being with them, but does not have the responsibility for disciplining or directing them. Greta has two adolescent stepchildren, one of whom lives with her and her partner. She has worked to establish a balance between being available to her stepchildren and not overstepping any boundaries: "I always felt that the best I could ever be was a friend to them, and I approached them with that kind of philosophy. And

I think in the long run, it's really paid off. They have a mother, you know, and I didn't want to take over that role even though my step-daughter lives with me." Greta enjoys outdoor activities like camping and hiking and was delighted to discover that her stepchildren shared her enthusiasms. A little to her surprise, she feels her stepchildren have added fun to her life. Not setting herself up as a parent also means that she does not feel responsible for her stepchildren's behaviour nor does she feel obliged to rescue them.

Adopting the friend role can be freeing. Peggy decided early on that she would try "to have a role of just being friends, being somebody they would find fun to be with, somebody who would take an interest in them, and do stuff with them." Peggy loves sewing and crafts. She has taught Mara and Jacob how to sew and often dreams up projects she can do with them. Her strategy seems to be paying off: "Just by virtue of the fact that I don't have to have full responsibility for them, I'm sometimes able to take things a little more lightly, or be the good guy for once instead of the bad guy."

The word "friendship" is a bit of a misnomer, because Couple stepmothers rarely experience the easy give and take and mutual support with their stepchildren that we associate with friendship. As discussed in Chapter 5, stepmothers rarely rely on their stepchildren, nor do they usually reveal much about themselves. The term "friendship" is shorthand for a friendly—rather than a problematic—relationship. Some stepmothers interpret "friend" as being like an advisor in the wings, someone who is available if their stepchildren want to talk. If their stepchildren do not approach them, they are not offended or hurt. As long as there is no animosity, they are content with a fairly arm's-length relationship. They are friendly, rather than friends. One stepmother has an amiable, but superficial, relationship with her eighteen-year-old stepdaughter, who lives with her mother and sees her father every second weekend. The stepmother and stepdaughter chat about everyday events, but the girl rarely volunteers any personal information, nor does she ask the stepmother much about herself. The stepmother is content with this distance because she has her own children to care for. When her stepdaughter asked for guidance in choosing her university program, the stepmother, who is a university professor, was pleased, because this was an indication that her stepdaughter valued her opinion.

Others equate friendship with having shared interests, values, and experiences with stepchildren. Stepmothers who are fairly close in age to their stepchildren or whose stepchildren were adults when they met often gravitate to this model. The relationship is more peer-like than parental. Priscilla's relationship with her stepchildren, Steven and Natalie, is like this. Their taste in music is similar and Natalie and Priscilla share a passion for animals: "Natalie and I don't have a mother-and-daughter relationship at all. It's always been much more of a sibling, well, older-sister, younger-sister, relationship."

Most Couple stepmothers see themselves as an older adult who takes an active interest in their stepchildren. They enjoy being able to add extras to their stepchildren's lives that might be missing otherwise; their financial contribution to the household will make it possible for their stepchildren to have figure skating lessons or a new computer. They take pleasure in introducing their stepchildren to new foods or wilderness camping or travel. One stepmother even described her ideal relationship with her stepchildren as a "fairy godmother." Her role is to provide treats for her stepchildren, whether taking them to movies or making their favourite cakes for birthdays.

Once Sheila's initial fear, that her stepsons would reject her, was dispelled, she began to look forward to her time with the two boys. In many ways, her relationships with her stepsons are similar to that with her younger brother, Patrick: "I like to compare the relationship I have with Daniel and Adrian with that of my younger brother. . . . The casual fooling around that you can do takes me back to the time I had with Patrick." Since Sheila and the boys share many interests, she characterizes their relationship as a friendship. Some weekends, Michael will be working at home, while Sheila and the boys are off kite flying or at a museum. At the same time, Sheila definitely feels like the adult in the situation, in her capacity as mentor. She is an avid reader, and she was astonished to learn that neither boy had ever been to a library: "I also see my role as exposing them to all sorts of things in life. . . . I'm starting to buy them classics. They've never read Dickens or Robert Louis Stevenson. I want to get them sort of male books, the heroes I read. They love them. They actually are very good readers, and they want to learn." Sheila is most satisfied when she can guide the boys' learning: "My ultimate role is really that of an educator, talking about issues, helping them open up and talk about themselves, which is very difficult for these two."

Couple stepmothers tend to shy away from disciplining their stepchildren. They situate themselves as a support to their partners, as someone with whom their partners can talk through issues, rather than being an initiator and enforcer of rules. One stepmother has learned that staying out of discipline makes for a more harmonious situation: "More and more I see that my husband needs somebody to talk to. I'm there when he's going through problems with them, but I don't get involved in disciplining them or chastising them." Sometimes this may mean holding back when they do not approve of what is happening. As one Couple stepmother described it, "My interest lay in not interfering."

While most Couple stepmothers have reasonably good relationships with their stepchildren and believe their stepchildren regard them fairly positively, a minority have strained or tense relationships with the children, often because of the children's divided loyalties. Perhaps because these women do not expect to love their stepchildren and vice versa, they become less distressed than other stepmothers if their stepchildren push them away. As well, since their main focus is their relationship with their partners, having a close relationship with their stepchildren is less critical for them than, for example, for Nuclear stepmothers.

At the same time, they are not satisfied to remain on the sidelines in their own house. Often these stepmothers find it useful to distinguish those areas where they can have legitimate power from those that they should avoid. They usually draw the boundary between being in charge of the household and being in charge of the children. It is okay to have an opinion about how the household is run, but not about disciplining stepchildren. They feel justified, for instance, asking their stepchildren to hang up their coats rather than drop them on the floor and requiring them to call if they will not be home for dinner, but they will not expect to dictate what their stepchildren's after-school activities should be. A rule of thumb used by a number of Couple stepmothers is that they should receive the same consideration from their stepchildren that they would from a housemate. The obvious difference between a stepfamily and housemates is that the stepmother is usually dealing with children, so she might have to be more directive than if she were living with another adult.

One Step Removed

Couple stepmothers' place in their stepchildren's lives hinges to a large extent on what their stepchildren will accept from them. Although a stepmother might want to introduce her stepchildren to Dickens, her stepchildren may turn up their noses. All stepmothers have to grapple with this problem, but Couple stepmothers often find it easier than some other stepmothers to live with a more distant relationship than they anticipated. They might wish to be friends with their stepchildren, but discover that their stepchildren regard them as unwanted intruders. This rejection is, of course, not pleasant, but Couple stepmothers' less ambitious expectations frequently shield them from hurt. There is a shorter fall to earth when one wants to be a friend than when one hopes to be a mother. Because their primary interest is their relationship with their partner, Couple stepmothers take their stepchildren's rebuffs less personally. Their more removed position also serves Couple stepmothers well in that it allows their stepchildren the time and room to approach them.

Just as Priscilla was ill-prepared to become a stepmother, it was apparent that her stepdaughter was also unready. When Priscilla and Terry married two years ago, Natalie was thirteen. Since she lived with her mother and only came over every second weekend, it took much longer for Priscilla to get to know her than it did with Steven. When her father told her he was remarrying, she was not happy: "[It was] obvious how she felt because she was just always downcast and sullen." On her visits, she refused to address Priscilla at all. Rather than pushing for a confrontation, Priscilla decided to leave her alone: "I just had a sense that if she could get over her anger at everybody, we would probably eventually get along. It wasn't just that I didn't want to waste my time with bashing my head up against a wall, but also a friend of mine's parents had split up and her father was living with a new wife who was bending over backwards to try and win my friend. Brenda couldn't stand these overtures. And I suspected that Natalie was intelligent enough to know when she was being wooed and I didn't want her to be turned off."

Natalie proved more obdurate than Priscilla anticipated, however. After about six months of being ignored, Priscilla began to worry: "I just felt like 'How can we go for years in this house without saying anything to each other?'" Eventually a solution presented itself. Priscilla loves horses. She had had her own horse when she was young and continued to ride whenever she had the chance. When she dropped by the stable one day, Natalie happened to be in the car. Natalie's eyes lit up when the owner asked her if she wanted to try riding. Seizing the opportunity, Priscilla offered Natalie riding lessons. Natalie has become a fanatical horse lover, and this has given them a common meeting ground: "This was safe, it was about an animal we both loved and it was just an optimistic sort of thing." Since Terry had no interest in riding, this activity was also exempt from any competition for his attention. Eventually their relationship expanded into other areas, and they now get along extremely well.

Priscilla was not distraught at first about Natalie's hostility because she was immersed in her relationship with Terry. She and Terry focused on being together and assumed everything would work out with the children. Priscilla now wonders whether they should have given more thought to Steven and Natalie's reactions. At the same time, their preoccupation with each other may have been an advantage: "I wonder if I don't sound like Terry and I were too selfish and blind because we hadn't thought about these things in the beginning. But, in a way, I'm glad we hadn't, because we would have spent a lot of time worrying about something that didn't turn out to be too much of a problem."

Supporting, Not Slaving

Given that Couple stepmothers believe biological parents should shoulder primary responsibility for their children, it is perhaps not surprising that they are less likely than other stepmothers to have sole charge of the household and child care. Couple stepmothers often have a more egalitarian division of domestic work with their partners than other stepmothers.[2] Rather than take the initiative with the children, they tend to act as supports to their partners. While Nuclear stepmothers may attempt to make up for the deficiencies of their partners by becoming the main parent, Couple stepmothers encourage their partners to be more involved fathers. Similarly, rather than directly disciplining or directing their stepchildren, they will advise their partners.

Although Couple stepmothers are generally satisfied with their role, there are stresses. Some become annoyed with their partner if they feel he is off-loading his responsibilities onto them. Even though the housework and child care are usually fairly equitably distributed, some Couple stepmothers sometimes find the extra tasks onerous. Either, like Priscilla, they had not anticipated how much their lives would be disrupted by their stepchildren, or they resent doing half the housework. Why should they have so much responsibility? The children are their partner's, not theirs! They may feel their partners are too willing to let the stepmother pick up a lot of the slack or do not acknowledge the huge adjustment the stepmother has made. The stepmothers may have stepped in too far too fast and may want to back out a little. It may take years to negotiate what they consider to be an equitable division of labour.

Couple stepmothers' main annoyance, however, is when they feel their relationship with their partners is being compromised. I have already described how stepfamily life creates less time for the couple, how the stepmother may spend her evenings alone while her partner reads what seems like endless stories to his children before he falls asleep in their bed, how the couple's sex life may be constrained by small children crawling into their bed, or how, when they finally have a moment to themselves, they are too exhausted to enjoy it. Since Couple stepmothers' raison d'être for being in the stepfamily is their partners, they may question what they are doing in the relationship. Most distressing is if their partners do not share their perspective. They do not want their partner to exclude or ignore his children, but by the same token, they do not want to be pushed aside or treated as second-class citizens.

When Karen first met Mordechai, his daughter Rivka, then age seven, lived with her mother in Israel and visited in the summers. Imagining that Rivka would be fairly peripheral to her life, Karen did not give much thought to becoming a stepmother. At the beginning, Karen and Mordechai lived like a childless couple. Karen was twenty-seven and just finishing her graduate studies in biochemistry, and Mordechai, then age thirty-eight, was a bio-chemist in the lab where she did her research. In addition to shar-ing professional interests, they both loved classical music and reading. For Karen the only irritant about her stepdaughter's visits was that Mordechai pretended he and Karen were just friends: "He would always treat our relationship in front of her platoni-cally. . . . I don't think Rivka was ever fooled by this facade, yet I used to resent her coming because it would naturally become a platonic relationship." After a few years of sleeping in the spare bedroom during Rivka's stays, Karen put her foot down. Now Rivka was upset: "She cried every night—why couldn't she stay in bed with us, basically. Every night she cried, 'Karen is there, how come I can't be there?'"

Rivka had always been very attached to her father and would often mention that she would like to live with him. At age twelve, she started serious lobbying. Although Karen "wasn't certain if I wanted her, I knew he wanted her, and I did everything to help him get her here." When Rivka moved in, it was clear she was only interested in her father: "She would exclude me by speaking Hebrew and of course he would want to cultivate her speaking Hebrew because he was afraid she would lose it." Although she felt like the interloper, Karen initially went along with this as she imagined Rivka (who spoke excellent English) would ease off. When she realized that Rivka was using Hebrew to exclude her, her acceptance soon curdled to resentment, particularly toward Mordechai, who did not consider Rivka's behaviour a problem. Karen's life had altered tremendously since Rivka had moved in, and she wanted Mordechai to acknowledge her position and con-front Rivka. It took him a couple of years to come around. Now, eight years later, Karen and Rivka are "perfect friends," but Karen's initial experience sharpened her belief that the relationship should come first: "I think your loyalties should be to your mate first, and to your children second. In a situation where you become the stepmum and his loyalty isn't to you first of all, it can take a while to get there. Right now, his loyalty is to me first, but it took years. That was the hardest thing to deal with."

The risk with the Couple model is that there may be no room for the children. Some stepmothers and their partners are so focused on their relationship that the children become overlooked. As well, if a stepmother feels insecure, jealous, and threatened, she may believe she has to guard her relationship with her partner by freezing out the children. She may discourage the children coming over, or while the children are there, she will organize it so the children have little time alone with their father. The role of the father is critical in determining whether this dynamic plays out. If he is an inattentive partner and father, the stepmother and her stepchildren will probably feel insecure and be more likely to jockey for position against one another. In this situation, the stepmother might be tempted to push her stepchildren out of the way by limiting their involvement with their father.

If, on the other hand, the father is both an active parent who takes responsibility for his children and a supportive partner, the stepmother will feel less inclined to protect her relationship with her partner. One might think from the description of Priscilla and Terry's passionate relationship that there would have been little room for his children, Steven and Natalie. This has not been the case. Terry has always been a dedicated father and has been scrupulous about spending time alone with his children. At the same time, he has been careful to include Priscilla in other ways. She has never felt threatened by her stepchildren's presence. On the contrary, she is delighted to have them in her life. In part this is because she genuinely likes them. If Terry had not been so skilled at balancing her needs with his children's, however, she might have been less enthusiastic.

Couple stepmothers are generally fairly satisfied. Concentrating on the couple relationship translates into fewer and more temperate expectations and thus a less devastating disillusionment. They also tend to have more varied relationships with their stepchildren than many other stepmothers. This fluidity makes it easier for them to respond to their stepchildren's wants and needs. Because they do not want to replicate the biological mother's role, there is usually less competition with her and thus fewer conflicts. In the end, their relationships provide a kind of buffer against vicissitudes of step-family life. Even if their relationships with their stepchildren are tense or difficult, they can imagine that one day they will have their partners to themselves. As Greta commented, "My mother always used to say to me, 'Don't lose sight that it's your relationship you need to be focusing on, because no matter what's going on with the children, they're going to grow up and go on their own.' That stuck with me. And I think my mother was really wise."

Chapter 12

The Extended Model: The More the Merrier

The final model is what I call an Extended Family model, because stepmothers who fit into this group view the stepfamily as an extended family. When we refer to extended families, we generally mean families that are more inclusive than the nuclear family, and encompass kin outside the household who have a less direct biological tie—cousins, aunts, and uncles. Stepmothers in the Extended model have an expansive view of kinship. For them, the stepfamily is an opportunity to enlarge and add to their family relationships. These women also have the most optimistic perspective of the stepfamily and are the only stepmothers to consider that stepfamily life can have advantages. While other stepmothers in other models have satisfying relationships with stepchildren and partners, and enjoy aspects of stepmotherhood, these women welcome the complex network of the stepfamily.[1]

Extended stepmothers who do not have their own children view stepchildren as serendipitous. Perhaps because the biological connection is less important to them than to some other stepmothers, they tend to welcome these children into their lives. They feel their stepchildren add a texture to their lives that would be otherwise lacking. Siobhan is one of the happiest and most contented stepmothers with whom I spoke. Now forty-six, she and her partner, Larry, who is also forty-six, have been together for thirteen years. Siobhan is a librarian and Larry is a United Church minister, and they met through their volunteer work with refugees. Larry had been separated from his first wife for two years when they met, and

Larry's two sons, Sam and Derek, lived half-time with him and half-time with their mother, Janet, with whom he had a good relationship. Siobhan and Larry planned to have children together, but Siobhan was unable to become pregnant. The two boys, now twenty-six and twenty-four, live on their own. Looking back on the years they were still at home, Siobhan feels lucky: "It has made our lives a lot more fun. Certainly when I look back on the days when the boys were with us, I really enjoyed them. They each had a marvellous sense of humour in different ways and you never knew what was going to happen next. . . . Having them really enriched my life. I'm really grateful to them for that. I wouldn't have had children in any sense without them."

Many of her happiest memories are of ordinary, everyday interactions: "I began to notice when Derek came home from school, if I was in the house, he would call out, 'I'm home' or 'Anybody home?' Then he'd bound upstairs and speak to me. Just very briefly, but he would always go up." In part these exchanges were satisfying to Siobhan, because they indicated how she had become part of her stepsons' world. Siobhan feels she and her stepsons are now closely connected, their lives gradually woven together through the accretion of shared meals, jokes, and family holidays.

Extended stepmothers with children from previous relationships, who already have complicated lives, also welcome their stepchildren. Josephine is now a stepmother for the second time and is related to children from three different families. She and her first husband, Kevin, had three children together. They divorced after fifteen years of marriage. Josephine was granted primary custody, and Kevin gradually drifted out of the children's lives so that she had sole care of the three children. Four years after her divorce, she met Stan, a widower with four children, whose wife had died of cancer. When Josephine and Stan married, they brought together nine people, seven of whom were adolescents. Stan died after six years of marriage and she assumed full responsibility for her stepchildren, as well as for her biological children.

Five years ago, she married again, this time to Brian, who had three children from a previous marriage. If you have followed this convoluted trail, you will have figured out that she is connected, either through step- or biological ties, to ten children. Josephine is currently sixty-seven, and all the children are adults, ranging in age from thirty to forty-three. She and Brian live on their own, but Josephine keeps in close contact with all ten of her biological and stepchildren. Many of them have their own families so that she is a grandmother to an even wider pool of children. Even though her life has been hectic—she worked at least part-time as a nurse throughout most of those years—she believes she would have lost out if she had not experienced all these "expanded relationships," as she calls them. Her pleasure has come both from her involvement with her stepchildren and from feeling she had a positive influence in their lives. For instance, Josephine and her middle stepdaughter from the second marriage, Elinor, share many interests. They laugh at the same jokes, swap books back and forth, and chat regularly on the phone. When Elinor is trying to make a decision, she will often call Josephine for advice.

Stepmothers who fit within the Extended model believe that not only do they benefit from this expanded network, but that their biological children and stepchildren do too. In contrast to Biological stepmothers who worry that their biological children may suffer from sharing their mother with stepsiblings, these stepmothers think their children profit from being involved with a wider circle of people. The Biological stepmothers view the stepfamily as a zero-sum game, where if one person gets more, someone else will receive less. Extended stepmothers, by contrast, consider that everyone wins in the stepfamily, because everyone gains additional support. Recently Josephine's biological daughter Katie described her view of her family. Josephine said, "Last week, [Katie] was talking about her relationships with her brothers and sisters. She said, 'Well, I always called them my brothers and sisters.

If it comes up, or it's necessary, I'll explain that these are my step-brothers, not my true brothers, my full brothers.' So she brought up this point herself. She said, 'That's how we feel about them, and if any of them need us, we're right there.' And I like that." Josephine was delighted because it confirmed her wish that a new supportive, extended family could be forged out of all the disparate—and potentially conflict-ridden—relationships.

Allies, Not Rivals

Stepmothers who fit within an Extended model are more likely than other stepmothers to have a friendly or amiable relationship with the biological mother. Rather than viewing the ex as the competition or someone to avoid at all costs, they usually aim for a civil, workable relationship. Their reasoning is that cooperation among adults creates a better environment for the children. The degree of closeness between the stepmother and ex-wife varies. Some are cordial, but fairly disengaged. They might both attend child-related events, such as school plays or dance recitals. If thrown together, they will chat politely, but not pursue contact beyond this. Others act like joint parents. The stepmother becomes almost an equal partner with the biological parents and is actively involved in many aspects of her stepchildren's lives. The stepmother and biological mother might together work out a plan to deal with a child's academic difficulties, might host a baby shower together for their daughter/stepdaughter, or the two households will celebrate the children's birthdays as a group. A handful of these stepmothers become friends with their partner's ex-wife. Their connection evolves beyond their shared involvement with the children. It is grounded in their mutual liking and may become quite separate from the stepfamily. The stepmother and biological mother may meet for lunch or go out shopping together without any intention to discuss the children.

Somewhat to Claire's surprise, she and her partner's ex-wife, Roxanne, have become friends. When Claire met her partner, Richard, three years ago, she was thirty-seven, as was he. Richard's marriage had ended less than a year ago, and he and Roxanne were still negotiating arrangements with the children and the house. Claire is a high-level executive in a bank, and by her own admission, works "ridiculously long hours." Becoming a stepmother has meant major adjustments and accommodations. Richard shares custody of his two children, Duncan, age ten, and Alisha, age seven, and the children divide their time equally between each parent's household. Richard and Roxanne's divorce was amicable and they are still friendly toward one another.

As a new stepmother, Claire was overwhelmed by the huge demands on her time and the loss of privacy. Without Roxanne, Claire's first year would have been rocky: "I'm involved in everything—discipline, going to school events, parent-teacher meetings—and I have to thank Roxanne for a lot of it. She's been quite wonderful, in fact. If she had been opposed to my integration into the children's lives, then it wouldn't have happened." Claire has become the third parent, and there is an easy, frequent communication between the two households: "Roxanne values my advice and I value hers. If we have a problem in our household, Richard and I will call over there and say, 'Well, does this happen over there? How do you think we should handle it?' Or we share information. Sometimes we'll phone over and say, 'Just thought you might like to know that we had this little success' or 'We're having this little problem so that if it spills over into your house, you'll know what's going on.' And that goes both ways."

Claire and Roxanne have become closer in the last six months since Roxanne became involved in a new relationship with Peter, a longtime friend of Richard's. Peter and his ex-wife were in the middle of an acrimonious separation and Roxanne had been a close friend of the ex-wife, so Peter and Roxanne decided to keep their relationship very quiet. Claire—as someone less entangled in the situation—became Roxanne's confidante. While she is amused to find herself in this position, Claire is happy to listen. If Roxanne's relationship with her new boyfriend is on track, both households will run more harmoniously. Her friendship with Roxanne has also benefited her relationship with Richard: "It might have been that Richard and I wouldn't have had as smooth a relationship, and the integration into spouses and the children would have suffered." Claire's attitude differs from that of many other stepmothers who feel threatened by the mother. Of course, Roxanne has been welcoming and not hostile as are some ex-wives, but even so, many other stepmothers could not tolerate such a constant presence of the ex-wife in their lives.

Of course, there are irritations. Claire and Roxanne are temperamentally opposites: Roxanne is an artist and free spirit and lives in a fairly spontaneous, haphazard way. Claire likes her life mapped out three months in advance. It drives Claire crazy when Roxanne calls on a Thursday evening wondering if they can switch that weekend's schedule so she and Peter can go out of town. Since they are friends, Claire will tell Roxanne that she is annoyed at Roxanne's lack of planning.

Many stepmothers have to put up with the biological mother erecting roadblocks to their relationships with their stepchildren. For their part, they often feel threatened by the fact of the biological mother's existence. Claire and Roxanne, by contrast, have been remarkably open and tolerant with one another: "Both Roxanne and I work very hard at it. We had lots of long talks about where did I fit into the picture and how should we do this . . . [It] is probably something that we should be very proud of."

It's the Weirdest Relationship

As you have probably deduced from Claire's, Josephine's, and Siobhan's stories, stepmothers who fit into this model view their stepchildren as kin. They are determinedly not mothers, however.

Their rationale for this is similar to stepmothers within the Couple model—they hope to bypass competition with the biological mother and avoid turning their stepchildren into the prize. Even if their partners are widowers, they do not presume to be the mother. With Stan's death, Josephine's four stepchildren were orphaned and Josephine became their only parent. Her relationships with her stepchildren are close—all of them call her "Mum" —but she would never refer to herself as their mother. She has helped keep their mother's memory alive: "I used to try to talk about their mother a bit, to keep her going. It was difficult with the youngest because she has a very short memory, she can hardly remember her [mother] at all. . . . [Their mother] was ill, and she really was hardly there for a while. I made a conscious effort to [talk about her], because I thought it was important."

These stepmothers distinguish between being a mother and doing "mothering" things. They will help their stepchildren shop for clothes, cook their favourite foods, and, if the stepchildren are receptive, be available to talk, but they never cross the line into claiming motherhood. At the same time, their stepchildren are very much part of their family. Most often they consider themselves as an additional parent. When Claire refers to joint parenting, she means she is a partner with the biological parents: "Pretty soon it evolved that in our house we're both parents. And that I have authority in my own right. If both parents are around, then we talk about it and impose a consequence. Or if only one of us is around, then whoever is there deals with it. And that is something that has turned out to be extremely healthy." Both parents are relieved to have Claire around: "They see me as another person that can take some of the burden. One more person to alternate taking time off work to be with a sick child. One more person to do some chauffeuring around, one more person to take some of the expense, one more person to love the children and give them attention."

While full parenting works for Claire and a few other stepmothers, more often Extended stepmothers play more ancillary roles. One stepmother facetiously referred to herself as a "one-step-removed-parent." These women are active participants in the care of their stepchildren, but the biological parents have the final authority. While Nuclear stepmothers view this lack of power as frustrating, Extended stepmothers often consider it liberating. They have the advantage of a close connection with children without all the responsibility. One stepmother drew a parallel between her relationship with her stepdaughter and that of a grandparent with his or her grandchildren: "I can enjoy her and we can do things together. We can have fun together. I'm not the one who has to carry all the extra worries as well with her. . . . One of the benefits is that you're not a prime player. . . . It's not quite as removed as being a grandparent. When I look at my parents and I see the way that they are with their grandchildren, all they do with their grandchildren is enjoy them."

Other stepmothers who have an Extended Family model cast their net farther in order to capture the right label for their relationships with stepchildren. While they do not consider themselves parents, their stepchildren feel like kin. They might characterize themselves as an aunt, or an older sister, or cousin. One stepmother settled on the cousin relationship as the best approximation of her ties to her stepchildren. She grew up in a large Italian family. Summers were spent with her cousins at her grandparents' farm. The children would often share a bed and run around together in a pack. As an adult, she and her cousins are still connected: "It's more of a familial relationship and I'm very used to that relationship with cousins because I have tons of female cousins who are approximately my age and older and younger, and we're all reasonably close to each other."

These kin labels rarely fit perfectly, however. Encapsulating the complexity of this bond is tricky. Even if stepmothers can find a term like aunt, or cousin, or grandparent, they usually qualify it. The woman quoted above, for instance, recognizes that the cousin analogy is imperfect, because she lives with her stepchildren and is responsible for them in ways that never would occur with her cousins. In reflecting on her relationship with her stepchildren, she concluded somewhat wryly, "It's really very interesting, isn't it. I mean, when you think of what a relationship is, it's the weirdest one in the world."

Flexibility

These stepmothers tend to have an elastic view of their relationships with stepchildren. While they might wish for a close tie with their stepchildren, they will recognize that trust may take time to develop. When Siobhan met her stepsons, Sam was thirteen and Derek eleven. Sam had been distressed by his parents' separation and continued to hope that they would remarry. Siobhan's arrival on the scene made his dream less likely. When Larry told the boys that he and Siobhan were getting married, Sam became sad. Derek, more engaged with his friends and sports, took the news in stride. Siobhan's heart went out to Sam, and her impulse was to console him. She could sense, however, that this would backfire, so she checked herself. With both boys, she reined herself in: "I knew enough to know that if I didn't handle it right, it could be a difficult situation. So I lowered my own expectations. I constantly talked to myself and told myself things like . . . 'This relationship will take a long time to develop and you can't push it. And eventually they will be your friends, but that may take a long time and right now you're just another woman in their lives who has nothing to do with them.'"

Her relationships with her stepchildren developed slowly. At thirteen, Derek was more interested in his friends than in getting to know his stepmother, and Sam actively pushed Siobhan away: "He didn't talk to me very much at all for the first year or two when we were living together. . . . He would introduce topics to establish the solidity of their family and talk about incidents they had shared as a family, that they had shared with his mother. At times I was conscious that he was bringing these things up to make a point, to shut me out, to remind me that I was the outsider."

After two years of this behaviour, most stepmothers would become discouraged, but Siobhan hung in: "If I started to react, I would talk to myself and say, 'Listen, this is a kid. What difference does it make in the long run? You're going to have a long relationship with him.'" Siobhan took comfort in the small signs that Sam and Derek were beginning to accept her into their family, whether it was Derek bounding up the stairs to tell her about his day or Sam asking for help with a school essay. Initially, the boys worried they would have to answer to a third parent, but Larry reassured them: "No, I'm the parent. If there ever is a situation where I have to be out of the household, then of course Siobhan would be in charge. But beyond that, you listen to your mother and you listen to me." Not having this disciplinary role left Siobhan free to "spoil" the boys in small ways, and they came to appreciate this: "They found it wasn't so bad if you have three adults who give you presents for Christmas and birthdays!"

Extended stepmothers' relationships with stepchildren often vary. Like Siobhan, they may take a long view, understanding that the relationship may be cool at first, then metamorphize into a friendship, and then finally develop into a family connection. As with other stepmothers, Extended stepmothers discover that the degree of intimacy they have with their stepchildren hinges to a large extent on what the stepchildren will tolerate. Siobhan would have liked a friendlier relationship with Sam at the beginning, but she sensed that any overtures would hinder their future relationship.

Chemistry is another critical ingredient for these stepmothers. They may hit it off with some stepchildren, but never bridge the gap with their siblings. Josephine, for instance, feels much closer to some of her stepchildren than others. Since she has known Brian's children (her second set of stepchildren) for only five years, her connection with them is less profound than with her first set of stepchildren where she had a pivotal role in their upbringing.

Brian's children were already adults when she met them and their allegiance is to their mother, while her first set of stepchildren have neither parent alive. Even within each group of stepchildren, her relationships vary. She feels particularly attached to one of her stepdaughters, Elinor. After Josephine's second husband, Stan, died, Elinor phoned Josephine every day and frequently dropped in to check on Josephine. When Josephine told Elinor she was marrying again, Elinor was delighted for her. Josephine said, "You just feel closer to some people. [Elinor] doesn't talk about her emotions very much, she's very much to herself, but I could really call on her, if I needed to." With Elinor's sister, Megan, the road has been rockier. Megan reacted badly to her father's remarriage to Josephine and then later blamed Josephine for Stan's death. She quit school as a teenager and left home, and Josephine had little contact with her for a number of years. Although they have re-established a relationship, Josephine holds her breath around Megan. Not only does she want to guard against old antagonisms flaring up again, she feels the need to protect herself.

At the same time, Josephine definitely has a stronger bond with her biological children from her first marriage. This makes sense to her. While stepmothers who adhere to a Nuclear model reproach themselves if they do not feel identically toward biological and stepchildren, Extended stepmothers accept these differing reactions. Josephine cares about her stepchildren and is concerned about their welfare, but she feels more at home with her biological children: "I find my own children more interesting, with the exception of Elinor, because I find her very interesting."

Extended stepmothers also accept the conditional nature of stepmother-stepchild relationships. One reason the stepmother quoted previously drew the analogy between her relationships with cousins and with stepchildren is that both have boundaries. There are limits to what she will discuss with her stepchildren, just as there are with her cousins. While she confided in her daughter that she finds Christmas a drag, she would not tell her stepchildren this in case they interpret it as a complaint about them: "There are certain things [the stepchildren and I] can't discuss because they are Angus's children. . . . The same kind of restrictions apply actually with cousins. For instance, that you cannot go to your cousin and start carrying on about your aunt, who is her mother."

You Need a Strong Relationship

Extended stepmothers place the couple relationship at the centre of the stepfamily. In contrast to Couple stepmothers, who often feel a need to protect their relationship with their partner from possible intrusions, Extended stepmothers see it as enhanced by the complex web of family relationships. Earlier, I quoted Claire, who thinks that her relationship with her partner developed more smoothly because his ex-wife was so welcoming. At the same time, her reason for becoming a stepmother was Richard, not a desire to acquire an instant family. She and Richard share many interests outside of his children: "We have a wonderful life during those times when the kids aren't around. We go on ski trips and we go to a lot of movies and to Bach concerts and the art gallery and the museum and to lectures on anthropology and all kinds of things. We browse in bookstores, we read books, we garden and cook and entertain." If her time with Richard gets eaten into by child demands, Claire becomes cranky. She would not want to alter the custody arrangement where the children split their time equally with each parent, because it allows her time with the children and with Richard.

These stepmothers consider a strong couple relationship essential, not only in sustaining the stepfamily, but for its own sake. It is what grounds the stepfamily. Josephine—who has been married three times, is a stepmother twice, and has three biological children and seven stepchildren—intimately knows the potential complications of stepfamilies. She believes that a strong couple bond is crucial for the stepfamily to prosper. Her advice to a new stepmother: "You should really want to marry the father for your own reasons. It's best if it's a very strong relationship, and that you want to be that person's wife very, very much. Because that closeness is going to bring you through anything that comes along."

Weaving a Web

Running through Extended stepmothers' reflections on their experiences is a particular philosophy about kinship. They consider their family the people with whom they feel connected, with whom they establish a link, and about whom they care. One Extended stepmother was taken aback when her stepson Luke informed her she was not part of his family. She knew he liked her so she felt more puzzled than rejected: "And his comment sort of stopped me for a second, and then I thought, 'Well, let's see what he means by this.' So I asked him and he said, 'Well, you can't be my family because you know, we're not blood.'" Luke's rationale is typical of how we conceptualize kinship in our culture. The stepmother's response to Luke offered an Extended family view: "I said, 'Well you know, sometimes families get defined in really different ways. You have friends and grandparents and you have all kinds of things that are in there. Family is really about people who care about each other and look out for each other.'" In other words, kinship is based more on what develops between people rather than on a biological connection. The stepmother's comments sparked her stepson to expand his notion about his family: "Then he said, 'Oh, so that means that—' and then he went through a bunch of names of people, 'they're all my family too?' And I said, 'Yeah, they are. I mean, aunts and uncles and all that kind of stuff.' But that conversation could have had a different outcome."

Extended stepmothers' understanding of kin is often capacious. They include extended family members and people who might not ordinarily be thought of as family, sometimes even their ex-spouses or their partner's ex-spouse. Although Siobhan only has one brother—that is, her nuclear family is small—she lists over thirty people as part of her family: "Larry and the boys, and my brother and his family, and I still have three aunts and two uncles in my mother's family alive. So certainly them and their spouses and all their children. So it's a pretty big family. I have some other cousins that are all on my mother's side of the family. I have some cousins on my father's side but they are like relatives more than family. The rest of us are very close. It's interesting too that the last summer we went to visit Larry's family . . . and I realized that, as we were getting close to where they lived, that I felt the same way. I felt the same excitement that I feel when I go home to visit my family. So, his family are my family now too." What's remarkable about this definition—in addition to the extensiveness of the network—is that almost none of these people live in the same region, or even country, as Siobhan, and she sees most of them only rarely. Siobhan's criterion for determining "family" is how close she feels to people. She considers her cousins on her mother's side "family," but her father's cousins "relatives" because they do not have the same degree of intimacy. Both sets of cousins live in the same community, so it is not proximity that creates the bond, nor blood, but connection and affinity.

Sometimes the links reach even farther. Josephine considers her ex-in-laws from her first marriage part of her family because they supported her when she was a single parent. She is grateful because at Christmas they gave presents not just to their grandchildren (Josephine's biological children) but to her stepchildren with whom they had no biological or legal ties. They also often invited both sets of children to family gatherings. She does not include her second set of ex-in-laws (Stan's parents), however, because after Stan died, they tried to undercut Josephine's efforts to create a family with her biological and stepchildren.

For stepmothers within an Extended model, choice plays a significant role in determining whom you count as family. Although she is unusual, Claire has absorbed Roxanne, her partner's ex-wife whom she calls her "wife-in-law," into her family, because of their reciprocal respect and reliance. Claire spreads her kinship net even wider: "My immediate family is Richard and the children, and my ex, and Richard's ex-wife, I might add. And I would also say my own parents and siblings and their spouses and children. And I would also say Richard's immediate family—his parents and his brothers and their spouses and children. And also it goes beyond that, Richard has a great-aunt who I feel is family." Not only does Claire include her ex-husband in her family, but she has added Richard's great-aunt, Martha, to the mix because she admires her, a feisty, active older woman who founded her own business in an era when this was a rarity.

Who Celebrates What Where?

Extended stepmothers tend to view holidays and other family events the way they regard kinship—the more the merrier. Although I have referred to family celebrations like Christmas and birthdays throughout the book, I have not particularly focused on them. These are often particularly fraught with tension in divorced and remarried families. A child's birthday party or graduation may turn unpleasant if former spouses harbour bitterness or there is hostility toward new partners. Even without overt antagonism, family events are complicated by divorce and remarriage. Where do the children celebrate Chinese New Year, Ramadan, Christmas, or Passover? Who goes to their birthday parties? Both parents? Stepparents too? Or does the child have two separate parties? When a stepchild gets married, who organizes the event? Where does everyone sit? Whose traditions get celebrated? With few guidelines or rules, everything is up for grabs.

Particularly at the beginning, family traditions often clash. One stepmother, accustomed to modest presents for birthdays and other holidays, was dismayed that her stepchildren expected and demanded substantial presents not just for Christmas and birthdays, but Easter, Valentine's Day, report cards, etc. When she proposed scaling back, she was branded as stingy by her stepchildren and their mother. This episode led to a rift with her stepchildren that took years to repair. Just as stepfamilies often take years to become a family, family traditions evolve over time. Remember the stepfamily that had two Christmas trees for the first few years in order to accommodate both families' decorations. Not all stepfamilies craft such elegant solutions, and stories about disastrous birthdays and holidays are legion.

How stepmothers want to mark holidays often reflects their ideology about family. One Couple stepmother, for instance, was appalled when she discovered she was expected to share Christmas day with her partner's ex-wife. Following their divorce, her partner and his ex-wife had continued spending Christmas together because of the children. The stepmother had anticipated her first Christmas alone with her new partner and here she was doling out mashed potatoes to his ex-wife. By contrast, an Extended stepmother was the one to suggest inviting her partner's ex-wife over for Thanksgiving dinner. She knew that her stepchildren's mother would be alone and that her stepchildren would feel guilty about this. For holiday meals, Josephine mixes people from her four different families (family of origin, first, second, and third marriages), as well as stray friends who are on their own. Another Extended stepmother has doubled the number of events she celebrates: "It's very playful. For instance, I'm Jewish and Gary [my partner] is not, so we now keep every festivity. My kids come over for Christmas, his kids are over for Hanukkah. Friday nights we have supper at home, then Sunday we go to church. It's incredible, but everything is so open that there's no room for jealousy, because everything is being taken into consideration."

Like the stepmother above, Extended stepmothers integrate many traditions into their new stepfamily. Not only do they assimilate their customs and their partner's family customs into the new family, but they create new ones specific to their family. Although Siobhan trod carefully with her stepsons, she felt she could still nurture them through food. While Larry is an excellent father, cooking is not his forte. Meals before Siobhan's arrival were sketchy. Siobhan loves to cook and found a receptive and appreciative audience in her stepsons. Coming from a large Irish household where eating and meals are central to family life, she brought those values to her stepfamily. Over the years, she introduced many of her family's special holiday cakes and breads. These have become such an integral part of the stepfamily that, when her stepson Derek went away to university, he asked her to mail him her Easter bread. Siobhan has also invented new traditions. When Sam and Derek were still at home, she would hold a big end-of-school-year party for all their friends, and at Easter she invited the neighbourhood children over for an egg hunt: "My stepsons were children I nurtured. Very definitely, and that made me feel really good . . . in terms of specific foods for specific times of the year or just decorating the house for specific times of the year or making a better celebration for their birthdays or for Christmas or whatever. Just a little bit of richness in life would have been lacking otherwise."

Extended stepmothers have a high tolerance for the complications of stepfamily life. How does this come about? Many were raised in large or extended families, where cousins or foster siblings were part of the fabric of everyday life. The ebb and flow of a big family is familiar, so that the stepfamily—with its multiple households and complex connections—is less of a shock. While most Extended stepmothers have had limited interaction with stepfamilies before becoming a stepmother, their experience in an extended family gives them a feel for stepfamily life. Even though Siobhan's immediate family is small, she grew up in a rural area where most of her neighbours were her relatives: "There were a lot of other children around, most of them were my first cousins. I was familiar with family settings where there would be a household full of people and all kinds of things going on at once. People may be scrapping and arguing and sounding as if they weren't getting along, but that was just part of life. . . . In that kind of situation you're used to a lot of different types of people in your life too, and you adjust very quickly to all of that. So suddenly having two children in my life who hadn't been there before was not a big thing."

Another stepmother, who does not have her own children, is amused that she adapted more quickly to the commotion of the stepfamily than her partner, the children's father: "Where I grew up, there was always somebody else. My mum had foster children, cousins, aunts, uncles. There was always someone staying over and it didn't matter. Whereas Jeremy [my partner] is from a two-kid family, and he's just not as, I guess I'd use the term, 'flexible.' "

Of course, all is not rosy and perfect for Extended stepmothers. They run up against many of the same obstacles as do other stepmothers. Their biggest frustration is when others do not share their extended perspective. While, like Siobhan, they can accept that their stepchildren may be wary initially, they become irritated when others hamper the evolution of an extended network. Josephine became angry at her second set of in-laws because they repeatedly reminded their grandchildren (Josephine's stepchildren) that Josephine was only a stepmother and not really a relative. Since the children's mother and father had both died, Josephine believed the children needed all possible love, and she could not fathom why her in-laws tried to poison the children's attachment to her.

Anita is furious with her stepchildren's mother, Carla. The children live primarily with Carla and are supposed to have two days a week with Anita and her partner, Bob. Often these visits are postponed or truncated because Carla will change dates at the last minute or demand that the children leave early. The children confided to their father that their mother insists their "real" family is her and her new husband. She is urging them to call their stepfather "Dad." The children feel torn, Bob is reluctant to make a fuss in case his ex-wife impedes his access even more, and Anita seethes impotently. Not only does she enjoy her stepdaughters, she can see how painful it is for Bob when another visit is cut short: "If Carla had her way, my understanding is that Bob wouldn't be able to see the children at all. She's done everything in her power to initially discourage that." Carla has also "forbidden" Anita to attend any events related to the children. Since Bob is reluctant to challenge his ex-wife, Anita is left at home while he goes off to the children's dance recitals, sports events, and school concerts. Anita said, "She said that she didn't want me ever to be at any functions that involved the kids. Anything at the school or whatever, she didn't want me there because I had nothing to do with the kids. I wasn't part of their life." Anita cannot fathom how the mother can be so blind to the advantages her children would gain from having two sets of adults concerned about them.

It sounds as though there is a clashing of models in this stepfamily. While the stepmother wants to widen the circle (Extended model), it appears that the mother wants to draw a tighter boundary and create a new family with herself and her new husband as the parents (Nuclear model). If the stepmother does not have support from others, it may be impossible to build an Extended stepfamily. The stepmother may see its merits, but if her partner is a disengaged father or the mother insists that her children stay within her orbit, the stepmother may be powerless.

Despite these irritations, stepmothers who fit within this Extended model generally are the happiest stepmothers. One reason may be that, compared with other stepmothers, many of their partners are involved fathers, and they thus experience fewer of the frustrations that other stepmothers have with their partners.[2] Their flexible notion of relationships may make them less vulnerable to disappointment if they cannot achieve their ideal relationship. They also do not attempt to bury the stepfamily or fight against it as some other stepmothers do. They are the stepfamily's defenders, advocating for the ways in which stepfamilies benefit everyone.

PART THREE

Letting Go, Stepping Back, Making Changes

Becoming a stepmother has a profound effect on almost all women. Their unquestioned assumptions about family life are exposed, ambivalent and sometimes violent feelings are stirred up, and their values clash with others in the stepfamily. Many stepmothers feel altered—sometimes profoundly—by their experiences. Some discover unknown reserves of strength. Others confront less admirable aspects of themselves. Over time, stepmothers' understanding and self-understanding often shift, and they develop new perspectives on themselves and on others in the stepfamily.

In this section, I describe experienced stepmothers' insights, and the kinds of adjustments they make that help ease and improve their situation. I devote one chapter to a group whose perspective on stepfamily life is particularly valuable—those stepmothers who are in this role for the second time, or who are also stepchildren. I have also included a chapter on finding outside help and support. Finally, I describe seven principles that characterize the values and actions of the happiest and most contented stepmothers.

Chapter 13

If I Only Knew Then What I Know Now

Survivors

Some stepmothers gain confidence through their experiences. They feel they have been tested many times and passed, perhaps not with A's, but with reasonably good marks. Looking back at the tumultuous early years, they are proud that they managed to weather the battles and still remain standing. One stepmother who had the major responsibility for five teenagers—her two from her first marriage and three stepchildren who were vociferously opposed to their father's remarriage—described the first five years as a war: "It was so daunting to me before I was remarried. I didn't think there was anyway for me to get through it and I respect myself a lot. . . . I learned that I can manage an incredibly complex household, full-time job, and all my outside things, and I could keep it all going. People come to our house and the fireplace is on, and the table is set and they think, 'This is amazing.'" This woman describes stepmothers as unsung heroes. She believes that stepmothers should band together and start a club for themselves where they would hand out "hero badges" to all its members.

Some stepmothers begin with trepidations about their ability to live up to the challenges of stepfamily life and are relieved when their fears do not materialize. Childless stepmothers, for instance, may discover that they enjoy their stepchildren and that the children respond positively in return. Interactions with stepchildren tap unsuspected talents. Joyce had been so unsure of her capacity to be a good mother that she had ruled out having children of her own. She and her parents had been at loggerheads for many years, and she worried that she would have similar kinds of conflicts with her own children. In her twenties, she had suffered through a long period of depression, and she was concerned that the stress of children would precipitate a relapse. When she met Karl, she was thirty-nine and resigned to being single. Discovering that he had three young children, ages ten, eight, and five, she backed away. Karl persevered. He encouraged her to meet his children, but she kept putting it off: "I just thought, why rush it? I think it's better to take it slowly." Because of her fears, Joyce took a long time to commit to the relationship.

Much to her surprise, she has realized that she is "actually quite good" with children. Karl increasingly turns to her for advice. Life is also more fun with stepchildren: "It's made me feel more positive about my capacity to be a parent and be with children. It's also shown me all the positive sides. I have a glimpse of how much work, but I also have a glimpse of how much pleasure and fun there is. One of the best things is just being more active, initiating things that I would never do on my own or even if I was just married. I'm always looking for fun things to do—play baseball in the summer, or Frisbee or go water-skiing." Joyce's life as a stepmother has its tensions. The children's mother has been antagonistic and tried to sour her relationship with her stepchildren, and Karl has pressured her to act like a mother to his children. Nevertheless, Joyce feels that she has "been really lucky with the way these kids have been toward me. . . . I can't even imagine now living without them." In the last few months Joyce has reconsidered her decision to have children and is now trying to become pregnant.

My Darker Side

Other stepmothers' self-revelations are less happy. They discover depths of negativity and ambivalence within themselves that they could never have imagined. Finding themselves caught in this cauldron of boiling anger, envy, hate, resentment, and bitterness can be scary. The intensity of their emotions shakes their self-confidence and makes them question their sense of themselves, particularly if they feel angry or hateful toward their stepchildren. Feeling spiteful or hostile toward their partner's ex-wife—even wishing she would die—causes much less soul-searching. With their stepchildren, they had imagined being loving and giving. Only a monster could have such negative reactions toward children. Although they may initially feel ashamed, some stepmothers are able to confront these feelings and gain new insights into themselves.

In Chapter 10, I described Kay, the "guilty" stepmother. She knew when she married Craig that she did not really warm to his two children, Jason and Brittany, but she tried to ignore these feelings, telling herself she would grow fonder of them. Unfortunately, her ambivalence deepened into dislike and even revulsion. She found herself recoiling if her stepson leaned up against her, becoming angry if her stepdaughter wanted to slip into her and Craig's bed in the morning (although she welcomed her own children), furious at cereal spilt on the kitchen table, fuming at her stepchildren's constant quarrelling. Her jaw ached from the effort not to snap at them. Kay was horrified by the intensity of her rage toward the two children, especially because she knew they liked her and wanted her to be their mother.

These emotions were at odds with how she had previously thought of herself. Kay is known as a tireless worker, the person everyone depends on. As a child, she was always the "good" child, the one who never created waves, was always reasonable and accommodating. Her feelings about her stepchildren caused her to question her motives in other situations. If someone praised her dedication to her work, her selflessness, she would wince inside: "I would never have envisioned that I would have these negative feelings about people, especially children. It's changed my perception of who I am. I'm not this saint that people think I am, or that somehow I led people to believe I was."

She began to redefine herself, and in the process she relinquished the notion that she could be a "saint." In the long run, accepting her darker side freed her to become a more complex person, someone who can be angry and fed up, as well as loving and giving. The process was a long time in coming and hard won. Kay almost left her marriage and spent a long time in therapy trying to sort it all out: "In a way it makes me more human, that I'm not this wonderful, good person all the time. I'm also allowed to be angry and resentful and all those things. I've never looked at myself more closely, would be the best way of understanding that."

Beginning to forgive herself also meant she felt more kindly toward her stepchildren. Part of her anger toward them stemmed from her inability to give them what they wanted. Their demands exposed her flaws. As she accepted her imperfections, she became less irritated with them. Through acknowledging the baser sides of themselves, some stepmothers start to let go of unrealistic expectations. While initially they may feel like failures for being unable to rescue their stepchildren, the realization that they cannot work miracles can be oddly liberating. This knowledge relieves them of the burden of attempting the impossible.

I Didn't Understand

Through experience, stepmothers often develop insight into themselves and their values. Sometimes, like Kay, their negative feelings force them to acknowledge previously buried aspects of themselves. Other times, particularly when faced with their powerlessness, stepmothers become aware of their own expectations about how people should act in families. Stepmothers often assume that what worked in their childhood families will automatically apply to the stepfamily. It can be a shock if their stepchildren do not want to spend their evenings chatting around the dinner table or if their partners dismiss manners as irrelevant. Joyce and Karl constantly bickered about the children during the first year of their marriage. Joyce thought that they should be more responsible around the house, or at least pick up after themselves. She believed Karl was too apt to let their homework slide. She also experienced the recurrent irritation for stepmothers—"Their table manners! Even at their current ages, they don't really know how to use a knife and fork properly. . . . It was driving me crazy because it was unpleasant to be at the table with kids who should be beyond the age where they spill every time they pick up a glass." Joyce's complaint was not with the children, with whom she enjoyed a companionable relationship, but with Karl, who had not taught his children properly.

Joyce realized the fighting was going nowhere: "And then I thought, 'I'm driving myself crazy, and it's not helpful to Karl.'" She came to the conclusion that "I was trying too much to do things with them the way I would do with my own child. And then I realized, these aren't my kids." This revelation prompted her to re-assess her values. As mentioned earlier, Joyce's relationship with her parents has been fractious. Although she still thinks her stepchildren need more consistent structure in their lives, she now can see how Karl's easygoing style may create a more loving atmosphere than the one in which she was raised.

Without ever consciously articulating their beliefs, many stepmothers start off with the assumptions that their stepchildren have been damaged by their parents' divorce, that non-divorced families are best and stepfamilies are only a poor substitute. Others anticipate that their relationships with stepchildren and their partner's ex-wife will be adversarial, or at least full of tension. When they discover that their stepchildren have adjusted well to living in two households, or if they do not receive a negative blast from the "ex," they may start to re-evaluate their preconceptions. Denise expected the worst. Denise's partner, Erik, has one daughter, Leesa, who is now seventeen. When Denise first met Erik nine years ago, Leesa lived with her mother, Barbara, in another region of the country. Because of the distance, Leesa would visit for long stretches in the summer and over winter break. The first summer after Erik and Denise married, Erik suggested that he and Denise pick up Leesa together. Denise was apprehensive, particularly about meeting Erik's ex-wife, Barbara. Erik had left his marriage for Denise, and Denise anticipated that Barbara would be bitter. Denise also worried she would be at a disadvantage with Barbara. She was twenty-five years old, eleven years younger than Erik and his ex-wife, and had grown up in a rural community, while Barbara came from an educated, wealthy background. Denise was just starting her career as a physiotherapist, while Barbara had established herself as a successful entrepreneur. Denise agreed to go with Erik, but she was very nervous as they knocked at Barbara's door: "My expectations were more negative than it has turned out. I think I thought maybe there would be a lot of resentment, that perhaps Barbara would be more sarcastic with me. The first night I met her was quite funny. We went to her house, and she said to Erik, 'You go up and play with Leesa upstairs, she wants to show you her room.' . . . She was very nice, just frank and said, 'I want to make sure Leesa knows she has a father and let's try to make sure we keep in contact' and 'Erik is bad at letter writing so I need your help to keep the connection going.'" Initially suspicious of Barbara's openness and friendliness, because she assumed Barbara had a malicious agenda, Denise gradually relaxed as she realized that Barbara wanted her as an ally in caring for Leesa. In the last few years, she and Barbara have become quite good friends. When Erik and Denise come to pick up Leesa, Denise and Barbara will go out for lunch on their own. Last year Barbara invited them to stay with her. Denise credits Barbara for their harmonious relationship: "I think when she sat me down that first night, she'd made a decision that we weren't going to get petty or try to undermine each other. . . . I think that I would have perhaps been more willing to fight and be difficult with Barbara, because I thought that was the role. And when I realized that it didn't have to be, we became friends."

Similarly, Denise imagined that Leesa would resent her new stepmother. During Leesa's visits, Denise kept her distance. When, at age twelve, Leesa announced she wanted to live with them, Denise panicked. She was certain that Leesa would try to drive a wedge between her father and her stepmother: "All through the whole first year, I thought, 'She's going to act up any minute now.' She didn't. She never did make any trouble. . . . I thought that maybe if she had emotional problems from her father leaving when she was younger, that they might come out then." When I asked Denise where these fears came from, she laughed. Leesa was an outgoing and even-tempered child who had never shown any signs of jealousy. Denise has subsequently concluded that she was projecting her fears onto the situation: "I had assumed that there'd be such resentment from the child, but Leesa doesn't seem to remember the time when her mother and father were together."

After two years of living with her father and stepmother, Leesa decided to return to her mother's because she wanted to go to high school with her best friends. Denise was surprised to discover how much she missed Leesa. Once she had let go of her biases, she had enjoyed having Leesa around. Erik's attitude also helped. While he has continued to maintain an amiable relationship with his ex-wife, he ensured that Denise was never left out or disregarded: "Erik is a sort of a relaxed person, and he tones things down. I probably would have made more of a fuss or errors, but Erik never made me feel like an outsider. Always I was the important one."

Erik's ex-wife remarried two years ago to a man with two young boys. During Denise and Erik's last visit to Barbara's, it was obvious that Leesa had become fond of her stepfather. Leesa and her stepfather were joking around together, and before Leesa went out with her friends, she gave all four adults—her mother, father, stepmother, stepfather—a big hug. Denise was concerned about Erik's reaction, but "he was really happy. We talked about that, and he said, 'That was so good to see, that was great!' So, no, he wasn't jealous, because I asked him did that hurt, and he said, 'No, it was really good.'" Leesa is delighted not to be the only child any more and has become attached to her two stepbrothers. Leesa believes that her life has been enhanced by her expanded family. She commented to Denise that she feels she has "the best of both worlds because I have two families who are really good."

As Denise spent more time with Erik, Leesa, and Barbara, she started shedding her preconceptions about divorce and stepfamilies. In doing so, she has shifted models. She started off firmly in the Couple camp—her relationship with Erik was her priority and Leesa was a side issue. Denise had never wanted children of her own and did not initially include Leesa as part of her family. Over time, her attitude shifted and she now sees the benefits of a large and expansive family (the Extended model). Neither Denise's brother nor her sister have children, so Denise's parents and siblings have also adopted Leesa into their family. An incident that occurred when Leesa was living with them showed Denise how far she had travelled: "When we went to parent-teacher night, one of the teachers said, 'Oh, yes, she's doing quite well, for someone from a broken home.' I couldn't believe it. I just said, 'Oh, but she has a happy home in both her homes.' I was quite shocked. . . . Before I was a stepmother, I probably would have said those foolish expressions like 'He comes from a broken family,' which really grates now when I hear it because it implies that the child has to be a wreck."

With Hindsight . . .

Stepmothers often believe that, if they were to start over again, they would take a very different approach—not that many are eager to repeat the experience. Looking back at their initial expectations, they ruefully acknowledge how little they understood about stepfamilies. Consequently, they made assumptions, the expectations described in Chapter 2, which created unhappiness for them and often led to strife with others. Compounding the negative effects of this ignorance was their certainty that they had a good grasp of the situation. Because of this, they did not seek out advice from more experienced stepmothers who might have warned them about the more obvious traps. One of the most useful insights for stepmothers is to realize that the stepfamily is not what they originally assumed it to be. This realization is both humbling and freeing. On the one hand, they have to admit they were mistaken, but, on the other, they are relieved of some of their impossible expectations.

No One's Perfect

In retrospect, stepmothers often feel they hobbled themselves with their initial expectations, and realize that they need to adjust these assumptions. Often they tried to be perfect stepmothers, which they equated with being a perfect mother. When they were unable to achieve this, they felt guilty. Their partner's and stepchildren's lukewarm responses to their efforts were also discouraging. By focusing on everyone else's needs, they neglected their own. As you have seen throughout the book, they often ended up resentful and burnt out.

Cheryl, now age forty-two, was a successful money manager when she met Victor, age forty-one, two years ago. His two young children were then ages seven and four and lived with him half-time. Cheryl routinely worked twelve- to fourteen-hour days and thought she could easily add on her new role as stepmother: "Looking at it with two years of hindsight . . . I realized that the expectations of myself have been quite unrealistic in the sense of expecting to be able to make it work. . . . I hadn't realized that it would be so hard, that's all. You know, after forty years of being effective and successful and able to live up to my expectations, this was just so completely different and so much more difficult on all the different levels. Just blew me away." After one year as a step-mother, Cheryl felt like she was drowning. She dreaded going home and her moods swings were mercurial. When she started locking herself in the bathroom to weep, she recognized some-thing needed to change. Her solution was to move to a four-day work week: "The decision to cut back wasn't so that I'd have more time to spend with them. It was so that I'd have more time to myself. It wasn't so that I could devote myself to becoming the perfect stepmother. It was to preserve my sanity."

Easing up often includes forgiving themselves. As stepmothers recognize that stepfamilies are complex, they accept their own complex reactions as understandable. They realize it is okay to feel trapped when every corner of their living space has been over-turned. Withdrawing is a natural response to living with sullen stepchildren, hostile ex-wives, or a partner who is only reluctantly supportive. Accepting ambivalent feelings allows stepmothers to stop chastising themselves. Some stepmothers make the distinc-tion between having negative feelings and acting on them: "I used to feel guilty because on Sunday evenings I'd feel relief when they went home. . . . I'm more accepting of those feelings. It doesn't make me a bad person. My measure of whether I'm being a good stepmother is how I treat those kids. I had to stop putting pressure on myself. I had to give myself a break."

Stepmothers also often realize that they demanded too much too soon from their partners and stepchildren. Often they had jumped right into parenting their stepchildren and quickly taken on a disciplinary role. Their stepchildren often resented this, and the stepmothers and stepchildren became locked in a contest of wills, with their partners caught in the middle. In previous chapters, I have described Betsy, the stepmother with a mission, and her frustration with her partner, Mick, for his lack of consistency with his children. Betsy now acknowledges how her zeal contributed to the tensions: "I expected too much out of all three of them. I really did. And unfair expectations of the kids. I walked in there and expected them, all of a sudden, to go from doing absolutely nothing all their lives to doing things when I asked them to." It was her stepdaughter, Olivia, who helped Betsy become aware of this. Although she and Olivia had the most furious battles in the household, they also talked most openly: "One thing Olivia brought up to me was that I was changing their family to what I thought family should be like. And I said, 'Yeah, you're right. That's exactly what I did. I'm sorry.'"

Betsy realized that her "inexperience and immaturity" had blinded her and she has become less demanding. Dinner is one instance. Betsy grew up in a family where dinner was served at exactly 5:30 every evening. She made a huge effort to carry on this tradition in her new stepfamily. While it was relatively easy for Betsy's mother, as a homemaker, to maintain this routine, Betsy, who works full-time, had to prepare the meal the night before and then rush home from work to have it on the table by 5:30. Often she would come in to find the kitchen strewn with dishes from breakfast and the children's after-school snacks. Mick would sometimes not arrive home until 6:30. By the time they sat down to eat, Betsy would be fuming. A couple of times, she stormed out of the house and left Mick and his children to eat on their own. Olivia's comments were a nudge to rethink the dinner policy. First she relaxed the 5:30 schedule, which was onerous for everyone. Dinner time is now flexible, structured around everyone's schedules. Her one fixed rule is that the children must clean up their dishes before she starts dinner preparation. Betsy knows that she has an advantage here because the children prefer her cooking—Mick's repertoire is limited and they have joked about endless dinners of Hamburger Helper before Betsy arrived: "Ninety-nine percent of the time now, I don't even start dinner until everybody's home. . . . If I get home and the kitchen's a mess because the dishes weren't done the night before, I just don't cook dinner. And if there's some sort of struggle going on over the dishes, it's easy. I've got a credit card, I can go out for dinner."

It's Not Me

Another hard lesson is not taking others' reactions personally. Over time, some stepmothers come to understand that their stepchildren's rebuffs and intransigence have little to do with them, that the children's coldness is a kind of loyalty to their mother or stems from a wish to have their parents re-united. When I asked stepmothers what they would tell new stepmothers, many advised: "Don't take things personally. If the children are cruel toward you, it may be for their own reasons, not because you're not a lovable person." Stepmothers often feel relieved by this insight. They can re-interpret their stepchildren's hostility as having less to do with them and more with what they represent. Slights from their stepchildren will sting less. Stepmothers may pull back from trying to win over stepchildren. At the same time, this recognition carries with it an acknowledgement of how little power and influence they have in the stepfamily. They may have to accept a more marginal role than they anticipated and would like. It can be hurtful to concede that they are peripheral to their stepchildren's lives, more a symbol than an actual presence.

A stepmother also may initially interpret her partner's preoccupation with his children as a rejection of her. I have described many scenes of stepmothers stewing alone in the living room while their partner reads his children bedtime stories, or feeling neglected while he drives the children to hockey practices, or resenting the way the children soak up all their father's time and energy. Over time, some stepmothers re-assess their partner's behaviour. After they have children and experience their own fierce attachment to their children, they can more easily understand and accept that their partner will defend his children from any criticisms the step-mother might offer, no matter how well-intentioned or perceptive her comments may be. Others realize that they felt in competition with their stepchildren for their partner's attention, because they believed that, if their partner gave too much to his children, there would be nothing left for them, a variation on the zero-sum thinking I described earlier. As one stepmother realized: "It gradually dawned on me that Matthew had the capacity to love a lot of people. I suppose our relationship strengthened really, and somehow there was more room for Anna [my stepdaughter] too. Also he needed my support. He would say, 'I found it difficult enough to cope with Anna and my feelings about that without you somehow creating problems that don't actually have to be there.'" Other stepmothers re-interpret their partner's inattention as stemming from his inability to balance everyone's needs rather than from any intention to neglect them. They might still criticize his abilities as a father but are less likely to take it personally.

Finally, many stepmothers become convinced of the wisdom of initiating more discussion in the stepfamily. As we have seen again and again, important issues are often never discussed in stepfamilies. Stepmothers feel they have to tiptoe around their stepchildren; their partner avoids contentious subjects with his children because of guilt; and the relationship between their partner and his ex-wife is often so strained that communication is minimal. All this can create a fog of misunderstandings and misinterpretations, as well as missed opportunities for finding out what everyone thinks, feels, wants, or needs.

On top of this, stepmothers and their partners seldom clarify whether they share similar aspirations for the stepfamily. Stepmothers' ideals for the stepfamily may diverge radically from their partner's, but because they have not discussed this ahead of time, stepmothers may feel hurt and disillusioned when they discover the gulf between their hopes for the stepfamily and their partner's. As we saw with Gail, a stepmother may dream of creating a warm, close-knit stepfamily, but discover her partner wants an arm's-length relationship with his children and is content with infrequent visits. Sometimes stepmothers are so blinded by optimism and love that they jump in without assessing whether this is what they want. They want to believe that everyone will live happily ever after, so they brush aside baleful looks from their stepchildren or their partner's habit of ignoring them when the children are around. In retrospect, stepmothers often wish that they had established rules at the outset with their partner, and believe that a clear structure would have helped the stepfamily develop more smoothly. Experienced stepmothers often advise prospective stepmothers to scrutinize the situation carefully: "Think while dating this person—observe the children, observe the relationship between the father and the children, and identify things that you like and don't like. And be clear. Don't expect to have everything your way, but be clear about the things that will really bother you if you don't get your way."

Many stepmothers acknowledge, however, that they would not have gained this knowledge without having gone through their experiences. Some believe that, even if they had been offered wise advice, they might not have listened, so confident were they that they knew what they were getting into. Stepmothers' realizations are often bittersweet. It can be painful to let go of their initial dreams and hopes. At the same time, it can be a relief to stop throwing themselves against a wall. While they might have aspired to a closer relationship with their stepchildren, they feel a certain measure of pride that they survived at all. Most learn that stepfamilies are a lot more complicated than they had anticipated, and, in the process, they often discover new dimensions in themselves as well. At best, their experience gives them an expanded awareness—of themselves, of their stepfamily, and of the possibilities for relationships.

Chapter 14

Changing Patterns

The longer a woman is a stepmother, the more contented she becomes usually. The first few years are often taxing and stressful. If a stepmother survives them, the stepfamily becomes less turbulent and she feels calmer and better able to weather the everyday demands of stepfamily life.[1] Of course, one reason that more experienced stepmothers may appear happier is that the more miserable stepmothers have already opted out. The divorce rate for remarriages is higher than for first marriages and subsequent marriages also tend to end more quickly than first marriages. Some stepmothers may leave early on if they are caught in an impossible situation. I suspect this may happen with those stepmothers who have pulled back from the stepfamily (the Retreat stepmothers). These women feel so lonely and isolated in the stepfamily that, unless they can alter the pattern, it is unlikely they will hang on for long. The long-term stepmothers might, therefore, be the "successful" ones, those who have managed to make their situation work. As we will see, this does not mean they magically live happily ever after, but, rather, that they learn to adapt or develop ways to modify patterns in the stepfamily.

Stepmothers believe that their stepchildren and partners also become more settled over time. Their stepchildren tend to become more receptive and less oppositional, while their partners become more engaged. Researchers who have studied stepchildren over a number of years support the stepmothers' observations. While children in stepfamilies tend to have more behavioural and emotional problems than children in non-divorced families, children in well-established stepfamilies start to behave more and more like children in non-divorced families.[2] As I have noted, a stepfamily can take many years to coalesce into a family and the initial stages can be rocky. The last chapter presented ways in which stepmothers change themselves. Stepmothers also often initiate external changes that help the stepfamily settle in and the stepmother feel more at home.

Realigning the Couple Relationship

Stepmothers often feel their relationship with their partner strengthens over time.[3] While a minority believe the couple relationship has been irreparably damaged and become increasingly estranged from their partner, most feel there is a rapprochement. Sometimes this comes about through stepmothers "educating" their partner. Initially, many stepmothers feel their partner is unaware of, or insensitive to, the enormous accommodations the stepmother has made. Their partner does not grasp that his spouse needs support and expects her to adapt immediately. Although some men respond to the stepmother's distress, usually it takes a long time for them to understand the stepmother's perspective, a process that often entails lengthy discussions and arguments.

One stepmother felt that her partner began to appreciate her perspective when her younger brother stayed with them for two weeks one summer. After tripping over the boy's running shoes, her partner complained about his sloppiness and inconsiderateness. The stepmother slyly asked how he would feel if her brother moved in full-time. Her partner looked aghast. The stepmother pointed out that living with his children was similar for her. She was fifteen years older than her brother and had doted on him when he was a baby. She could forgive his faults. Her stepchildren, by contrast, felt like strangers and not very hospitable strangers at that. Although the couple continued to wrangle, the stepmother felt that her partner had become more empathetic. Most step-mothers do not have the advantage of such a pointed lesson, and, more often than not, their partner's education is protracted.

Stepmothers, for their part, learn to be more diplomatic. At first, when they feel ignored and trampled on, they often react by list-ing all their partner's and his children's faults. Predictably, their partners will respond by cataloging the stepmother's shortcom-ings. Back and forth they go. Eventually, some stepmothers tire of this pattern. They start to bite their tongue or choose less accusa-tory language to frame their frustrations. This stepping back often happens in tandem with another change—the stepmother letting go of unrealistic expectations. As the stepmother becomes slower to pounce, her partner often becomes more amenable to listening.

In the previous chapter, we saw how Joyce discovered unex-pected reserves of skill with children. Despite this, she had seri-ously thought about leaving her marriage after the first year, because she felt that Karl dismissed her frustrations: "He has said things like, 'Well, you don't know anything about kids.' You know, because I haven't had kids." His barbs hurt, in part because they mirrored her own doubts about her maternal abilities. Joyce retal-iated by criticizing Karl's inability to be consistent with his chil-dren, which she believed resulted in the children's poor manners and messy habits. Karl counterattacked. After many months of this battling, Joyce decided to tone down her comments about the children, particularly since her anger was really directed at Karl. As she stepped back, Karl also altered his combative stance: "I think he sees that I'm not trying to control things . . . that I have some genuine concerns and that I'm not putting him or the kids down. I'm just making suggestions and I think he's much more recep-tive." Now that Joyce and Karl have more temperate discussions, he has come to appreciate her perspective: "It took a long time for Karl to realize that this was an adjustment for me to step into this life. . . . It was hard, it was really difficult for me in some ways."

Stepmothers also step back as they encourage their partners to become more active fathers. I have described a number of step-mothers who had assumed most of the parenting responsibilities, while their partners either remained disengaged or retreated. Stepmothers often push their partners to become more involved, less to escape the work themselves, but more because they believe their partners and their children will benefit from increased close-ness. As one stepmother explained: "My father is very special to me. And I want Courtney to have that with her dad. So I encour-age that." Some stepmothers also sense their stepchildren want a closer connection with their fathers. Even if a stepmother has a good relationship with her stepchildren, this may not compensate for their distant relationship with their father. These stepmothers attempt to teach their partners the kinds of emotional skills that are usually associated with mothers. They become "father coaches," urging their partners to spend more time with the chil-dren, recommending activities that the fathers can do with their children, and explaining to the men how their children feel or why they are reacting in a particular way. Sometimes their partners are unaware of their blind spots and need to be coaxed into paying attention to their children. As Courtney's stepmother explained: "He didn't listen to her. He wasn't really there with her so I had to do a lot of pushing and pulling sort of psychically in the back-ground—letting him be with her, encouraging him to be with her and to be her father." Some stepmothers observe their partners evolve into more engaged fathers over time as they learn to be more attuned to their children.

From the stepmothers' perspective, their ideal relationship with their partners is a partnership, where they listen to each other and work in tandem to resolve problems, where each person's contri-bution is acknowledged and valued. Stepmothers want to be con-sulted and included in decisions that affect them. A minority of stepmothers have this kind of relationship from the outset and it provides a powerful buffer against problems with children or ex-wives. Paulette told me: "Richard and I can talk about our kids without getting totally defensive or upset. If he had a problem with one of my kids, if I had a problem with his, the bristles don't stand up. . . . We're able to understand what the other partner is saying and agree. I think that's a big area that makes it work."

For most stepmothers, however, achieving an equal couple relationship takes time. Some never achieve this. Establishing an equitable partnership may be a bigger challenge for couples in stepfamilies since a family predates the couple relationship, the father-child bond can overshadow the couple bond, and stepmothers are often outsiders at the beginning. It is hard for stepmothers to assume an equal footing when the culture of the family is still foreign to them. Some men are so accustomed to acting independently that they may need a great deal of prompting in order to consider the stepmother. Usually both parties have to learn how to talk and listen to each other. As the stepmother steps back and mutes her criticism and her partner becomes more understanding of her perspective, a space is cleared in the relationship where the couple can begin making mutual decisions. Mutual does not mean that both have equivalent say over every issue, but that each person feels he or she has been consulted.

The way a couple negotiates the decision for a stepchild to move in full-time is often revealing. Stepfamilies are more fluid than non-divorced families, and there is often a lot of movement between households. In my study, a sizable group of the stepmothers started off with stepchildren staying only on weekends or for short periods and then found themselves full-time stepmothers, sometimes with two or three days' notice. Particularly as children become adolescents, they can decide independently whether they want to move in with their fathers.[4] Of all the women I interviewed, only one stepmother refused her teenaged stepdaughter's request to move in full-time. This stepmother had a good relationship with her stepdaughter, but her partner was poor at balancing everyone's needs and he would often ignore the stepmother when his daughter was around. Since the stepmother and her partner lived in a one-bedroom apartment and already had a baby of their own, the stepmother could cite lack of space as an excuse. Her relationship with her stepdaughter was apparently not damaged and the two remained on good terms.

Most stepmothers, however, support their stepchildren moving in because they believe that they cannot deny their partner and his children the opportunity to live together. They may recognize that their lives will be radically altered, but feel the relationship between their partners and their children should take precedence. Even Patricia, whose stepdaughter, Amy, treated her abominably, was prepared to allow Amy to move back if Amy were willing to agree to some basic house rules. Understandably, stepmothers want to be part of the decision. If their partners present the move as a fait accompli, stepmothers are generally hurt and often infuriated. This is their house and they believe they deserve a say in how it is run.

Over time, most stepmothers come to believe that the couple relationship should have a central place in the stepfamily. One stepmother was determined not to make the same mistake in her second marriage as she had in her first: "One of the reasons that my first marriage broke up is that I put all my energy into my children and there was nothing left over for the primary relationship in my life. I've learned that it's important for the primary relationship to have importance, because your kids leave. I know this now, but I didn't realize it until I was in this relationship."

While stepmothers who fit within the Couple and Extended models understand from the outset that the couple relationship needs to be protected, other stepmothers come to this insight as their relationship becomes swamped by the stepfamily. Often they start to create time for the couple. One stepmother set aside two hours a week for her and her partner: "Sunday morning was our time. Nobody interfered. It was the only chance I could get to read. So every Sunday morning the kids could not disturb us until 10. That meant time to ourselves—it didn't mean we were even talking." Other couples go on vacation without the children or arrange for a babysitter so they have an occasional evening out on their own. Some stepmothers realize that they need a kind of metaphorical time out, a break from their constant bickering. Recognizing how wrangling over stepchildren or the ex has infected and spoiled the couple relationship, they may attempt to separate these issues from their relationship with their partner.

A Corner of One's Own

One way stepmothers compensate for feeling overrun is to claim a space for themselves. Having a place of their own can be critical in feeling they have a stake in this house. Some stepmothers convince their partners to move to a new house that will accommodate the expanded family and will not contain the history of the previous family. Others renovate. Repainting helps some stepmothers put their stamp on their house. Sometimes stepmothers set aside a room or even a desk for themselves. Even if a stepmother rarely uses her corner, she has a sense of security from knowing that it exists.

Moving or redecorating requires money, and this is often in short supply in stepfamilies. Some stepmothers have to bear with the ex-wife's decorating scheme for a long time. One stepmother moved into her partner's house where he had lived with his first wife. He was supporting two households on his salary, and redecorating was out of the question. This woman's stepchildren also resisted any changes to their house. When she hung up one of her paintings in the dining room, they complained. The first wife loved pastels and floral designs, while the stepmother craved white walls and uncluttered rooms. The pink-flowered wallpaper and chintz-covered furniture in the living room were a constant irritation. The stepmother's solution was to paint a small back room and put in her own furniture: "Once I got my own space it was a 100 percent improvement. . . . My advice to anybody is when you move into another house that is not your own, you have to create your own space. Not the whole house, because that takes a really long time to do, but take one room, one corner, one something, and turn it into your own place. And this is where I used to go if I got frustrated."

My Time

Some stepmothers respond to the increased demands on their energy by making time for themselves. One reason they encourage their partners to be more active is so they will have a break. One stepmother became weary after months of entertaining her stepchildren every weekend. As a lawyer, she worked extremely long days during the week and wanted calm on the weekends. With two young stepchildren and often their friends as well, however, the house was always bursting with activity. She helped her partner enroll the children in gym classes every Saturday morning and suggested that he take them out for breakfast before class. She stayed home in her dressing gown and enjoyed the solitude. Everyone was happy with this solution: "I said, 'I would really like to have some quiet time at home.' And a few times they insisted I come too when they were going for walks, but that's happening less and less because they also want to have more and more time with their dad."

Other stepmothers, like Cheryl, cut back their hours at work. Rearranging visitation schedules can also relieve pressure. Some stepmothers inherit a situation where their stepchildren switch between their parents' houses on alternate days. With these daily moves, the stepmother never has time off. As soon as the children leave, she begins preparing for them to return. Not only do stepmothers feel exhausted by this, but they believe their stepchildren suffer from the constant shifts. Not all visitation schedules are so choppy, but stepmothers often find short stays disruptive—for instance, if the children are with them for one night during the week and one night on the weekend. They may propose reworking the schedule so that the children's visits are bunched together. Although the children are with them the same amount of time, the stepmother has bigger chunks of free time and the children have greater stability in their lives.

It can be difficult for stepmothers to balance their needs against their stepchildren's and partner's desires. Stepmothers who have troubled relationships with their stepchildren may wish their stepchildren were never around and may absent themselves when their stepchildren are present. As in Kay's situation, this can create additional tensions with their partner, who may believe the stepmother is shirking her responsibilities. On the other side, stepmothers who like their stepchildren may feel selfish when they want some solitude. One woman has been an enthusiastic stepmother to her two teenaged stepchildren and is delighted to have them in her life. Her partner and stepchildren are outgoing and very physically affectionate with one another, while she is a self-described introvert who "did not come from a hugging family." Overwhelmed at first by the exuberance of her new family, she would retreat to her bedroom to unwind after work: "When I moved in with George and the kids, I found that there were always people around. I would go up to the bedroom, whether it was to write, to just read, or just get away. . . . And I regret that because I would shut the door and kind of isolate myself without thinking about it. So I've got that pattern set. Like when I come home from work, I'll often still do that. Change my clothes and close the door, spend an hour by myself." In retrospect, she knows that she created a certain distance, but she also knows she could have not managed without checking out. Many stepmothers try to find the right mix between being available and preserving their sanity.

Who Should Pay for What?

Throughout the book, I have described how friction about money can be a stressor in stepfamilies. The stepmother may resent that her salary is helping to support her partner's ex-wife, particularly if this woman appears determined to make the step-mother's life miserable. She may also be furious if her partner lavishes money on his children without consulting her. There is often just less money in stepfamilies. One salary may be divided across two, or even three, households. The stepmother may see her standard of living contract after joining the stepfamily. Instead of being used for travelling or going out to eat, her income may disappear into orthodontic bills and new school clothes for the children.

For some stepmothers, however, money is not a issue. While a large income may give the stepfamily some room to manoeuvre so that they do not have to scrimp and can afford a spacious house, having this financial cushion seems to be less important than how the couple negotiates money. There is usually little friction when a couple has similar values about money. Most stepmothers believe that their partners should contribute financially to their children's well-being. If they share their partners' views about what is reasonable support, they are often happy to pitch in as well. As I discussed earlier, some stepmothers gain a lot of satisfaction from feeling they are giving their stepchildren advantages the children would not have otherwise. It also makes a difference if the step-mother's contribution is recognized. Most stepmothers do not expect their stepchildren to notice that their stepmother is paying for their piano lessons, but they do want some acknowledgement from their partner. Having input into decisions about money that directly concern them is another important piece in a harmonious financial situation. If all these circumstances are present, pooling finances can work well.

When the stepmother and her partner are at odds over money, however, it is often wiser to keep the stepmother's income separate from her partner's. It is much easier to watch your partner buy expensive presents for his children if your money is not involved. Daphne and her partner, Mitchell, have always had separate accounts: "My money goes for expenses in the household, like the taxes and the bills, and for my own expenses. He pays for the children's activities." Recently, she became annoyed when her eighteen-year-old stepdaughter, Brianna, decided that she did not like her brand-new glasses and convinced her father to buy her an even more expensive second pair: "The first pair was $350 plus the lenses and the second pair was $400 plus. And that's the kind of wastefulness that I resent." When Daphne suggested that Brianna could have lived with the original pair for at least six months, Mitchell disagreed with her: "He said that the way she looks at this stage in her life is very important." Daphne was able to let go of her annoyance by reminding herself it was not her business how Mitchell spent money on his children: "It's one of those things that is very irritating but it isn't my place to be irritated. I mean it's not my money, she's not my daughter." Like Daphne, some stepmothers learn to stay out of transactions that do not directly affect them. The stepmother may think that her stepchildren receive too much allowance but recognize that this is her partner's decision.

Separate finances also make sense if there is a contentious relationship with a partner's ex-wife. Some mothers will attempt to have the stepmother's income considered in deciding child support payments, and the stepmother will discover that, although she has no legal rights in relation to her stepchildren, she may have financial obligations.[5] One stepmother had been married to her partner for eight years when his ex-wife decided to take him back to court after her second marriage split up and she ran into financial difficulties. The whole experience was very traumatic: "It was like going through the divorce all over again. . . . My income brought into consideration, but I was not allowed to go to the examinations for discovery and I was not allowed to go to the court situation with the lawyers and the two parties. All of a sudden I thought, 'Wait a minute, I thought I had some rights in this situation.' But in fact I didn't have any rights at all." The stepmother consulted with several lawyers, who told her that, indeed, she could be required to support her partner's wife. In the end, the ex-wife lost her case, but the stepmother felt bitter toward her not only for this action, but also because the mother manipulated her youngest son: "The youngest was in a very torn situation, because he was very loyal and protective toward his mother, and she had him operate like a spy in the situation. He didn't really realize what he was doing, I'm sure, but he was told to find out what we had. . . . It was a terrible position for him to be in, and it made us realize that we couldn't discuss our financial situation when he was in the room."

Some stepmothers keep their finances separate from the start, when they are advised by lawyers not to contribute anything to their stepchildren's upkeep so they will not be required to submit their income if the mother takes her ex-husband to court. One stepmother's partner is still not divorced from his first wife because they are caught up in protracted and unpleasant financial negotiations. The stepmother and her partner have been renting a house and would like to buy one together, but are worried about the implications: "We try to be careful about not presenting my income as a resource to her. . . . I've talked to a lawyer, because I want to be protected. And the lawyer said, 'If you buy anything, put it in your name and make sure that all the documentation shows that you're the sole owner as much as possible.'" Although some stepmothers resent having to be so rigid about finances, it is worse to discover that they have no control over how their money is spent.

A New Broom

Stepmothers often consider their new households chaotic or poorly organized. They respond by establishing new rules and household routines. Having a structure can be a relief for everyone—not just the stepmother—because everyone now knows when dinner will be, where they can find clean laundry, and whose turn it is to do the dishes. At the same time, stepmothers often realize that they need to separate out those areas in which they have legitimate power from those they should stay out of. A useful guide is whether an issue directly affects them. Many stepmothers evolve to a position where they have authority over how the house is run but not over their stepchildren's behaviour. It is reasonable to expect their stepchildren to pick up dirty dishes off the living room floor, because this infringes on the common living space, but unreasonable to insist the children practise the violin. Stepmothers who initially are enthusiastic about taking charge of the household often back off later. They learn to avoid laying down the law with their stepchildren, because of the resistance this provokes. They move into a more advisory role, where they talk through issues with their partners. Unless the children are very young, experienced stepmothers generally shy away from disciplining their stepchildren.[6]

Gradual changes are usually more easily tolerated than a radical overhaul. As Betsy discovered, although the stepmother may be less frustrated if the house is clean and tidy, she may have to contend with a rebellion from her stepchildren and partner. What works best is if the stepmother and her partner first agree on a plan and then present it jointly to the children. Even if the children know the stepmother is the instigator, they will see their father's support for the initiative. Without their partner's backing, a stepmother's grand plans often founder.

Sometimes You Don't Hit It Off

An important shift for many stepmothers is accepting that their stepfamilies will never be what they had hoped they would be. While this may be disappointing, as it represents the loss of their initial dreams, persisting only brings continued unhappiness. It may be painful to acknowledge their stepchildren will never regard them as a mother, but facing repeated rejections is even more difficult. Stepmothers often shift models as a result of their disillusionment. Some start off believing that they will recreate a Nuclear family. The negative response of others—or even of themselves—forces them to re-evaluate this ideal and move toward the Couple or the Biological model, or if their situation is particularly grim, into Retreat. Letting go of their initial vision for the stepfamily can also be liberating. They may have approached the stepfamily with suspicion and then discover that the stepfamily has advantages. Denise, whom I described in the last chapter, believed at first that she had to protect her relationship with her partner from possible outside attacks (Couple model). She was then disarmed by the friendly welcome she received from her stepdaughter and her stepchildren's mother. Now she believes her life has been enhanced by her relationships with both of them (Extended model).

One of the biggest challenges for a stepmother is admitting that her relationship with a stepchild is a failure. Stepmothers usually arrive at this stage only after considerable self-recrimination and many attempts to mend the rift. It may be hard for stepmothers to relinquish the idea that they must like their stepchildren because this belief is closely tied to our cherished notions about how women interact with children. Like the stepmother quoted in Chapter 3, who asserted that a stepmother can learn to love her stepchildren if she just keeps trying, stepmothers often feel that they should keep trying to repair their troubled relationships with stepchildren. It can be a relief to realize they cannot turn this relationship around, that no matter what they try, they will not pry open that locked door.

Even more radically, some stepmothers acknowledge (although usually only to themselves) that they do not like their stepchild. For Rosanna, her stepdaughter Ginger's attitude of "me, me, me" was grating. It was easy to respond warmly to Ginger's older sister, Vickie, but Ginger's unquenchable need for attention from her father and her constant requests for this and that special treat set Rosanna on edge. While Vickie was laid back like her father, Ginger was like her mother, who kept trying to draw her ex-husband back into her orbit. At first Rosanna tried to conquer her dislike: "I tried too hard at first. I really tried too hard. And it was too depressing because when you try hard and things don't work, you get really depressed." She now views her relationships with her stepchildren as she does friendships. Some people hit it off and others do not: "I don't think it's good to try to force a relationship. I mean, if you don't like the kid and you don't click, then you don't click."

Extending the Olive Branch

Of all the stepmother's relationships in the stepfamily, the one with her partner's wife tends to evolve the least over time. Since stepfamilies in which the stepmother and the mother have a civil relationship tend to be more harmonious, it is generally in the stepmother's interest to cultivate a good working relationship with the mother, where they can at least converse politely and perhaps consult about the children. Stepmothers who develop a cooperative relationship with their stepchildren's mother often see it as beneficial, not just for the children, but for them too. Not all stepmothers are so willing to extend themselves and connect with the mother, however. Even if they are, they sometimes face formidable barriers.

Reasonable stepmother-ex-wife relationships seem to flourish best under three conditions: one, the stepmother not wanting to mother her stepchildren; two, the mother viewing the stepmother as an ally rather than as a threat; and three, the biological parents having relatively open communication. Stepmothers have direct control only over the first. Stepmothers who do not attempt to mother their stepchildren are less likely to view their stepchildren's mother as an adversary and also be more tolerant of the mother's foibles. Some stepmothers discover that when they adopt a cordial approach with the mother, she often reciprocates. They may even be able to thaw the mother's wariness.

Sometimes the mother is the one to extend the olive branch. The stepmother will initially distrust this gesture, but her predecessor's friendliness will disarm her. Other times, even if a stepmother wants an amicable relationship with her stepchildren's mother, she may be stymied if the ex-wife views her as the enemy. Similarly, if the stepmother's partner and his ex-wife have a poisonous relationship, the anger and tension between the two ex-spouses may preclude the stepmother establishing any relationship with the mother. Occasionally a stepmother can circumvent the ex-spouses' hostility and link directly with the mother. The success of this tactic depends on the goodwill of both the stepmother and mother, which may be in short supply if there is a great deal of conflict in the stepfamily.

Some stepmothers also acknowledge that what they know about their stepchildren's mother is filtered through others, usually their partners, but also their in-laws or their stepchildren. Since her partner's views of the ex-wife are sometimes negative in the extreme, the stepmother can remind herself that her impression of the ex may be distorted. As one stepmother realized: "I've tried to keep an open mind, that as a person, I don't know her. I only know what [my partner] has told me and of course that's going to be slanted, so I try to keep that in perspective." Although her relationship with the ex-wife may still be strained, the stepmother will interpret her partner's comments with a grain of salt, recognizing that the ex-wife might not be quite the harridan she has been painted to be.[7]

Creating a Family Album

Stepfamilies often form their identities through creating family traditions. Some spring up spontaneously. In Chapter 5, I described Sheila's first encounter with her stepsons on a camping trip. This weekend was so successful that the boys asked to return to the same site the next summer. The camping weekend has become an annual pilgrimage with fixed rituals, including stopping at the same restaurant for dinner on the way home. Not only have these trips enabled Sheila to become closer to her stepsons, they have created a common store of memories. When her stepson Daniel refers to the time the bear tore through their campsite, Sheila is part of the story too.

Having shared experiences helps everyone feel more connected to one another and to the stepfamily. Developing family stories and traditions takes time, of course, but the stepmother can help coax them along. Some stepmothers initiate new customs in their stepfamilies. Timing is crucial. Some events may not succeed, because they are introduced too quickly. As described with the stepfamily who needed two Christmas trees for the first few years, children may need the comfort of holding on to familiar patterns for a while. Innovations can also fail because they do not suit the culture of the new family. In Chapter 2, we saw the frustration of a stepmother who wanted her stepfamily to re-enact the same lengthy family dinners she had enjoyed as a child. Until she abandoned this practice, she was often left alone in the kitchen after dinner, surrounded by a mountain of dirty dishes. The trick is both to honour past traditions and to develop new ones that fit with the stepfamily.[8]

We have heard about Hillary as she vented her irritations about being a childless stepmother with two rambunctious children, an intrusive ex-wife, and a partner who was a slave to his children. Two years in, Hillary feels the situation has eased. She attributes this to the many changes they have undertaken. Altering their living space was a big one. Stefan lived in an apartment after his divorce, so when he and Hillary married, he moved into Hillary's house, which was tiny. There was no bedroom for Peter and Emily, so they slept in Hillary's study. Although Hillary was happy to have the children in her life, she began to feel "smothered and invaded" in her own house. Something had to give: "I insisted that if we were going to continue to live together, the four of us, that we had to get a bigger house. There was just no way I was going to continue to live that way." In order to afford the kind of house they wanted, they had to move outside the city. For Hillary, the inconvenience of commuting has been offset by the luxury of space. The children each have their own bedroom and share a bathroom, and their mess is confined to that space. Hillary has her own study—which is off-limits to the children—where she can retreat when she needs time alone: "It's a much happier atmosphere, partly because I'm not hassled all the time."

Hillary also insisted that they rework some of the household routines. Stefan catered to all his children's desires and they had become like little pashas, expecting every whim to be satisfied. She convinced Stefan that it was reasonable for an eleven-year-old and an eight-year-old to have chores. The children must now keep their rooms tidy and set the table for dinner. Hillary thinks they could have even more responsibility, but decided to concede that battle. When Hillary and Stefan first started living together, it was tacitly assumed that she would conform to Stefan's household rules, many of which had originated with his ex-wife. Now she and Stefan work more as partners: "I always felt I was screaming to get my rules heard and now we have developed our own rules as a couple."

Hillary has settled comfortably into the Couple model. It took a long time to get to this point. She struggled with having less power than she wanted, and Stefan often reacted defensively to Hillary's suggestions. Hillary believes they both have shifted. She now acknowledges "clear boundaries" to what she can and cannot do: "I can't say to the kids, 'I think you shouldn't be driven everywhere. I think you should learn how to take public transit.' Their parents drive the kids everywhere. I don't agree with that but I don't have any influence here." Stefan also now requires more from his children: "There is more of a blend of our styles now. Stefan will be firmer with them than he used to be, so I don't have to feel like I'm this bad stepmother who's always saying we have to have expectations and structure here. So we've modified one another's styles." Hillary and Stefan jointly present any new rule to the children. Hillary believes that their unified decision-making gives her greater authority in the children's eyes.

Hillary also now reacts less personally to her stepchildren's ambivalence. She knows that their mother exerts tremendous pressure on them to be loyal to her and that this creates a conflict for both children, particularly for Emily, the eldest. At first, if the children ignored Hillary or were distant when they returned from their mother's, Hillary would get upset. Now that she recognizes the dynamic, she is less affected. She is also more apt to raise issues directly with Peter and Emily: "One thing that bothered me for a long time was when the kids would phone the house and I would answer. They would say, 'Is Dad there?' It was really hurtful to me that they didn't want to chat with me. I would tell Stefan this, but it took me a long time to realize I could tell them myself."

As Hillary has felt more accepted and listened to, particularly by Stefan, she has relaxed. She is more likely to let an issue slide instead of fretting about it. Stefan's ex-wife, Marika, is still a thorn in Hillary's side, but the fact of Marika's existence torments her less as she feels more secure. Each summer she and Stefan and the children have taken a holiday together and these have drawn everyone closer together. The children had never been on a train, so last summer Hillary arranged a week-long trip to Quebec City by train, which was a big success. While Emily is somewhat standoffish and becoming more so as she enters adolescence, Hillary's relationship with Peter, now ten, offsets this: "He's a very sweet caring individual. . . . We are probably the most compatible. He will say things to me like 'I haven't given you my famous bonecrushing hug today. Can I do that?' Or 'Dad and I made up a new hug. Can I show it to you?'"

Hillary believes that while her family's solutions might not work for everyone, changing the household routines, moving to a more spacious house, and talking more openly have all contributed to a more harmonious situation. Compromise has also been key. Many experienced stepmothers have learned to weigh their own needs against accepting that this family may never become what they had hoped. The "Serenity Prayer" could have been written by an experienced stepmother: "Grant me the serenity to accept the things I cannot change; courage to change the things I can; and wisdom to know the difference."

Chapter 15

The Triumph of Experience over Hope:
Seasoned Stepmothers

Given the many trials of living in a stepfamily, it may seem aston-
ishing that some women willingly submit themselves a second
time. As divorce has become more prevalent, so have "serial marriages," where people marry and divorce multiple times.[1] The
chances are now greater that a woman might become a stepmother twice or even three times. Given the higher divorce and
remarriage rate, it is also more likely that women becoming stepmothers now or in the future will have been stepchildren themselves. Many of the women I interviewed, particularly long-time
stepmothers, had grown up when divorce and remarriage were
less common. Nevertheless, 16 of the 104 had been part of a stepfamily before, either as a stepchild or a stepmother, or they had
half-siblings, that is, at least one of their parents had children from
another relationship. Although this is a small group, I devote a
chapter to them because they have a lot of wisdom, gained
through experience, which can be helpful to novice stepmothers.

Growing up in a stepfamily or having previous experience as a
stepmother has a significant influence on the way stepmothers
conceptualize their role. The effect is less marked if their parents
remarried when they were adults and had already left home, or if
they had half-siblings as a child, that is, either one or both of their
parents had children from a previous relationship. The latter group
may be least affected by the dynamics of a stepfamily because they
lived with both their parents, so that their family seemed like a
non-divorced family. Their half-siblings, whose parents had split

up and were thus stepchildren, would probably have had quite a different perspective on the same family. In one interview, a stepmother initially told me that she did not know any stepfamilies. Later, she mentioned her half-sister, who is fifteen years older than she is. Only then did it strike her that she herself was a member of a stepfamily. When this woman was a child, her half-sister lived in another city and visited sporadically. Because of the age difference and lack of contact, her sister seemed more like a cousin than a close relative.

Nevertheless, all the women who had been part of a stepfamily—whether directly or more indirectly—shared two attributes: none wanted to be mothers in their new stepfamily, nor did they aspire to re-create a nuclear family with their stepfamily. Jessica's parents had divorced when she was two and her mother remarried when Jessica was five. Jessica, now forty-six, has an excellent relationship with her stepfather and in many ways feels a greater debt to him than to either of her biological parents. Her father opted out early on, and her mother was often self-interested and self-involved. When she became a stepmother, she modelled herself on her stepfather: "I thought I would be just a super stepmother . . . what my stepfather had been to me. Which was a really loving, caring, kind, supportive other adult in my life. My stepfather never tried to take my father's place. And, you know, we're best friends."

Unlike many inexperienced stepmothers, Jessica does not equate stepmothering with mothering or rescuing. Her partner, René, has pressured her to be more like a mother with his two teenaged children. Her response is that her two stepchildren "already have a perfectly good mother who lives down the street." Inspired by her stepfather, Jessica has aimed for a light touch. She jokes around with both stepchildren and enjoys spoiling them in small ways. After her stepson left for university, Jessica sent him cards and treats for Halloween and Valentine's Day. She was pleased when her stepdaughter recently sought her advice about a conflict with a friend at school, but she would never push the girl to confide in her.

Lucy, whose father died when she was eight and whose mother remarried two years later, has taken an even more radical position. She refuses even to call herself a stepmother, because of the association with motherhood. Although Lucy became very attached to her stepfather—"He was a very dear person to me, extremely, extremely"—at the beginning she was upset at him and at her mother and refused to acknowledge his presence. She is grateful that her stepfather kept his distance and let her approach him: "Actually, at the very beginning when he married my mum, I called him uncle. It took me some time to say, 'He is my stepfather,' to accept him." Lucy's quarrel with the term "stepmother" is that it presumes a kind of connection that may not exist and that it also pits the stepmother and biological mother against one another: "My problem with the concept of stepmother is that it forces on the child and on the stepmother a role that's really not right for either one. It's not fair . . . it forces the stepparent and the child to compare."

Lucy, age forty-two, had two children in her early twenties who are now away at university. Her partner, Anthony, while the same age as Lucy, did not have his two children until his late thirties. When Lucy met him six years ago, her children were preparing to leave home. His children, Sam and Elizabeth, were six and four. Lucy was ambivalent about whether she wanted to start over with birthday parties, sleep-overs, science projects, and the routines imposed by living with young children. Although Lucy now works full-time as a teacher, her children had been her priority. When they were little, she took a five-year leave from work in order to stay home with them. Anthony's ex-wife, Ruth, by contrast, lives for her work as a medical researcher in a university. She puts in long days in her lab and is often away at conferences. Out of necessity, Anthony became the primary parent in his first marriage. His fantasy was that Lucy would gradually replace Ruth and they would parent together. While Lucy admires his dedication—"One of the reasons I fell in love with him is because he's a wonderful father"—she wanted to avoid what she considers a trap. It was more difficult to resist her stepdaughter, Elizabeth: "At age five she said, 'I would like to call you Mummy.' And I explained, 'You have a mummy, and she is your mummy and you spend every second week with her.' At first she felt rejected. Then we talked a lot and she said, 'I think you're right.'" Lucy knew that Elizabeth's mother would hit the roof if she discovered that Elizabeth was calling someone else "Mummy," that it would stir up unpleasantness not only between Lucy and the biological mother, but probably between Elizabeth and her mother too. Based on Lucy's own very positive experience with her step-father, her ideal relationship with her stepchildren is that of an aunt. She feels connected and concerned about them and includes them as part of her family, along with Anthony and her two biological children: "I'm the mother to two of them and then a close aunt, a close relative to the other two. The love and the relationship is there. . . . I feel this keeps it clean and clear. So nobody gets confused and nobody has to get jealous."

Binocular Vision

Stepmothers who were also stepchildren tend to recount positive, rather than negative, memories of their stepparents. This is true for women who became stepchildren whether as children or as adults. The quality they prize most in a stepparent is kindness. Although they may not have shown their appreciation when they were children, in retrospect they value stepparents who were sup-portive, caring, and considerate. If their stepparents treated them respectfully and with tact, they are also grateful. Their ideal is a stepparent who knows when to be available and when to stand back. They are scornful of stepparents who are mean, unfair, cold, and distant. Memories of stepparents criticizing, belittling, or ridi-culing them still rankle many years later.

Only one stepmother had the kind of evil stepmother found in fairy tales. Ellen's mother died when Ellen was three. As an only child, she and her father, Jack, became very close while they were on their own. It was wrenching for Ellen when he remarried four years later, particularly since her new stepmother "acted and pretended—in her words and actions—as though I didn't exist." It became worse after Ellen's half-brother and half-sister were born. Like Cinderella's stepmother, Ellen's stepmother openly favoured her own children over Ellen. When her stepmother was pregnant, Ellen overheard her tell a friend that "I've always pretended that Jack was never married before, that this is his first marriage and his first baby. I don't count Ellen as part of the family." At Christmas Ellen's half-sister and half-brother would receive a mountain of toys, while Ellen would have only new socks and underwear to unwrap. The stepmother's constant message to Ellen was that she was a miserable, rotten person who would never amount to anything. This discounting and discrimination was enormously hurtful to Ellen, and she feels her stepmother's mistreatment left significant emotional scars: "I really had no self-respect. I always used to think that I must be the person who takes all the suffering for other people so that other people can have happy lives, and God'll dump it all on me, so I'll be the one that has to bear all the problems. And I'm sure it's all because of her."

Just as in the fairy tales, Ellen's father does not really figure in her stepchild story. His presence is shadowy. Why did he not object when his wife bought such meagre presents for his daughter? Why did he not protect Ellen from her stepmother's cruelty? As an adult, Ellen has become close again to her father. While she is still bitter toward her stepmother, she does not carry any grudges toward him for his lack of support. Ellen did have one ally in the situation, her half-sister, who spoke up about her mother's unjust and biased behaviour, but Ellen felt bereft most of her childhood and adolescence.

When Ellen met Bill through a mutual friend at work, she was immediately attracted to him. On hearing that he had two children, however, she refused to consider dating him. Ellen, at that time thirty-seven, had decided early on that she was too flawed to have her own children. Her memories of her stepfamily were so painful that she could not contemplate living in one again. Bill persisted. Eventually she agreed to meet his two children, Leslie, then age seven, and Adrienna, age four. While there were no miracles, the first encounter went more smoothly than she had anticipated. They spent the day at the beach and when Ellen said goodbye to the children, Adrienna gave her a hug. Ellen was frank with Bill about her misgivings. He reassured her that she did not have to take on anything she did not choose to do.

Stepfamily life has been both easier and more difficult than Ellen imagined. Ellen, an actuary, likes life to be orderly and precise. This has caused friction with her stepchildren who are used to their father's more easygoing style: "I'm very strict. I insist on the rules being followed. . . . I want it done, I want it done now, and I want it done this way." At the same time, her memories of her stepmother are a powerful incentive to bite her tongue, rather than say derogatory or hurtful things to her stepchildren: "My first rule of being a stepmother is to think what my own stepmother would have done and then do exactly the opposite, because she was a real bitch."

Initially Leslie and Adrienna lived with their mother and came to their father's twice a month. Bill and his ex-wife were locked in a nasty custody battle that ended with Bill being granted joint custody. Then four years later, his ex-wife decided to move away to go to university and told Bill she wanted him to take the children full-time. Ellen landed in a place she had dreaded—being a full-time stepmother. Her elder stepdaughter, Leslie, found the transition particularly difficult. She idealized her mother and frequently compared Ellen's cooking negatively to her mother's. Ellen's instinctive reaction was to point out that at least she was there while Leslie's mother had run off, but memories of her own stepmother helped her control her frustration. Now, seven years into stepmotherhood,

Ellen still feels ambivalent. She counts down the days each year before the children leave for their summer vacation with their mother. At the same time, she knows the children appreciate the order she has brought into their lives: "Leslie has said, 'Boy, when I get married and have kids, I'm just going to bring them over here with you to babysit when they're one and I'll pick them up when they're fourteen. I'll know that you'll look after them.' That's one of the best compliments she could give me. They know they can trust me to do what they need done, and to look after them properly and keep them safe and warm."

Stepmothers who were also stepchildren admire stepparents who do not discriminate between stepchildren and biological children. While these women did not want their stepparents to supplant their parents, they were thankful if their stepparents did not accentuate the differences between them and their step-siblings and treated both groups equitably. Zoe, who lived with her mother, stepfather, and his two children from the time she was seven, still appreciates how scrupulous her stepfather was. One time when Zoe was a teenager, he promised her that she could borrow his car. Zoe's stepbrother wanted it the same evening. When his father refused, the boy tried to win his father over by arguing that his claim should take precedence because he was the son and Zoe was only the stepdaughter: "My step-father looked at him and said, 'Well, she's just as much my child as you are.' And he made me feel like I was a part of him. And I'm still really close to him." Although many stepmothers try to be even-handed with both their stepchildren and biological children, stepmothers with the dual lens of stepmother and stepchildren are hyper-aware of this issue. With their own stepchildren, they are sensitive to situations where the children might feel slighted. Zoe, now age twenty-six, has a two-year-old daughter and a six-year-old stepdaughter. She is meticulous about making sure that, if she buys a treat for her daughter, she buys the same thing for her stepdaughter.

At the same time, when these stepmothers praise their step-parents, none comment that their stepparent *loved* them as a parent. They focus on the stepparent's actions, not their feelings. They might appreciate that their stepparents had identical house rules for both them and their stepsiblings, but they do not expect that their stepparents would have felt the same way toward them as they did toward their own children. Perhaps this is because their own feelings for stepparents and biological parents also differed. This distinction should provide some relief and consolation to those stepmothers who are ashamed if they do not have identical feelings for both stepchildren and biological children. Instead, these women can concentrate on acting fairly and not worry that they are wicked for feeling more connected to their biological children.

Stepmothers who were stepchildren also draw on their emotional experiences as stepchildren to help them understand and respond to their stepchildren. This empathy is particularly useful if their stepchildren reject them or are unfriendly. Recognizing how mixed up they felt as stepchildren allows them to take their own stepchildren's reactions in stride. Yawen, age twenty-six, became a stepmother four years ago. A year after that, her father remarried, to a woman only twelve years older than she was. Yawen was surprised at how agitated she felt about the presence of this new woman in her father's life. When she became pregnant last year, she could empathize with her teenaged stepdaughter's reaction: "I knew [the news about the pregnancy] was going to be tough on her. . . . Your relationship with your parents is probably the only exclusive one you can count on. Sharing my parents is something I never expected to have to do, ever. And the idea of some baby going around calling my father 'Daddy,' I would have difficulty with that."

As I listened to these women reflect on their experience as stepchildren, Lucy's ideal of a kindly aunt sounded better and better as a model for stepmothers. An aunt is someone to whom you are related, with whom you have a shared connection, but without the intensity of a mother-child bond. Aunts are often well-disposed toward their nieces and nephews, interested in their welfare, and concerned and caring, but they usually do not demand or even want the mutual devotion usually present between parents and children.

Second Time Around

The stepmothers I interviewed who were on their second go around as stepmothers tended to focus on more painful experiences than stepmothers who were stepchildren. This may be because their memories were coloured by the failure of their previous relationship. All the women who were stepmothers for the second time believed they had had fairly good relationships with their stepchildren from their first stepfamily. Most stayed in contact with the children after the relationship broke up. A few even had stepchildren living with them after they split up with their partners. If they did not continue to see their stepchildren, it was usually because of the bitter relationship with their ex-partner. Sometimes these women manoeuvred around this impediment by seeing the children via the first wife, with whom they had more in common now that they were both ex-wives. In general, while their relationships with their partners were severed, their relationships with their stepchildren were not. A small subset—notably the Extended family stepmothers—still considered their first set of stepchildren part of their family, along with their second set and their biological children. Over time, however, their relationship with their former stepchildren became more distant.

These women had a sharp, often painful, sense of unfulfilled hopes and expectations from their first experience as stepmothers. Their regrets and sadness were, not unexpectedly, strongest in relation to their partners because these relationships had not survived. There were also unrealized aspirations in relation to their first set of stepchildren. Most had embarked with what they now viewed as overly optimistic expectations. Like many stepmothers, they had believed they would become mothers to their stepchildren. They had often assumed the primary domestic responsibility and felt very attached to their stepchildren. Ending their relationship with their partner exposed the folly of this ambition.

Second time around, their ideals were less lofty. None aspired to be a mother and they discouraged others in their new stepfamily from foisting that role on them. Rather than jumping in immediately, they were cautious and held back. They wanted to see what would transpire with their stepchildren and gave the relationship space to develop slowly. Their approach complemented the advice of stepmothers who were also stepchildren about not forcing the relationship.

In their second stepfamily, they regarded the stepparent-stepchild relationship as having necessary limits. While, in their first stepfamily, they might have imagined they could have acted as a mother to their stepchildren, they had learned that no matter how much they might they care for and about their stepchildren, they could not claim a parent's privilege. They also learned that it was unwise to pour all their energy into this boundaried relationship. Although this position was often initially self-protective (in order to ward off further hurt), they also felt it was a safeguard for their stepchildren. On the one hand, the stepmother was not promising something she could not deliver, and on the other, she was not demanding something that might create a conflict for the children. While these second-time-around stepmothers were available and involved with their stepchildren, they were careful to avoid casting themselves as indispensable. In this, they were most like Couple stepmothers. They believed the parents should parent. They would support their partners, but they would not take primary responsibility for the children. One woman was a stepmother to three children in her twenties. When, ten years later, she started again with two new stepchildren, she decided, "I've learned limits. I've learned that it's okay to say no. . . . I think I've learned that you're never going to be a hero anyway, so it's not going to make that much difference. It probably builds a respect for you too, by setting down what you will and will not do."

Glenda, age thirty, has been married to Axel, who is thirteen years older than she is, for a year and a half. Axel's two children, John and Matthew, who are now nine and twelve, live primarily with their mother and stay with their father on weekends, holidays, and for one month in the summer. When Glenda and Axel initially talked of marriage, she warned him she would set limits: "Axel at first took it as a bad thing when I said, 'I am not going to love kids that are not my own like that again.' And he was like, 'So, you're not going to love my kids.' I said, 'No, I'm not going to love them the way I will love my own. I will love your kids and care for your kids and be there in terms of safety and everything, but they're not mine and somebody else controls them in terms of my access to them.'"

Glenda came to this stance through experience. When she was twenty-three, she had moved in with Dave, who had two very young children, ages two and three. Dave and his ex-wife had just arranged for joint custody and he was supposed to have his children living with him half-time. Dave owned a number of car dealerships and routinely worked twelve- to fourteen-hour days. At that time Glenda had just graduated from university and was at loose ends about her career direction. She quickly fell into caring for the children: "I became like the second mum. They were almost babies when I first met them. . . . I made their first Halloween costumes, took them out to Halloween, and did their birthdays. I did everything. Took them to their first nursery school."

Dave and Glenda's relationship fell apart and three years later, he walked out. Dave refused Glenda any contact with his children, in part, Glenda feels, because her bond with the children "was so close that their father actually resented the relationship." Because Glenda was *only* a stepmother, she had no legal rights in relation to the children. Glenda was devastated by the breakup, primarily because of the loss of the children. The two children, then five and six, were a "mess." Glenda had been their parent for more than half their lives. Now she had abruptly disappeared. Dave's ex-wife Arlene was sympathetic to Glenda, because Dave had walked out on her too. She and Glenda had worked in tandem as parents and she appreciated Glenda's commitment to her children. She proposed that Glenda visit the children at her house. Dave was livid when he discovered the arrangement and threatened to withhold Arlene's child support. Realizing that continuing to see the children might cause them more turmoil than separating from them, because they would have to lie to their father, Glenda decided to taper the relationship off gradually. When she was offered a job in an advertising agency in another city, a natural break presented itself. Except for sending the children cards and presents for their birthdays and Christmas, she now rarely has contact with them. Glenda still regrets the outcome. Her experience also left her shaken, because she discovered that no matter how much she had done for her stepchildren, how much she cared about them, she did not have any power: "And that was a big lesson for me, and I think that every stepmother is going to go through that because you don't make the decisions, you have no rights over these kids if you happen to break up with your husband."

Not only would she not place herself in the same untenable position again, she feels it is unfair to children to try to be their mother, because who knows what might happen. Going into her second stepfamily, Glenda's attitude was: "Absolutely no expectations whatsoever at all." If a relationship developed, she would welcome it, but she would not force it. Before she and Axel got married, she talked to his two boys and told them she hoped that they would be friends. She was prepared that this might not happen. As it turned out, Glenda likes the two boys and feels this is reciprocated. Nevertheless, part of her remains detached: "I am pleasantly surprised and really pleased that we have a nice relationship. I expect that when they're at my house, they will be polite to me and courteous to me, but I don't expect them to phone on my birthday, I don't expect them to buy me Christmas gifts, I don't expect those things. They do it now because they choose to."

Before committing themselves to another stepfamily, these second-time-around stepmothers studied the new situation thoroughly and dispassionately. They needed to reassure themselves that this was what they really wanted. They were much more likely to thrash out expectations with their partners than they had been in their first stepfamilies. Rather than flinging herself into marriage with Axel, Glenda took her time. She wanted to get to know not only Axel and his children, but Axel's ex-wife as well, since her relationship with Dave's ex-wife had been critical to Glenda's survival. When Axel's ex-wife, Laurel, refused to meet with Glenda, she knew Laurel would be more of an irritant than an ally, and this has turned out to be the case. Glenda knew she wanted children of her own and clarified this with Axel before they married. Although initially she planned to get pregnant right away, she decided to hold off for a little while: "So I said [to Axel], 'Well, I'll wait two or three years just to make sure that everything's lined up and there's a good relationship established between the boys and me, rather than them being introduced to a new baby right away.' "

Stepmothers also situate themselves in a different place second time around. In their first stepfamilies, they tended to plunge into parenting, but they are now content to support their partners. If they find themselves slipping into a parental role, they will extricate themselves quickly. The first summer Glenda's second set of stepchildren came for their month-long stay, she ended up taking caring of them most of the time. It alarmed her that, despite her resolve, she had once again put herself in the middle: "I felt I was doing everything—I was making their dinners, I was packing their lunches, I was getting them to camp. I was doing all the motherly roles and resenting it because I'm not the mother. . . . It wasn't forced upon me, I just did it. And I think that a lot of stepmothers do just do it. Once you do it, it's hard to reverse it."

After the boys left, Glenda told Axel that next time he had to be more involved. She had enjoyed having the boys there, but it was his responsibility to care for them. The boys' next scheduled visit was for ten days over the Christmas break. A month before they arrived, Glenda reminded Axel to start planning. The visit was a great success. Axel took the boys skiing and snowboarding on his own. Glenda made herself less available by going out more with friends. A couple of evenings when Glenda came in, Axel and his sons were having an uproarious time in the kitchen making dinner. Glenda noticed that the boys were delighted to have their father to themselves. Some stepmothers' partners push the stepmothers to leap into the breach, but these women hold fast. They are willing to be involved with their stepchildren, but within limits. Glenda feels her more-removed position has paid off. She has kept her autonomy and, at the same time, has a companionable relationship with the boys, which seems to suit them fine.

Second-time-around stepmothers also place more value on the couple relationship. Reflecting back on their previous relationship, seasoned stepmothers often wonder if the breakup of their first relationship occurred in part because it became lost in the stepfamily. Determined that this will not occur again, they are vigilant about protecting and nurturing their time with their partners. Like Extended and Couple stepmothers, they also adopt a long view, recognizing that the children will eventually leave and they will be on their own. As one second-time-around stepmother reflected, "Life doesn't end when these kids go away to university. And our life doesn't totally revolve around them either. We're not afraid to have a life apart from them."

What can we learn from these women? Although there are obvious differences between the stepmothers who were stepchildren and the second-time-around stepmothers, their perspectives are complementary. If we blend the two, an ideal stepmother emerges. She is a kindly presence who does not assume or presume to be a parent. She is available, but does not situate herself at the centre, nor does she demand that her stepchildren respond to her with loyalty. She will help and support but she will not take full responsibility for this stepfamily. On the one hand, this stance gives the children room to approach their stepmother at their own pace, and on the other, it eases the stepmother's expectations of herself. It also encourages the fathers to become more active and involved. Recognizing that they do not have the power of a biological parent, stepmothers do not attempt to be one. Although it may be initially frustrating to accept these limitations, it can also be liberating because stepmothers no longer bear responsibility for that which they cannot alter.

Chapter 16

Looking for Help

Feeling at their wits' end and reluctant to confide in family or friends, many stepmothers seek outside guidance. Often it feels less threatening to pour out their troubles to a stranger who is perhaps less likely to be judgmental. Some stepmothers opt for therapy for themselves, or they go with their partners, or with the whole family. Other members of their stepfamily, such as their stepchildren, may have a separate therapist. Stepmothers also use other services—for instance, talking to their family doctors or joining a parenting group for stepfamilies. Many create their own informal support networks through talking with other stepmothers or seek out self-help literature.

Outside help can be enormously valuable when stepmothers have an opportunity to unburden themselves, find an empathetic ear, or develop new insights into themselves and their situations. Unfortunately, some stepmothers receive misguided advice that reinforces, or even exacerbates, existing problems. In this chapter, I describe the kinds of assistance that are most beneficial and contrast these with help that creates further complications. I suggest how stepmothers can find therapists, resources, and supports that may help them.

An Outsider's Perspective: Finding Professional Help

Many of the women I interviewed had either been in therapy themselves or someone else in the stepfamily had sought counselling related to stepfamily issues.[1] Some stepfamilies availed themselves of multiple forms of therapy. The stepmother would have her own therapist, her stepchild would see another, and the whole family would meet for family therapy. Even before she became a stepmother, Veronique had consulted a psychologist. When she met John, Veronique was thirty-two, childless and lived a nomadic, carefree life. An arts administrator, she typically chose short-term contracts that allowed her to live in cities in Canada, the United States, and Europe. She loved the travel associated with her work, and when not on the road, would be out most evenings at concerts or art events. John had two young daughters, Robin and Maggie, ages seven and five, who lived half-time with him. He was a devoted father and Veronique knew that, if she were to commit to a long-term relationship with him, she would have to become more rooted. Veronique found a therapist who was well known as a stepfamily and divorce expert. After about eight meetings with the therapist where she weighed her options, Veronique decided that she would rather be with John than have the freedom to pick up and move. Her therapist recommended that she and John have a few sessions together. Veronique found these joint meetings very helpful because she and John each stated what they expected and wanted from the other and then they jointly worked out ground rules about who would do what in the stepfamily.

Although her initial meetings with the therapist enabled Veronique to bypass many of the pitfalls for beginning stepmothers, she still felt overwhelmed by the magnitude of the changes in her life. About a year after she and John started living together, she heard about a parenting group for stepfamilies and cajoled John into going. Her motivation this time was support. She did not know any other stepmothers and hoped to discover whether others had had similar problems adjusting. Around the same time, John and his ex-wife were contacted by the school principal about their youngest child, Maggie, who was not fitting in easily at school. After being assessed, Maggie started weekly meetings with the school counsellor and was able to express some of her distress at all the changes that had occurred in her life.

Within a two-year period, this stepfamily had been involved in four kinds of therapy, each addressing a different issue. None of these therapeutic encounters had been motivated by a crisis. Stepmothers like Veronique rely on therapy or counselling as a source of guidance. Feeling ill-equipped for their new situation, they want to gain an understanding of stepfamilies. Rather than wait until they feel desperate, they hope therapy will help forestall potential problems. After her sessions with the psychologist, Veronique felt more confident about becoming a stepmother: "I found it really helpful, just to be dealing with someone not in a crisis situation. I hadn't even moved in, although we were certainly dealing with the kids together at that point. Just to work through some of the stuff around our relationship and to have that sorted out."

Stepmothers like Veronique want concrete information. It is therefore essential that the professional they consult be knowledgeable about stepfamilies and their dynamics. Veronique's therapist offered her the kind of advice many stepmothers take years to learn: "She was really clear from the start saying, 'If you don't find your space in this whole configuration right from the start, you're going to be lost.'" Veronique had moved into the house where John lived with his daughters. In order to establish her own territory, she set aside one room in the house as her study. It was a tiny space, tucked up in the attic, but it was hers. Veronique has been designing and making jewellery as a hobby for years and this room became her studio. Both Robin and Maggie were keen to make their own jewellery, which pleased Veronique because it gave her an opportunity to connect more with her stepdaughters: "Sometimes the kids are just a hoot. I really like making jewellery and doing artwork and having somebody to do it with. Because they're just learning, I can be the expert or the teacher. And that's fun too." If Veronique is in her room, the girls will often gravitate there and hang over her shoulder watching her work. Her study has become more cluttered and crowded than almost any other corner of the house. Nevertheless, the therapist's counsel that Veronique mark out her own space allowed her to feel that she had some autonomy in this family.

Many more stepmothers seek therapy because they are unable to manage. They feel isolated, disregarded, powerless. They need an ally, someone who will listen without judging. Therapy becomes a place where they can express the resentments and anger that they hesitate to show publicly. These women are searching for what is missing in their situations—support and acceptance. They need a therapist who will acknowledge and validate their experiences. As these stepmothers voice their pent-up feelings, they often begin to reclaim a sense of control and relax unrealistic expectations of themselves and others.

Professional counselling can help couples when their relation-ships have become frayed or when conflict dominates all their interactions. By the time a couple arrives in the therapist's office, they may no longer be listening to each other. For couple therapy to be successful, each person must feel that his or her perspective is recognized and understood. Since many issues are not discussed in stepfamilies, assumptions and expectations pile up. The therapist can play a critical role in helping each person articulate what he or she wants from the other. While couples in non-divorced families also struggle with these problems, they are often intensified in the stepfamily because of its complicated structure. Therapy can pro-vide a neutral arena for the couple where they can listen to one another without overreacting or attacking.

Couple therapy can also help the couple address disagreements over children. As I have discussed, typically the stepmother believes her partner is too lax with his children, while he argues that she is too demanding and rigid. Here the therapist may take a more practical approach—for instance, moving the stepmother out of the centre and encouraging the father to become more active. The ideal outcome is if each person begins to comprehend and have empathy for the other's position. One stepmother believes couple counselling saved her marriage: "It allowed us both to just air everything that we couldn't really air. I couldn't say anything to Robert without him getting defensive and then I would get defensive and it would erupt into something it really wasn't about. . . . I totally recommend counselling."

Family therapy can help address tensions and conflicts that have built up in the stepfamily—for instance, when a stepmother and her stepchildren are at an impasse or when a stepmother and her partner cannot deal with an aggressive child. Who goes for therapy depends on the dynamics of the stepfamily. Sometimes the stepmother, her partner, his ex-wife, her new partner, and the children all show up, ready to pitch in and develop a workable plan. Other times, only part of the stepfamily will attend. If a stepmother's partner and his ex-wife cannot be in the same room without blowing up, it is wiser that they be seen separately. Since members of stepfamilies themselves are often uninformed about stepfamily dynamics, it can be helpful if the therapist describes common problems in stepfamilies, such as loyalty conflicts or boundary definition. It is often encouraging for people to discover that their splintered situation is not an anomaly and that it will take a while for them to gel as a family.

Family therapy can also provide a safe venue for stepfamily members to start to talk to one another. In my clinical practice with divorced families and stepfamilies, for instance, I have found that children are often reluctant to tell their parents that they feel pulled in two directions by their parents' competing demands for loyalty. They love their parents and do not want to hurt their parents' feelings or risk losing them. A therapist can assist the children in telling their parents they need them to cooperate more and fight less.

Although only a handful of the stepmothers I talked to joined a parenting group for stepfamilies, all found it worthwhile. Hearing about other people's trials made them feel less isolated, as did encountering stepparents who face similar frustrations. Group members could both support and commiserate with one another. Veronique credits her group with restoring her sense of humour, which she was in danger of losing:"This couple was talking about his ex-wife and he says,'Well, it's never going to be over.When the kids are bigger, when they get married, or graduation, there'll always be other things to deal with. . . . It's never over while they're still alive.' And it's true. It was particularly funny because the thought had crossed my mind too."

When Therapy Doesn't Work

Treatment for stepfamilies seems to founder on two shoals: an unwillingness on the part of some to commit to make changes and the inadequacies of the professionals. Some stepmothers feel they have an uphill battle persuading others that therapy is warranted. Usually it is their partners who drag their feet, although sometimes their stepchildren or the children's mother are unenthusiastic participants. A stepmother may see a need for couple therapy, but her partner will dismiss her concerns. Another feels her stepchild would benefit from counselling, but her partner will refuse to consider it.While, in general, women are more likely to go for therapy than men, in stepfamilies, the father's cooperation is crucial because of his key position in the family. Without his participation, it is often impossible for the stepmother to initiate any changes.

Some stepmothers think that their partners deny the severity of their children's problems out of guilt. Others believe their partners will not commit to therapy because they want to avoid the necessary painful self-examination. One stepmother thought her eight-year-old stepson, Darren, should have counselling after his mother left town without any warning. Although Darren did not express any hurt feelings, the stepmother could see how bereft he felt. She tried to convince her partner to talk to his son, but in keeping with his usual pattern of avoiding emotion, he shied away from the topic. The stepmother could not broach the subject herself because Darren was sensitive to any hints that she was criticizing his mother. When the stepmother suggested that counselling might be a good idea, her partner "wasn't for this at all," she says. "I didn't push it very hard. He doesn't really see the value of a lot of counselling. And I can't imagine getting him involved, which would have to happen, if we were to go with Darren. We'd all have to go as a family and it would be like pulling teeth to get him to go along."

Another stepmother insisted her partner go to counselling with her and his children. He had pretty much relinquished his parental responsibilities, and, while she had reasonable relationships with her three adolescent stepchildren, she sensed their resentment at having to answer to her. She spent a lot of time locating a knowledgeable therapist, so she was dismayed when her partner threw away the opportunity. They had to cancel a number of appointments because he scheduled business meetings at the same time, twice he forgot to show up, and when he did come, the therapist would have to remind him of what they had discussed previously. The sessions gradually dwindled away. It can be hugely frustrating for a stepmother when she believes that therapy would benefit the stepfamily, yet nothing happens because of her partner's reluctance to be involved. Some stepmothers end up going for individual counselling, now dealing with the additional issue of their annoyance at their partners.

Therapists who are uninformed about stepfamily dynamics may also hinder the stepfamily's ability to deal with problems. Assuming that stepfamilies are just like non-divorced families headed by two biological parents, these therapists may offer inappropriate, and even harmful, guidance. They may recommend that a stepmother act more like a mother or they may treat a new stepfamily as though it were a fully formed family. Telling a stepmother that she should work harder at acting like her stepchildren's mother may only add to the stepmother's guilt and stir up more conflict with stepchildren. Even self-proclaimed experts about stepfamilies are no guarantee of success. Some stepmothers found that these therapists offered advice too quickly, rather than attempting to understand the stepfamily's perspective.

Throughout the book you have encountered Martha, the step-mother who considered herself the quintessential wicked step-mother. Knowing that she—and the rest of the family—was in dire need of help, Martha went looking. It took her and Wilf five tries to find a therapist who was able to help them. When Martha met Wilf, he had been a widower for two years and was struggling to care for his three children, then aged twelve, ten, and eight. As a social worker who worked in an AIDS hospice, Martha quickly picked up that all three children—and particularly Alicia, the youngest child—were still in shock after their mother's death. Wilf also worried that his children never mentioned their mother. Within six months of their marriage, Martha and Wilf started hunting for a therapist. They first attempted family therapy with two therapists who were known as experts about stepfamilies. It was a disaster. Martha wanted some suggestions about how to approach her stepchildren. Instead she and Wilf felt they were being blamed: "[Therapy] certainly was not helpful to us at the time. What happened is both Wilf and I felt that we were being told that we were bad people for getting married, that what we had done to these children was just terrible. It was a little late—what were we to do at that point? . . . We ended up feeling very guilty."

Thinking that the children might be more forthcoming if they were not present, Wilf and Martha enrolled them in a group for children whose parents had died. Another failure. While Alicia benefited from meeting other children in similar circumstances, the boys, Sean and Mark, now fourteen and twelve, refused to speak: "The leader told us that she had never had a more difficult group and that [Sean and Mark] controlled the group with their anger." Finally the therapist recommended that the boys withdraw. Martha felt even more discouraged and she "ended up blaming myself—that the reason they didn't open up was because I made them go."

Martha and Wilf next elected for couple counselling, reasoning that if they could develop a plan together, then perhaps this would ease life at home. Martha's relationships with her stepchildren had become even chillier and she dreaded going home at the end of the day. Whenever she thought about her situation, her stomach would knot up. She wanted some direction about how to address their problems, but, instead, she and Wilf felt they were educating the psychologist. After a few sessions, they stopped going. On the positive side, at least they did not feel more monstrous at the end of this round.

Their fourth experience was the worst. This time they selected a child psychiatrist who saw them first as a couple. The therapist advised Martha to be more motherly to her stepchildren, particularly to her stepdaughter, Alicia. Martha had initially imagined she and Alicia would have the same kind of closeness that she had with her own daughter, Sarah. She invited Alicia along on their weekend shopping excursions and suggested that Alicia join Sarah's Girl Guide troop where Martha was a leader. Alicia brushed away all Martha's proposals. After repeated rejections, Martha gave up. Despite the therapist's recommendation, Martha was unwilling to be turned down again.

Martha also wanted some ideas about how to handle Alicia's habit of going through Martha's clothes and makeup and taking small items. Even when Martha's belongings were found in her bedroom, Alicia denied she had taken them and continued to pilfer. Martha was shocked by the therapist's response: "She went on about how she'd let her own daughters come in and use her clothes and her makeup and they shared all this and she thought this was all wonderful—'We're one big happy family.' . . . She didn't understand," Martha said with a laugh, "so we didn't stay there very long." Luckily, Martha and Wilf were now far enough along in their stepfamily to recognize that this woman had no understanding of stepfamilies, and they did not return for a second session. Nevertheless, it was hard for Martha not to interpret the therapist's comments as a criticism.

By this time, three years into the stepfamily, Martha and Wilf were in despair. Tensions at home had not eased, and Martha felt more alienated from her stepchildren. For the fifth time, they threw themselves into the fray, this time back to family therapy. All their previous therapists had pushed Martha to mother her stepchildren: "One of the mistakes, in hindsight, all the therapists made was to encourage me in the mother role. Because their mother had died, it was more natural for people to assume that I should play the mother role." Their fifth therapist first met with Martha and Wilf as a couple and then with Wilf and his children. She recommended that they not meet as a whole family because she believed that, because of all the antagonisms, "we were not ready for this. In fact, she never brought us all in together." After consulting with everyone in the family, the therapist advised Martha to do less: "The most significant thing that she did was to take me out of the parental role and said, 'Wilf is the parent of these children and needs to parent these children.'" The therapist suggested Martha be "a friend, just a friend." She should be kind and available and see herself as someone who would provide treats for her stepchildren but not direct them. Martha stepped out of the disciplinarian role and Wilf took more responsibility in the household and for his children. It was clear from the children's response that they had craved this closer relationship with their father.

Martha's relationships with her stepchildren are still not great. Her interaction with her middle stepson, Mark, is now friendly, but communication is still strained with Sean and Alicia. The main improvement is that she no longer feels compelled to impose the kind of motherly attention on her stepchildren that neither she nor they enjoyed. Martha wonders if her stepfamily might have progressed more smoothly if she had received better guidance from the beginning. While she was too ready to jump in and take over, the therapists' advice only reinforced this tendency.

Professional help can thus be a mixed blessing. The most effective therapists first listen to, and empathize with, the stepfamily's struggles. They also help clarify communication within the stepfamily by creating a safe space in which people can begin to articulate feelings and expectations that have often been suppressed. Finally, by situating the stepfamily's problems within the larger context of stepfamily dynamics, they help normalize the family's struggles. Ignorant therapists, on the other hand, can exacerbate an already troubled situation. Stepmothers discover that they must choose their guidance carefully.

In looking for a therapist, stepmothers should try to be clear what they want from therapy. Advice and guidance? Information? Support and empathy? For a stepmother like Veronique who did not know any other stepmothers, a support group for stepparents was invaluable. Another stepmother may need an empathetic therapist who can help her sort out her ambivalent feelings toward her stepchildren. In conjunction with their therapist, stepmothers should determine who should attend. As in Martha's situation, for instance, if there is a lot of antagonism, it may be better for just the couple to be seen at first. Stepmothers should also look for therapists who are knowledgeable about stepfamilies and stepfamily dynamics. It is reasonable to ask what kind of experience and training the therapist has in this area. If there is a local stepfamily association or a family services centre, they may have a list of names of clinicians who specialize in this area. Since the needs of stepfamilies vary tremendously, stepmothers should be wary of therapists who believe there is a single way for stepfamilies to interact and that there are simple answers to stepfamilies' complex problems.

Self-Help Literature: I Need All the Help I Can Get

Very early in Sheila's relationship with Michael, before she ever met her stepsons or she and Michael started living together, she started looking for guidance: "I wanted to read about stepmothers because I only knew about the bad things. I didn't know anybody who had been in that situation and I didn't know if there was anything I needed to know about it." At the same time, she questioned why she was doing this: "I know my mother never read a book about how to be a mother when she had me, so why should I spend time and money learning how to be a stepmother?" Her anxiety won out over her ambivalence, however, and she purchased a couple of books that she studied carefully. Not only did the books help Sheila understand and define her role in the stepfamily, but she passed them along to her partner as well: "They were useful to Michael because I put bookmarks in and underlined things to show him my role, his role, his kids' role. I felt it was as much an education for him as it was for me."

Self-help books and articles are a huge source of support and insight for many stepmothers. Some use these materials as an adjunct to counselling, while, for others, they are their primary source of information. While most gravitate to books about stepfamilies, self-help books on parenting in general, on gender differences, and communication skills can also be illuminating. For one stepmother, who is a lawyer, her books on mediation offered her the best practical advice for dealing with her stepchildren.

It is not always easy to find the right materials, however. Books may be difficult to locate. Sometimes the information is simplistic or does not reflect the stepmother's experience. One stepmother was offended by a book entitled, *Second Wife, Second Best*. She has a good relationship with the first wife and considers herself an equal with her partner, and she felt the title perpetuated a negative stereotype of stepmothers.

Self-help materials can help stepmothers sort out their role and place in the stepfamily. Once they feel more settled, they will set the information aside. Sheila, for instance, read books assiduously at the beginning. When I asked which ones she would recommend, however, she could not recall the titles, because it had been almost three years since she had consulted them. Other stepmothers do not seek out information about stepfamilies until they find themselves out of their depth. They are initially confident, and only later realize how unprepared they are. One stepmother who became an avid reader of books and articles about stepfamilies doubts whether she would have been receptive at first: "There's nobody out there who can tell you what to expect. Family and friends chuckled at the idea of me dealing with kids. My mum and dad were a little bit concerned. But at the beginning I was so happy and in love—nothing was a problem!"

Self-help books and articles are most valuable when they act as a kind of mirror, reflecting back the stepmother's experience. It can be a relief for stepmothers to discover that their trials are not unique. A stepmother who considers herself evil for her jealousy of her partner's attention to his children, for instance, may be comforted to read that this is a common reaction. Self-help materials can also offer insight. Some childless stepmothers rely on child development books to give them standards by which to judge their stepchildren's behaviour. They may realize, for instance, that it is reasonable to expect a ten-year-old child to learn table manners, but not reasonable to expect this of a four-year-old.

Stepmothers may also learn new approaches or strategies for dealing with their stepchildren. One stepmother, feeling desperate, reached out for guidance in every direction. She and her partner went for couple counselling, she had therapy for herself, and she scoured the bookstores: "I read a lot of books about stepmothers. I found almost every one useful because it was so new to me. I must have read about half a dozen. Also books generally about kids—how to talk so kids will listen and how to listen so they'll talk. I was just trying to understand what it's all about. It was really helpful to see that it wasn't just me." Reading helped her be less harsh on herself—to let go of the idea that she had failed because she could not remake her stepchildren into perfect children. Although she doubts that self-help books would have dissuaded her from marrying her partner, she wonders whether some knowledge might have helped her avoid the more obvious traps. Her advice to new stepmothers: "I would say—think long and hard before you [become a step-mother]. Do a lot of reading about the pitfalls, both in that rela-tionship [with stepchildren] and also in the relationship with your spouse."

For a list of relevant readings, see the Appendix.

Support Networks: You Can Let Your Hair Down

Encountering other stepmothers is often a huge relief. Some stepmothers feel they can finally speak freely. One stepmother described why she was more open with a stepmother she had just met than with her family and friends: "You can really let your hair down and say things that if I'd said to my friend or to a family member, they just couldn't see it in the same light. Maybe they would think you were being cruel or overly sensitive or overly emotional." Although many stepmothers initially do not know any other stepmothers, often later they actively seek them out. One stepmother noticed that she was immediately drawn to any stepmothers she encountered: "Nobody understands the life of a stepmother. I found myself looking for stepmothers or grav-itating toward them. I was at a dinner party last summer and one person there was a stepmum. Well, do you think I talked to any-body else? No!"

Trading stories and commiserating with another stepmother can be exhilarating. Finally, someone who nods understandingly when you describe how your stepson ignores you or your partner's ex-wife spreads lies about you destroying her marriage. It can be com-forting to discover that others are afflicted with jealousy and rage or reassuring to hear that others have worse struggles than you do. One stepmother was delighted to meet two other stepmothers at her workplace: "There are a few people in my office who are in the same situation, and we exchange stories. Boy, does that make you feel better! Because you realize we have it really great compared to some situations. And you see some things better in theirs. But everybody's got a story." Stepmothers sometimes band together into a kind of informal club where they can speak frankly, or they develop support networks with other stepmothers.

Stepmothers who do not know other stepmothers often hunger to meet women in similar situations. All the women I interviewed knew I was a stepmother. When I offered to talk about my experiences and the research findings after we finished our interview, they leapt at the chance, curious to find out whether their experiences were typical. Some women called later to say it was therapeutic to tell their story, that this was the first time they had spoken openly. After hearing that other stepmothers had similar reactions and feelings, it felt as though a weight had been lifted off their shoulders.

While most of the stepmothers met other stepmothers through social networks, many communities have self-help support groups for stepmothers and stepfamilies. In order to help stepmothers find these kinds of useful resources, I have developed a website where I describe organizations and associations for stepmothers and stepfamilies and provide links to these groups: http://faculty. msvu.ca/elizabethchurch.

Most of this chapter has focused on professional therapy. Of course, therapy is not a panacea. It can make a huge difference to stepmothers and their families when they are unable to resolve their problems on their own, but it can also add to their problems. Self-help literature and more informal support networks can also be really valuable to stepmothers, offering them new perspectives on their situation. In their advice to new stepmothers, stepmothers often mention connecting with other stepmothers. Since Veronique was such an avid consumer of outside help, I was interested in her recommendations for stepmothers. Top of her list was

"Find some other people who are in the same situation and get yourself an informal network of people to vent with or hear from or get advice from."

Over time, most stepmothers realize they need outside support, whether it is through conversations with other stepmothers, from books and articles, or from professionals. Trying to go it alone takes a toll. It is not always easy to locate the correct assistance, however, and stepmothers need to proceed cautiously. It may take repeated attempts before they find something that works for their situation. Finding the right help can provide enormous relief, releasing stepmothers from guilt, anger, resentment, and from feeling alone in their struggles.

Chapter 17

The Seven Principles

There are no simple answers to the question of how to be a good stepmother. Stepmothers begin with disparate expectations, face a variety of challenges, and traverse many different paths in their quests to be good stepmothers. What is relevant to one situation will not work in another. Being a stepmother is an evolving and complicated business and stepmothers' experiences cannot be compressed into a single set of rules. By recounting the stories of the stepmothers who took part in my study, my hope is that stepmothers will recognize their experiences and that this recognition will give them new insights into, and understanding about, their own situations.

While there is no set of rules for stepmothering, from my research I have identified seven principles that guided the actions of the happiest stepmothers I interviewed.

1. Accept that you do not know.
2. Know yourself.
3. Recognize what you cannot do.
4. Recognize what you can do.
5. Take the long view.
6. Start the conversation.
7. Embrace the weirdness.

At first glance, these principles may seem like bromides, and indeed, some have been around in various forms for thousands of years. Like many apparently obvious maxims, these principles are not easy to discover or to live by. Stepmothers often reach these insights only through painful self-examination, extensive discussion, and consultation with others. For some readers, these precepts may be old news. This chapter is intended for stepmothers who want guidance on how to move forward.

1. Accept That You Do Not Know

The Greek philosopher Socrates' famous claim that all he knew was that he knew nothing is relevant for stepmothers today.[1] Stepmothers' initial expectations often get them into trouble. They project their hopes and beliefs onto their stepfamily and become hurt, disappointed, and bitter. At the root of their expectations is a confidence that they have a good understanding of this situation. Only later do they realize how misplaced their assumptions were. Except for stepmothers who have lived in stepfamilies before, most stepmothers have minimal knowledge about stepfamilies. By acknowledging their ignorance, stepmothers become more open and less likely to insist that the stepfamily conform to their ideals.

Even if a stepmother has a good grasp of how stepfamilies interact in general, her new stepfamily is an unknown culture with its own history and traditions. A stepmother who imposes her values onto the new situation does so at her peril. Accepting that she does not know permits her to ease in and take the temperature of this family before initiating any changes. A wise stepmother has few expectations about how her stepfamily should behave.

The corollary to this is to recognize that others may not know either. Stepmothers often become trapped by the expectations of others—their partners, in-laws, and even their therapists—who push them into mothering their stepchildren. Stepmothers often accede, even if this runs counter to their own inclinations. Resisting the pressures of others allows the stepmother to proceed more cautiously and the stepfamily to develop more gradually.

2. Know Yourself

Stepmothers are often so ashamed of their ambivalent or angry feelings toward stepchildren that they try to deny them, even to themselves. Rather than burying these emotions, stepmothers should expose and inspect them, because these reactions may be a good indication that something is awry. Guilt, for instance, is often a sign that unrealistic expectations are at work. Either the stepmother is bowing to pressures from outside or is forcing herself into an untenable position. Resentment often masks feelings of being disregarded and overlooked. Similarly, jealousy and envy often have their roots in insecurity and powerlessness.

The danger in not heeding these signals is that the stepmother may unconsciously enact them. A stepmother who cannot admit to her rage, jealousy, guilt, resentment, or wounded feelings may unwittingly inflict her frustrations on the situation. Rather than seeking to understand why she feels so unhappy, she may attempt to overcome these feelings by eliminating the apparent source—usually her stepchildren, but sometimes her in-laws or her stepchildren's mother. With her stepchildren, for example, she may limit the time the children can visit, constantly pick on their faults, and criticize them to her partner. She may cut off contact with her in-laws, compete with her stepchildren's mother, or act in mean-spirited ways that only redouble her shame. One consequence of ignoring these powerful feelings is that the negative patterns of interaction often escalate, thus adding to the stepmother's problems.

If stepmothers acknowledge their unpleasant, often uncomfortable feelings, they can start to examine how and why they arose. This enhanced self-knowledge is often the first step in addressing the stepfamily's problems. Talking to other stepmothers, reading self-help materials, or engaging in therapy can all be helpful in developing self-understanding. This process can be lengthy. Martha, for example, only began to see with her fifth therapist how she had boxed herself in by trying to become a mother to her stepchildren.

Even if a stepmother can make few concrete improvements, acknowledging and accepting her reactions can create enough emotional distance that she will be less likely to act them out. Similarly, understanding why others treat her with coldness or hostility may help to moderate the stepmother's hurt feelings. If a stepmother feels miserable, there is a high probability that others in her stepfamily do too. Recognizing that others are struggling often makes stepmothers feel more forgiving and less personally attacked.

By recommending that stepmothers know themselves, I am not proposing that they accept responsibility for all the problems in the stepfamily, nor that they put up with rudeness or contempt. Rather, I am suggesting that, without self-examination, stepmothers are often fated to remain mired in their problems. Self-understanding will not solve all problems, but it can help stepmothers evaluate how they arrived at this place.

3. Recognize What You Cannot Do

Stepmothers often throw themselves into stepmothering with great enthusiasm or aspire to be fairy godmothers. When their mission fails, they feel hurt and unappreciated. Most stepmothers take on too much responsibility at the beginning. With experience, they learn to step back and do less. They realize that they cannot perform miracles. No matter how much time and energy a stepmother commits, and despite her best intentions, she cannot make her stepfamily work without support from others. If her stepchildren refuse her admittance into their lives, if her partner does not back her up, or if her stepchildren's mother forces the children to choose between her and the stepmother, the stepmother can do little.

Although it may be painful to acknowledge her limited influence, the stepmother can then assess exactly what is and what is not possible. She may have to live with a circumscribed role in the life of the stepfamily, or accept that her relationships with her stepchildren will never be intimate or even friendly. She also can relinquish the belief that she is the one responsible for the success of her stepfamily and transfer responsibility back to those who do have authority, usually her partner and her stepchildren's mother. The challenge is for the stepmother not to regard this shift as a personal failure, but as a systemic issue, related to the structure of her stepfamily.

Stepmothers must tread very cautiously in certain areas. Motherhood is one of these. Only in very rare circumstances can a stepmother step into the mother's place—for instance, if the mother is absent and the stepchildren are very young. Even if stepchildren believe their stepmother is their mother, however, this is a chancy strategy. At the same time, a stepmother should not demand of herself that she love her stepchildren as she loves her biological children. Women who have the dual lenses of stepmother and stepchild do not expect that stepparents will, or should, love their stepchildren as a mother would.

Some stepmothers adopt a more removed stance from the beginning. Paradoxically, waiting on the sidelines often means that these stepmothers are more likely to be welcomed in than stepmothers who leap in uninvited. Holding back and not assuming that a relationship exists from the beginning allows stepchildren to make the first step toward the stepmother. It is prudent to wait and see what will unfold rather than jumping in at the beginning and then being forced to retreat.

4. Recognize What You Can Do

Although many stepmothers end up with a more circumscribed role than they had originally anticipated, most can identify some space in which they can act. A useful guide for stepmothers is to distinguish between areas where they have legitimate authority and those they should avoid. Generally, it is best to leave the disciplining of stepchildren to the biological parents. A stepmother can, however, support her partner and encourage him to be more involved with his children. This path usually benefits everyone— the children and their father become closer and the stepmother no longer has to carry the whole burden. While a stepmother may not be able to organize the household exactly as she would wish, she does not have to be a doormat. It is reasonable to expect to be treated civilly and to have influence over how the household is run, particularly as it affects her.

While stepmothers can rarely be mothers to their stepchildren, they can often have a significant influence in their stepchildren's lives. The ideal is the Extended stepfamily, where family members work cooperatively to create an expanded network of kin. The stepmother is a supportive, caring, involved, interested presence in her stepchildren's lives, similar to a close aunt or older cousin. The Couple model, where the stepmother is friendly and available without considering her stepchildren part of her family, is another workable solution, particularly if her stepchildren are older or their main allegiance is to their mother. Sometimes neither of these is possible, and the stepmother must settle for less.

Stepmothers need to determine where they belong in the step-family. Although many stepmothers start off believing they will range freely within the stepfamily, they adapt to having a smaller sphere of influence. A stepmother may be gratified, for example, when her stepsons become eager readers as a result of her encouragement or when her stepchildren solicit her opinion about which university to attend. The stepmother's influence may not be visible for many years. One stepmother whose stepchildren were hostile and rude during their adolescence was pleased when, ten years later, her stepson credited her with his commitment to the environmental movement. While these may appear small accomplishments, for stepmothers, they are signs of their membership in this family.

5. Take the Long View

Stepfamilies are works in progress. As noted, stepfamilies can take as many as ten to twelve years to become a family. Stepmothers who understand this are often the happiest. Recognizing that it may take time for the stepfamily to coalesce, for their stepchildren to warm up, or for them to locate their space in this family relieves the pressure to conjure up instant solutions. A stepmother who envisions the stepfamily stretching over many years will be less likely to try to fix everything immediately.

Believing that their relationships with stepchildren will grow over time allows stepmothers to let connections develop without forcing them. Stepchildren's initial unfriendliness will be set within the context of a long-term relationship. It is easier for a stepmother to tolerate being ignored by her stepchild if she can imagine their relationship developing over many years. Hanging in for the long term also often yields success—most of the stepmothers in my study felt that their situations improved over time. On the other side, if it does not, miserable stepmothers can console themselves by reminding themselves that their stepchildren will eventually grow up and leave home.

6. Start the Conversation

As I have noted, much is left unsaid in stepfamilies. Stepmothers are wary about stating their feelings to stepchildren because the relationship feels so fragile, many of their partners avoid challenging their children because they feel guilty, the children are reluctant to speak freely because of loyalty issues, couples fail to discuss their expectations for the relationship and the family, and relationships between ex-spouses are so acrimonious that communication is negligible. In this atmosphere, stepmothers often feel they are boxing with shadows. Misunderstandings flourish, crucial issues never get addressed, let alone resolved, and people feel inconsequential and overlooked.

Although starting the conversation may feel risky, airing issues often helps to clarify them and may lead toward solutions. If a stepmother ascertains that her partner wants her to assume responsibility for the household but she believes it should be shared, at least their disagreement is in the open and they can begin negotiating. If the stepmother and the mother speak directly to one another, they can clear up misunderstandings and build some bridges for future discussions. When stepmothers reassure stepchildren that they have no intention of attempting to replace their mother, tensions are often eased.

Sometimes when stepmothers take the chance and initiate conversation, they meet resistance. Their stepchildren may turn away or their stepchildren's mother may rebuff their overtures. Stepmothers' fears that they will be attacked—or be accused of wickedness—rarely materialize, however. Usually the worst they encounter is silence. Sometimes the response is a long time in coming or arrives only indirectly. In Chapter 10, I described how Leah suggested to her stepson, Mark, that he might feel more comfortable calling her by name rather than feeling compelled to refer to her as his mother. Although Mark did not acknowledge her comment, he switched to calling her Leah and their relationship has become friendlier.

It is advisable that stepmothers not divulge everything to everyone. Before a stepmother unleashes her angry and wounded feelings on her stepfamily, she should first understand her reactions. A support network outside the stepfamily is enormously beneficial here. If a stepmother is not heard inside the stepfamily, she needs people outside the stepfamily with whom she can sort out her feelings. This person can be a friend, family member, another stepmother, or a professional. This kind of discussion is equally necessary as initiating conversation within the stepfamily. While easy, relaxed communication among stepfamily members is the ideal, this rarely happens in stepfamilies without some gentle coaxing.

Stepmothers who screw up their courage to start the conversation often discover that others are grateful to be invited to speak.

7. Embrace the Weirdness

One stepmother characterized the stepmother-stepchild relationship as the "weirdest one in the world." This woman went on to observe that in stepfamilies, "you step lightly, but you're bonded forever." What makes the stepfamily so weird is precisely the tension this woman articulates—you are connected to these people, but you have to step cautiously because you are in unfamiliar territory and cannot assume or presume you understand where you are treading.

Fortunate stepmothers find ways to live comfortably within this paradox. Rather than considering the stepfamily a poor substitute for the non-divorced two-parent family, they appreciate the advantages of a stepfamily, whether it is the chance to be around children, to be linked with an expanded group of people, or to have a front-seat view on the culture of another family. They recognize the stepfamily's strengths, that its looser ties and complex network of relationships offer people another model of how to interact. It is the rare stepmother who grasps this from the beginning, however, and stepmothers often have to shed their prejudices before they learn to love the stepfamily. Like Denise's stepdaughter, Leesa, they come to believe that stepfamilies might be "the best of both worlds because they now have two families."

The genesis of this project was my desire to understand the experience of being a stepmother. Throughout the process of researching and writing this book, I became aware that "understanding stepmothers" happens on many levels. Not only was I attempting to understand stepmothers, but the women I interviewed were themselves trying to make sense of their situations. At the same time, many felt isolated and lonely because others did not seem to grasp or understand their struggles. They craved a sympathetic response from their partners, family and friends, but this was frequently not forthcoming. I was also impressed with their under-standing and compassion for others. Often they would forgive their stepchildren's initial coolness and would be instructing their part-ner on how to interpret, and attend to, his children's feelings.

As I puzzled over the diversity of reactions among the stepmoth-ers—why one wanted to be a mother to her stepchildren, while another was content to be a friend—I began to reflect on what we mean when we say someone is "family." The stepmothers used a variety of criteria to define their stepfamilies—the biological link, sharing a household, connection through marriage, and liking. I learned that there are multiple ways to be related. At the same time as my thinking about families evolved, so did my stepfamily. Since I started this project, both my stepchildren have had children of their own. My stepson has a four-year-old daughter, and my stepdaugh-ter had a son last year. My two daughters were eleven and nine when they became aunts. Naturally, they were not ready to become aunts in the way we usually think of that relationship. Neither was I, with two relatively young children, ready to think of myself as a grandmother. I was content to continue to be "Elizabeth," as my stepchildren have always called me, but my stepson's partner, who is from Taiwan, seemed to want a more official title for me. Her first language, Mandarin, has a more complex vocabulary for family relationships than does English. There are separate words for pater-nal grandmother and maternal grandmother, but even Mandarin could not produce a word for "paternal stepgrandmother." My stepdaughter proposed that I be called "Abba," the name devised by a niece when she could not manage "Elizabeth" and subsequently adopted by many of my nieces. I was delighted by her suggestion because this name reflects the special relationship I have with these young children who are an integral part of my expanding family. My experience and my research have taught me that we are all connected and that this peculiar web of relationships we call a step-family enriches all of our lives.

Appendix

Background to Study

One hundred and four stepmothers participated in the study. The study was advertised via family physicians who informed their patients about the study, media interviews, and notices and talks to community organizations. The group of women who volunteered represented a fairly homogenous sample of white, middle-class and professional-class Canadian women. In order to qualify for the study, the stepmother had to be living with a man who had children from a previous relationship. I included women who were co-habiting as well as those who were legally married, since many couples choose to co-habit after divorcing. Both residential stepmothers (those who had stepchildren living with them at least half-time) and nonresidential stepmothers were included: 71 percent had had at least one stepchild live with them half-time or longer for some period of time since they had become a stepmother, while 29 percent were "weekend" stepmothers or had never lived with their stepchildren. I looked for a mix of breadth of experience: 21 percent had been a stepmother for two or less years, 34 percent for between three and five years, and 45 percent for six or more years.

At the time these women became stepmothers, most had stepchildren under the age of eighteen: forty-nine had at least one preschool stepchild (average age of these women's stepchildren was 5.8 years), thirty-six had stepchildren ages seven and older (average age 10.2), fifteen had stepchildren who were adolescents or older (average age fifteen), and four had only adult stepchildren (average age of adult stepchildren was twenty-seven years). I was interested in how having children of one's own affects stepmothers' experience. The participants were almost evenly divided between those who had their own children and those who were childless: 55 percent had biological children, while 45 percent did not. Of the stepmothers who had children, about half (52 percent) had children from a previous relationship and the rest became mothers after they were stepmothers.

Since most stepmothers in Canada and the United States are nonresidential stepmothers, the participants in this study are not typical. They may represent a group of engaged, involved stepmothers, however. Stepmothers who rarely see their stepchildren perhaps would not volunteer for a study or may not identify themselves as stepmothers.

I interviewed each stepmother individually about her experience. The interviews, which lasted between one and a half to three hours, focused on stepmothers' experiences and perceptions of their role. Although the interviews were framed by a series of questions, I invited the stepmothers to raise any issues that they thought were relevant. The interviews often covered a lot of territory. I explored their relationships with various members of their stepfamily, including stepchildren, partners, partners' ex-wives, and in-laws. I was interested in how they believed their own backgrounds and values had influenced their expectations prior to becoming a stepmother and whether these expectations had shifted over time. Stepmothers were encouraged to identify both the positive and negative aspects of stepmothering. At the end of each interview, I asked the stepmothers to give their definitions of a good mother and a good stepmother (the questions were alternated so that half defined a good mother first and the other half a good stepmother first). The stepmothers knew that I was a stepmother myself and were eager to hear about my—and other stepmothers'—experience after the interview was over. Many said that the interview was the first time they had felt free to express their feelings and thoughts about being a stepmother.

The interviews were audiotaped and transcribed, and I spent many hours sifting through the transcripts, trying to pull out recurring themes. Once a list of common themes was generated, all the interviews were coded using these categories and the context for the themes was identified. Jealousy, for instance, was a theme that frequently appeared among the stepmothers. As I coded it throughout the stepmothers' interviews, I could identify who the stepmothers felt jealous of and in which situations it was most likely to occur. I found that stepmothers were more likely to feel jealous of their stepchildren when they felt their partners were not paying attention to their needs.

One of my initial questions was why it was so hard to be a stepmother. While stepmothers struggled with many aspects of their role, seven main sources of stress reappeared over and over in their interviews. These seven stresses became the basis of the chapters in Part One. As I analyzed the transcripts, I became aware that the stepmothers were operating from a diverse variety of assumptions about their roles. I identified five different approaches to stepmothering, which became the Nuclear, Biological, Retreat, Couple, and Extended models. A working definition, specifying the main characteristics of each model, was developed. Using these definitions as a guide, a research assistant independently read through the transcripts of two-thirds of the interviews and assigned each stepmother to a model. There was an 80 percent agreement between my designation and the research assistant's, which suggests that these models represent relatively distinct ideas. I then examined the stepmothers in each model as a group in order to identify commonalities among these women. I also did case studies of two stepmothers within each model as a way of uncovering more of the details and subtleties of their experience.

Throughout the process of the analysis, it became abundantly clear to me that being a stepmother was not a static state, but that the stepmothers evolved over time and often gained a great deal of insight, and even wisdom, about how to be a stepmother. Chapters 13, 14, and 17 reflect their acquired knowledge. I chose to depict the stepmothers' experience through their stories because this seemed to capture the diversity and complexity of contemporary stepmothering.

Endnotes

Introduction

1 L. Bumpass, K. Raley, and J. Sweet, "The Changing Character of Stepfamilies: The Implications of Cohabitation and Nonmarital Childbearing," *Demography* 32 (1995): 425–436. M. Coleman, L. Ganong, and M. Fine, "Reinvestigating Remarriage: Another Decade of Progress," *Journal of Marriage and the Family* 62 (2000): 1288–1307. H. Juby, N. Marcil-Gratton, and C. Le Bourdais, "A Step Further in Family Life: The Emergence of the Blended Family," *Report on the Demographic Situation in Canada 2000: Current Demographic Analysis* (Ottawa: Statistics Canada, 2001). N. Marcil-Gratton, *Growing Up with Mom and Dad? The Intricate Family Life Courses of Canadian Children* (Ottawa: Statistics Canada, 1998), Catalogue 89-566-XIE. Vanier Institute of the Family, *Profiling Canada's Families* (Ottawa: Vanier Institute of the Family, 1994).

2 A.-M. Ambert, "Being a Stepparent: Live-in and Visiting Stepchildren," *Journal of Marriage and the Family* 48 (1986): 795–804. C.G. Barnes, P. Thompson, G. Daniel, and N. Burchardt, *Growing Up in Stepfamilies* (Oxford: Oxford University Press, 1998). A. Bernstein, "Gender and Stepfamily Life: A Review," *Journal of Feminist Family Therapy* 1, no. 4 (1989): 1–27. M. Crosbie-Burnett, A. Skyles, and J. Becker-Haven, "Exploring Stepfamilies from a Feminist Perspective," in S. Dornbusch and M. Strober (eds.), *Feminism, Children and the New Families* (New York: Guilford Press, 1988). L. Ganong, and

299

M. Coleman, *Remarried Family Relationships* (Thousand Oaks, CA: Sage, 1994). L. Nielson. "Stepmothers: Why So Much Stress? A Review of the Research," *Journal of Divorce and Remarriage* 30 (1999): 115–148. D. Whitsett and H. Land, "Role Strain, Coping, and Marital Satisfaction of Stepparents," *Families in Society: The Journal of Contemporary Human Services* 73 (1992): 79–92.

3 Perhaps one reason that stepfathers and stepfather families (stepfamilies with a biological mother and a stepfather) have been studied more thoroughly than stepmothers and stepmother families (where there is a biological father and stepmother) is that the former are more common than the latter, because women are more often awarded custody of their children.

Chapter 1: The Wickedest of Them All: The Image of the Wicked Stepmother

1 A. Dundes, *Cinderella: A Folklore Casebook* (New York: Garland, 1982). M.R. Cox, *Cinderella: Three Hundred and Forty-Five Variants* (London: Folklore Society, 1892). J. Ellis, *One Fairy Story Too Many: The Brothers Grimm and Their Tales* (Chicago, IL: University of Chicago Press, 1983). N. Philip, *The Cinderella Story* (London: Penguin, 1989). M. Ury, "Stepmother Tales in Japan," *Children's Literature* 9 (1981): 61–72. V. Vatuk and S. Vatuk, "The Lustful Stepmother in the Folklore of Northwestern India," *Journal of South Asia Literature* 11 (1975): 19–43. J.D. Yohannan, *Joseph and Potiphar's Wife in World Literature: An Anthology of the Story of the Chaste Youth and the Lustful Stepmother* (New York: New Directions, 1968). J. Zipes, *Fairy Tales and the Art of Subversion* (New York: Methuen, 1988).

2 J. Garner, *Politically Correct Bedtime Stories* (New York: Macmillan, 1994).

3 D. Noy, "Wicked Stepmothers in Roman Society and Imagination," *Journal of Family History* 16 (1991): 345–361. P. Watson, *Ancient Stepmothers: Myth, Misogyny, and Reality* (Leiden, The Netherlands: E.J. Brill, 1995).

Endnotes

4 M. Tatar, *Off with Their Heads: Fairy Tales and the Culture of Childhood* (Princeton, NJ: Princeton University Press, 1992).

5 K. Stone, "Fairy Tales for Adults: Walt Disney's Americanization of the Märchen," in N. Burlakoff and C. Lindel (eds.), *Folklore on Two Continents: Essays in Honor of Linda Dégh* (Bloomington, IN: Trickster Press, 1980): 40–48.

6 "The Tale of Hildur, the Good Stepmother," in *Adventures, Outlaws and Past Events: Icelandic Folktales III*, A. Boucher (trans.) (Reykjavik, Iceland: Icelandic Review, 1977): 19–28. M. Rudolph, *The Good Stepmother* (New York: Simon & Schuster, 1992). J. Cruickshank (Producer) and A. Tennant (Director), *It Takes Two*. [Motion Picture]. United States: Warner Brothers, 1995.

Chapter 2: Crashing Mirrors: Unrealistic Initial Expectations

1 Coleman, Ganong, and Fine, "Reinvestigating Remarriage: Another Decade of Progress." E.M. Hetherington and M. Stanley-Hagan, "Parenting in Divorced and Remarried Families," in M. Bornstein (ed.), *Handbook of Parenting* 2nd ed., vol. 3 (Mahwah, NJ: Lawrence Erlbaum, 2002): 287–315. E.B. Visher and J.S. Visher, *Old Loyalties, New Ties: Therapeutic Strategies with Stepfamilies* (New York: Brunner/ Mazel, 1988).

Chapter 3: Motherhood: The Impossible Ideal

1 At the end of every interview, stepmothers were asked to define a "good mother" and a "good stepmother." (The questions were alternated so that half defined a good mother first and half a good stepmother first.) Forty-two percent said that a good stepmother should be the same thing as a good mother. The order of the questions did not influence their response. Neither did having children of their own: stepmothers with biological children equated good stepmothering with mothering as often as those without children. At the

301

same time, 90 percent of the stepmothers stated in their interviews that they recognized they could never be a mother to their stepchildren, because the children already had a mother, even if she was dead.

2 M. McMahon, *Engendering Motherhood: Identity and Self-Transformation in Women's Lives* (New York: Guilford, 1995).

3 E. Badinter, *The Myth of Motherhood: An Historical View of the Maternal Instinct* (R. DeGaris, trans.) (London: Souvenir Press, 1981). S. Thurer, *The Myths of Motherhood* (New York: Houghton Mifflin, 1994).

4 P. Caplan, *The New Don't Blame Mother: Mending the Mother-Daughter Relationship* (New York: Routledge, 2000). D. Eyer, *Motherguilt: How Our Culture Blames Mothers for What's Wrong with Society* (New York: Times Books, 1996). J. Flax. "Mothers and Daughters Revisited," in J. van Mens-Verhulst, K. Schrues, and L. Woertman (eds.), *Daughtering and Mothering* (London: Routledge, 1993): 146–56.

5 M. di Leonardo, "The Female World of Cards and Holidays: Women, Families and the Work of Kinship," in B. Thorne and M. Yalom (eds.), *Rethinking the Family: Some Feminist Questions* (rev. ed.) (Boston: Northeastern University Press, 1992): 246–61.

6 Sixty-two percent of the stepmothers reported that they had the primary responsibility for the household, 35 percent said that the housework was shared, and 3 percent said that their partners did most of it. These figures are congruent with other studies that show that the division of household work in stepfamilies is still based on traditional gender roles, with women doing more than men, although men contribute more than in first marriages. Coleman, Ganong, and Fine, "Reinvestigating Remarriage: Another Decade of Progress."

Chapter 4: Who's the Real Mother in this Family? Dealing with the "Ex"

1 Statistics Canada, *Census Questions 2001* (Ottawa: Statistics Canada, 2001). Statistics Canada, *Census 1996: Questions and Reasons Why Questions Were Asked* (Ottawa: Statistics Canada, 1996).

2 E. Church, "Poisoned Apples: Stepmothers' Experience of Envy and Jealousy," *Journal of Feminist Family Therapy* 11 (1999): 1–18.

3 Stepmothers who saw themselves in a mother role with their stepchildren were more likely to compare themselves to the ex-wife than were stepmothers who did not cast themselves in this role: 47 percent of the former group in contrast to 22 percent of the latter group.

Chapter 5: Walking on Eggshells: Relationships with Stepchildren

1 Fifty-eight percent of the stepmothers identified positive aspects to their relationships with their stepchildren and only 20 percent had very troubled and problematic relationships with stepchildren.

2 Sixty percent of the stepmothers reported that they felt there was a tentative quality to their relationships with stepchildren and consciously held back from saying or doing certain things. Half (53 percent) of these women also believed that they had good relationships with their stepchildren.

3 About three-quarters (77 percent) of the stepmothers reported feeling powerlessness in their stepfamily, some more acutely than others.

4 C.L. Johnson, "Kinship and Gender," in D. Demo, K. Allen, and M. Fine (eds.), *Handbook of Family Diversity* (New York: Oxford, 2000): 128–48. C.L. Johnson, *Ex Familia: Grandparents, Parents and Children Adjust to Divorce* (New Brunswick, NJ: Rutgers University Press, 1988).

5 E.M. Hetherington and W. Clingempeel, "Coping with Marital Transitions: A Family Systems Perspective," *Monographs of the Society for Research in Child Development* 57 (1992). Hetherington and Stanley-Hagan, "Parenting in Divorced and Remarried Families."

6 D. Ephron, *Funny Sauce* (New York: Penguin, 1986): 159.

7 Fifty-five percent of the stepmothers had biological children of their own, 29 percent from a previous relationship and 28 percent from their current relationship. These numbers add to more than 55 percent because two stepmothers had children from both previous and current relationships.

Chapter 6: Unsupportive Partners, Awkward Fathers

1 Sixty-six percent described their partners as unsupportive. Of these, about half felt completely unsupported, and the other half were mixed, viewing their partners as supportive in some ways and unsupportive in other ways. Stepmothers who felt unsupported were more likely to assert that living in a stepfamily had negatively affected the couple relationship.

2 Seventy percent were critical of their partner's parenting, while twenty-three stepmothers (22 percent) praised their partners as fathers. Only four stepmothers described what could be considered abusive behaviour by their partners, such as belittling, sarcastic comments to the children, excessively harsh punishment, or openly favouring one child over another.

   Stepmothers' perception of their partners as incompetent fathers was similar to the findings of a British study of stepfamilies: G.G. Barnes, P. Thompson, G. Daniel, and N. Burchardt, *Growing up in Stepfamilies* (Oxford: Oxford University Press, 1998).

3 Fathers who do not have custody become increasingly distant from their children over time: only 25 percent see their children at least weekly and 33 percent never see their children or visit only a few times a year. F. Furstenberg, "Childcare after Divorce and Remarriage," in M. Hetherington and J. Aratesh (eds.), *Impact of Divorce, Single Parenting, and Stepparenting on Children* (Hillsdale, NJ: Erlbaum, 1988): 245–61. Hetherington and Stanley-Hagan, "Parenting in Divorced and Remarried Families."

4 About one-third (32 percent) reported that part of their initial attraction to their partner was that he had children. Many of these same women (62 percent) were critical of their partners as fathers.

5 Forty-one percent believed their partner's inability to be firm resulted from feelings of guilt.

6 As was the case with housework, the majority of the stepmothers (65 percent) were responsible for the general organization of the house-

hold. Fathers were more active in caring for their children, but even here, 44 percent of the stepmothers reported they had primary responsibility for child care, and only 13 percent reported that their partner did most of the child care. The rest believed it was shared.

7 About a third (35 percent) of stepmothers found the extra household responsibilities onerous.

8 About two-thirds (65 percent) felt their relationship had suffered by being part of a stepfamily, and only five asserted that their stepchildren had had little or no effect on the couple relationship.

The research on the effect of children on remarriage relationships is mixed. Some studies find that marital quality is lower, while others find no differences. Generally, there is more tension, and disagreements usually focus on children. Some studies have found that marital quality is lower when both partners have children from prior marriages. Coleman, Ganong, and Fine, "Reinvestigating Remarriage: Another Decade of Progress." J. Gold, D. Bubenzer, and J. West, "The Presence of Children and Blended Family Marital Intimacy," *Journal of Divorce and Remarriage,* 19 (1993): 97–108. C. Hobart, "Conflict in Remarriage," *Journal of Divorce and Remarriage,* 15 (1991): 69–86.

Chapter 7: The Childless Stepmother: Will It Ever Be My Turn?

1 At the time of their interviews, forty-six stepmothers did not have biological children. About a quarter were planning to have children in the future, while the rest were not.

2 McMahon, *Engendering Motherhood.*

3 Only one of the forty-six childless stepmothers' partners was more enthusiastic about having children than they were.

4 Of the twenty-nine stepmothers who had children with their partners, seventeen (59 percent) had one child, nine (31 percent) had two children, and three (10 percent) had three children.

5 About one-quarter (24 percent) of the childless stepmothers' partners decided unilaterally that they did not want more children.

6 B. Wilson and S. Clarke, "Remarriages: A Demographic Profile," *Journal of Family Issues* 13 (1992): 123–40.

Introduction to Part Two: Becoming a Stepmother: Five Models

1 See the Appendix for a description of the process of identifying the five models.

Chapter 8: The Nuclear Model: We're Not *Really* a Stepfamily

1 D. Schneider, *American Kinship: A Cultural Account* (2nd ed.) (Chicago: University of Chicago, 1980). D. Schneider and R. Smith, *Class Differences and Sex Roles in American Kinship and Family Structure* (Englewood Cliffs, NJ: Prentice Hall, 1973).

2 Twenty-three stepmothers fit within the Nuclear model and twenty-two of them had stepchildren living with them at least half-time. Compared with the other four models, the Nuclear step-mothers were significantly more likely to live full-time with their stepchildren (Chi-Square= 9.509, p<.025).

3 Ganong and Coleman, *Remarried Family Relationships*.

4 M. Coleman and L. Ganong, "Insiders' and Outsiders' Beliefs about Stepfamilies: Assessment and Implications for Practice," in D. Huntley (ed.), *Understanding Stepfamilies: Implications for Assessment and Treatment* (Alexandria, VA: American Counseling Association, 1995): 101–112. M. Coleman, L. Ganong, and C. Goodwin, "The Presentation of Stepfamilies in Marriage and Family Textbooks," *Family Relations* 43 (1994): 289–97. S. Gamache, "Confronting Nuclear Family Bias in Stepfamily Research," *Marriage and Family Review* 26 (1997): 41–69. L. Ganong and M. Coleman, "How Society Views Stepfamilies," *Marriage and Family Review* 26 (1997): 85–106.

5 Ninety-five percent of the Nuclear stepmothers were in charge of organizing and managing the household compared to 44% of the other stepmothers. Similarly, 91% did most of the housework—the cooking, cleaning, laundry, etc.—in contrast to 42% of the others.

With childcare, 87% of these women had the primary responsibility, compared with 25% of the rest of the stepmothers.

6 Almost half (48%) said that they wished the ex-wife would die or disappear compared with 8% of the rest of the stepmothers.

Chapter 9: The Biological Model: What's Mine Is Mine and What's Yours Is Yours

1 Eighteen stepmothers fit into the Biological model.

2 P. Papernow, *Becoming a Step-Family: Patterns of Development in Remarried Families* (San Francisco: Jossey-Bass, 1993). P. Papernow, "The Stepfamily Cycle: An Experimental Model of Stepfamily Development," *Family Relations* 33 (1984): 355–63.Visher and Visher, *Old Loyalties, New Ties*. E.Visher, J.Visher, and K. Pasley, "Stepfamily Therapy from the Client's Perspective," *Marriage and Family Review* 26 (1997): 191–213.

3 Sixty-three percent felt guilty about their stepchildren, compared to 34 percent of the rest of the stepmothers.

4 Like Nuclear stepmothers, Biological stepmothers were in charge of running the household: 82 percent reported that they were the main organizers of the household, and 66 percent said they did most of the household work. They were less likely to have the primary responsibility for child care: 44 percent reported that they did most of the child care.

5 Eighty-nine percent were very critical of their partners as fathers, compared with 64 percent of the other stepmothers.

6 Ninety-five percent believed their relationship with their partners had been negatively affected by having stepchildren, compared to 58 percent of the other stepmothers.

Chapter 10: The Retreat Model: I Had to Opt Out

1 Four of the 104 stepmothers had retreated completely. Many others had retreated partially from their initial position and were less

involved in the stepfamily. Other studies have also found that many stepmothers pull back, at least somewhat, when they realize that their expectations for their relationships with stepchildren will not be fulfilled. Bernstein, "Gender and Stepfamily Life." Coleman, Ganong, and Fine, "Reinvestigating Remarriage: Another Decade of Progress." A. Orchard and K. Solberg, "Expectations of the Stepmother Role," *Journal of Divorce and Remarriage* 31 (1999): 107–23.

Chapter 11: The Couple Model: Friendship, Not Kinship

1 Thirty-one stepmothers fit within the Couple model.
2 Only 14 percent of Couple stepmothers reported that they had the main responsibility for child care, while 72 percent believed that child care was shared equitably with their partners. With housework, about a third (39 percent) were in charge of the household, and about half (53 percent) shared the housework with their partners.

Chapter 12: The Extended Model: The More the Merrier

1 Twenty-eight stepmothers fit into the Extended model.
2 Forty-four percent of the Extended stepmothers described their partners as involved, committed fathers, compared with 25 percent of the other stepmothers.

Chapter 14: Changing Patterns

1 Longitudinal studies of stepfamilies have shown that, if the couple makes it through the initial high-risk years of stepfamily life, marital satisfaction increases and remarried couples' stress level starts to approximate that of first-married couples. J. Bray and J. Kelly, *Stepfamilies: Love, Marriage and Parenting in the First Decade* (New York: Broadway, 1998). M. Hetherington and J. Kelly, *For Better or for Worse: Divorce Reconsidered* (New York: Norton, 2002).
2 About one-quarter to about one-third of children in stepfamilies

experience emotional and behavioural problems, compared to about one in ten children in non-divorced families. The longer the children live in their stepfamilies and the more stable the stepfamilies become, the more the children in stepfamilies start to look like children in non-divorced families. It appears that, after a difficult initial adjustment period, most children do fine in stepfamilies. E.M. Hetherington and J. Aratesh (eds.), *Impact of Divorce, Single Parenting and Stepparenting on Children* (Hillsdale, NJ: Erlbaum, 1988). E.M. Hetherington and K.M. Jodl, "Stepfamilies as Settings for Child Development." Paper presented at the National Symposium on Stepfamilies, Pennsylvania State University, University Park, 1993.

3 About two-thirds of the stepmothers who initially perceived their partners as unsupportive believed that, over time, their partners became more understanding of the stepmother's position.

4 A third had at least one stepchild move in or out of their residence at least once. Often these changes were made informally, and the custody arrangement was not legally altered. On paper, it may have appeared that the mother had sole custody, but some or all of the children were living with their father. This finding is similar to a study of adolescents in Canadian stepfamilies that found that a third had changed residence at least once. P. Gross, *Kinship Structures in Remarriage Families*. Unpublished doctoral dissertation, University of Toronto, 1985.

5 In the United States, according to common law, stepparents do not have a financial responsibility for their stepchildren. However, they can be held financially responsible for their stepchildren following a marital separation if it can be shown that they acted as a parent to the children during the marriage or if it can be shown that a child would be "financially harmed by the change." M. Engel, "Do I Have an Obligation to Support My Stepchildren?" in *Stepfamily Association of America* (2000). Retrieved 23 September 2003 from http://www. saafamilies.org/education/articles/$/engel-5.htm. M. Mahoney, *Step-families and the Law* (Ann Arbor, MI: University of Michigan, 1994). M. Mason, S. Harrison-Jay, G. Svare, and N. Wolfinger, "Stepparents:

De Facto Parents or Legal Strangers?" *Journal of Family Issues* 23 (2002): 507–22.

In Canada, the Manitoba Court of Appeal recently upheld the financial obligation of a stepfather to support his stepchild after his common-law relationship broke up. The court ruled that the stepfather had a legal obligation to support his stepdaughter because he had been providing support during the time he had lived with her. D. Gambrill, "Stands in the Place of a Parent," in *Law Times* (2002). Retrieved 23 September 2003 from http://www.canadalawbook.ca/headlines/headline249_arc.html.

6 There is some evidence that stepchildren will reject stepparents who attempt to discipline them, particularly early on in the relationship, and that stepmothers who stay away from disciplining their stepchildren tend to have better health. Coleman, Ganong, and Fine, "Reinvestigating Remarriage: Another Decade of Progress." E.M. Hetherington and M. Stanley-Hagan, "Diversity Among Stepfamilies," in D. Demo, K. Allen, and M. Fine (eds.), *Handbook of Family Diversity* (New York: Oxford, 2000): 173–96.

7 About a fifth of the stepmothers observed that their knowledge of their partner's ex-wife was derived primarily from their partner's opinions, which were often negative.

Other studies have shown that divorced fathers tend to describe their ex-wives in highly devaluing terms, even after they have remarried. D. Schuldberg and S. Guisinger, "Divorced Fathers Describe Their Former Wives: Devaluation and Contrast," in S. Volgy (ed.), *Women and Divorce/Men and Divorce: Gender Differences in Separation, Divorce and Remarriage* (New York: Haworth Press, 1991): 61–76.

8 Research on family rituals in stepfamilies has shown that the most successful rituals highlight the interplay of old and new rituals and bring all the family members together. D. Braithwaite, L. Baxter, and A. Harper, "The Role of Rituals in the Management of the Dialectical Tension of 'Old' and 'New' in Blended Families," *Communication Studies* 49 (1998): 101–120.

Chapter 15: The Triumph of Experience over Hope: Seasoned Stepmothers

1 Coleman, Ganong, and Fine, "Reinvestigating Remarriage: Another Decade of Progress."

Chapter 16: Looking for Help

1 Fifty-two percent of the stepmothers reported that either they or someone else in their stepfamily had gone to therapy to address issues related to the stepfamily: 20 percent had had individual counselling, 22 percent couple counselling, 19 percent family therapy, three participated in parenting groups, two consulted with family doctors, and 19 percent reported that their stepchildren had also been in therapy. Forty-two percent of these women had participated in more than one kind of therapy.

Chapter 17: The Seven Principles

1 Plato, *The Last Days of Socrates: Euthyphro/Apology/Crito/Phaedo*. H. Tredennick (trans.) (London: Penguin, 1995).

Suggested Further Reading

Books about divorce and stepfamilies

Ahrons, C. *The Good Divorce: Keeping Your Family Together When your Marriage Comes Apart.* New York: HarperCollins, 1994.
Guide to how to achieve "good" divorces and remarriages that benefit everyone in the family.

Bray, J., and Kelly, J. *Stepfamilies: Love, Marriage and Parenting in the First Decade.* New York: Broadway, 1998.
Based on a nine-year study of stepfamilies, this book describes how stepfamilies evolve and develop over time.

Ephron, P. *Funny Sauce.* New York: Penguin, 1986.
Funny and perceptive account of Ephron's own experience as a stepmother.

Hetherington, M., and Kelly, J. *For Better or for Worse: Divorce Reconsidered.* New York: Norton, 2002.
Mavis Hetherington, one of the foremost researchers in the United States on divorce and remarriage, has gathered her findings from three longitudinal studies into an informative overview of the long-term effects of divorce and remarriage.

Maddox, Brenda. *The Half-Parent: Living with Other People's Children.* New York: M. Evans, 1975.

Account of author's often painful experiences as a stepmother.

Maglin, N. B., and Schniedewind, N. (eds.). *Women and Stepfamilies: Voices of Anger and Love.* Philadelphia: Temple University Press, 1989.

Collection of essays by stepmothers about their experience.

Books on parenting and general relationship skills

Faber, A., and Mazlish, E. *How to Talk So Kids Will Listen and Listen So Kids Will Talk.* New York: HarperCollins, 1999.

Sensible advice for parents about how to communicate effectively with their children.

Fisher, R., and Ury, W. *Getting to Yes: Negotiating Agreement without Giving In.* New York: Penguin, 1991.

Although this book is a primer on negotiation, its principles can be applied to many situations where people are trying to reach an agreement.

Gordon, T. *Parent Effectiveness Training.* New York: Three Rivers Press, 2000.

Guide for parents about how to develop positive relationships with their children.

Acknowledgements

I have been fortunate to have the support of many people during the research and writing of this book.

I owe an enormous debt to the all the stepmothers who shared their stories and whose insights informed and expanded my understanding of what it means to be a stepmother. For obvious reasons, I cannot thank them by name.

Roberta Dwyer and Raylene Smith provided valuable research assistance. Memorial University generously granted me support for my research, including a sabbatical leave.

I am grateful to Lori Chapman, Babs Church, Evan Church, Matthew Church, and Karen Teff for their thoughtful advice and sympathetic reading of early drafts of the manuscript.

My editor, Lynne Missen, has been an enthusiastic and responsive guide to a neophyte writer.

My daughters, Lucy and Elinor Barker, cheerfully sent me off to the office during the long process of writing this book.

I have relied on my husband, William Barker, at every step on the way—for his intelligence, critical insights, and unflagging encouragement.

315

Acknowledgements

Finally, I would like to thank my stepchildren, Anthony and Madeleine Barker, without whom this project never would have been conceived and whose amused tolerance freed me to carry on.